Security

Security is a vital subject of study in the twenty-first century and a central theme in many social science disciplines. This volume provides a comparative analysis of the ways in which the concept of security is theorized and studied across different disciplines. The book has two objectives: first, to explore the growing diversity of theories, paradigms, and methods developed to study security; and, second, to initiate a multidisciplinary dialogue about the ontological, epistemological, paradigmatic, and normative aspects of security studies in social sciences. Readers across nine fields are invited to reflect on their conceptualizations of security and to consider how an interdisciplinary dialogue can stimulate and enrich the understanding of security in our contemporary world. Analytically sharp yet easy to read, this is a cutting-edge volume exploring what security is and what it means in today's world.

PHILIPPE BOURBEAU is Temporary University Lecturer in the Department of Politics and International Studies at the University of Cambridge.

Security

Dialogue across Disciplines

Edited by

PHILIPPE BOURBEAU

CAMBRIDGE
UNIVERSITY PRESS

University Printing House, Cambridge CB2 8BS, United Kingdom

Cambridge University Press is part of the University of Cambridge.

It furthers the University's mission by disseminating knowledge in the pursuit of education, learning and research at the highest international levels of excellence.

www.cambridge.org
Information on this title: www.cambridge.org/9781107514737

© Cambridge University Press 2015

This publication is in copyright. Subject to statutory exception and to the provisions of relevant collective licensing agreements, no reproduction of any part may take place without the written permission of Cambridge University Press.

First published 2015

Printed in the United Kingdom by Clays, St Ives plc

A catalogue record for this publication is available from the British Library

Library of Congress Cataloging in Publication data
Security (Cambridge University Press)
Security : dialogue across disciplines / edited by Philippe Bourbeau.
    pages cm
Includes bibliographical references and index.
ISBN 978-1-107-10740-3 (Hardback) – ISBN 978-1-107-51473-7 (Paperback)
1. Security, International. 2. National security. 3. Security, Internal. 4. Human security. 5. Economic security. I. Bourbeau, Philippe II. Title.
JZ5588.S42855 2015
355'.033–dc23   2015016103

ISBN 978-1-107-10740-3 Hardback
ISBN 978-1-107-51473-7 Paperback

Cambridge University Press has no responsibility for the persistence or accuracy of URLs for external or third-party internet websites referred to in this publication, and does not guarantee that any content on such websites is, or will remain, accurate or appropriate.

Contents

Notes on contributors	*page*	vii
Acknowledgments		xi
1	A multidisciplinary dialogue on security *Philippe Bourbeau*	1
2	Philosophy: The concepts of security, fear, liberty, and the state *Jonathan Herington*	22
3	Anthropology/ies: Moving beyond disciplinary approaches to security *Daniel M. Goldstein*	45
4	Geography: Securing places and spaces of securitization *Philippe Le Billon*	62
5	Sociology: Security and insecurities *Lisa Stampnitzky and Greggor Mattson*	90
6	International relations: Celebrating eclectic dynamism in security studies *Philippe Bourbeau, Thierry Balzacq, and Myriam Dunn Cavelty*	111
7	Psychology: The phenomenology of human security *Thomas C. O'Brien and Linda R. Tropp*	137
8	International political economy: Conceptual affinities and substantive differences with security studies *Ronen Palan and Hannah Petersen*	156

| 9 | Criminology: Reimagining Security
Jan Froestad, Clifford Shearing, and Melani Van der Merwe | 177 |
| 10 | International law: Between legalism and securitization
Wouter Werner | 196 |

| *References* | 219 |
| *Index* | 282 |

Notes on contributors

THIERRY BALZACQ is Professor in the Department of Political Science and holder of the Tocqueville Chair in Security Policies at the University of Namur, Belgium. He his also the Scientific Director of the Institute for Strategic Research at the French Ministry of Defense in Paris. He has authored and/or edited more than ten books, including *Traité de Relations Internationales*, coedited with F. Ramel (2013).

PHILIPPE BOURBEAU is Temporary University Lecturer in the Department of Politics and International Studies at the University of Cambridge, United Kingdom. He is the author of *The Securitization of Migration: A Study of Movement and Order* (2011). His research, focusing on security, migration, and resilience, has been published in *International Studies Review*; *Journal of Ethnic and Migration Studies*; *Millennium: Journal of International Studies*; *Resilience: International Policies, Practices and Discourses*; *Critique internationale*; and *Revue européenne des migrations internationales*.

MYRIAM DUNN CAVELTY is Deputy for Research and Teaching at the Center for Security Studies, ETH Zurich, Switzerland. Her research focuses on the politics of risk and uncertainty in security politics and changing conceptions of (inter-)national security due to cyber issues in specific. She is the coeditor of the *Routledge Handbook of Security Studies*, and her articles have been published in International Political Sociology, *Security Dialogue, Cambridge Review of International Affairs* among others.

JAN FROESTAD is Associate Professor in the Department of Administration and Organization Theory at the University of Bergen, Norway. His research interests cover studies of normality, deviance, and disability; conditions for generalization of social trust; and the governance of security and conflict management. He is the coauthor of *Security Governance, Policing, and Local Capacity* (2012).

DANIEL M. GOLDSTEIN is Professor in the Department of Anthropology at Rutgers University, United States. He is the author of three books: *The Spectacular City: Violence and Performance in Urban Bolivia* (2004); *Outlawed: Between Security and Rights in a Bolivian City* (2012); and Owners of the Sidewalk: Security and Survival in the Informal City (2016). He is the co-editor (with Enrique D. Arias) of the collection *Violent Democracies in Latin America*. A political and legal anthropologist, Professor Goldstein specializes in the anthropology of security; his current research examines undocumented workers' vulnerabilities and responses in a context of securitized migration in the United States.

JONATHAN HERINGTON is Assistant Professor in the Department of Philosophy at Kansas State University. His research focuses on applied questions in moral and political philosophy, with a special emphasis on public health ethics and the concept, value, and practice of security. He has published work in the *Review of International Studies*, *Health Policy and Planning*, and the *Hastings Center Report*.

PHILIPPE LE BILLON is Professor at the University of British Columbia with the Department of Geography and Liu Institute for Global Issues. Working on linkages among environment, development, and security, he has published widely on natural resources and armed conflicts, the political economy of war, resource governance, and corruption. His two latest books are *Oil* (2012 with Gavin Bridge) and *Wars of Plunder: Conflicts, Profits and the Politics of Resources* (2013).

GREGGOR MATTSON is Associate Professor of Sociology and Law and Society at Oberlin College. He earned an MPhil at Oxford University and a PhD at the University of California, Berkeley. He is the author of the forthcoming book, The Cultural Politics of European Prostitution Reform and, with Claude Fischer, of a review article on the relative impacts of domestic insecurity in the United States, "Is America Fragmenting?"

THOMAS C. O'BRIEN is a graduate student in Social Psychology and in the Psychology of Peace and Violence Program at the University of Massachusetts Amherst, United States. He graduated from Washington University in St. Louis with an A.B. in Psychology and Jewish, Islamic and Near Eastern Studies. Before attending the University of Massachusetts Amherst, he interned for the International Center for

Journalists in Washington, D.C. His research focuses on the psychology of intergroup relations, including factors that may motivate public support for foreign policies and the ways that peace activism may affect public opinion.

RONEN PALAN is Professor of International Political Economy at City University London, United Kingdom. He was a founding editor of the *Review of International Political Economy*. He is the author of, among others, *Offshore World* (2003) and *Tax Havens: How Globalization Really Works* (2010) (coauthored with Richard Murphy and Christian Chavagneux) and the editor of *Global Political Economy: Contemporary Theories* (2012) and co-editor with Sandra Halperin of *Legacies of Empire* (2015).

HANNAH PETERSEN is PhD candidate at the Department of International Politics at City University London, United Kingdom, working on energy security and risk theory in International Political Economy. She has previously studied in Konstanz University, Sciences Po Paris, Sheffield University, was a visiting fellows at Harvard University, and worked research assistant at the German Institute of International and Security Affairs.

CLIFFORD SHEARING is a Professor at the Griffith Criminology Institute, Griffith University, Australia as well as in the Law Faculty at the University of Cape Town, South Africa. He holds an Adjunct Professorship in the School of Criminology at the University of Montreal, Canada. Recent books include *Imagining Security* (2007), *Lengthening the Arm of the Law* (2009), *The New Collaborative Governance* (2012), *Where's the Chicken?* (2012), *Security Governance, Policing, and Local Capacity* (2013), and *Security and the Anthropocene* (2016).

LISA STAMPNITZKY is Lecturer in Politics at the University of Sheffield and earned her PhD in sociology at the University of California, Berkeley. She is the author of *Disciplining Terror: How Experts Invented "Terrorism"* (2013), as well as a number of articles and book chapters on political violence. Her current research focuses on public justifications of torture in the war on terror.

LINDA R. TROPP is Professor of Social Psychology at the University of Massachusetts Amherst, United States. Her research concerns how members of different groups approach and experience contact with each other, and how group differences in status and power affect cross-group relations. She is the co-author of *When Groups Meet: The Dynamics of Intergroup Contact* (2011), editor of the *Oxford Handbook of Intergroup Conflict* (2012), and co-editor of *Moving beyond Prejudice Reduction: Pathways to Positive Intergroup Relations* (2011) and *Improving Intergroup Relations* (2008).

MELANI VAN DER MERWE is a PhD candidate in criminal justice at the University of Cape Town, South Africa. She received a B.A. in criminology, anthropology and psychology from the University of Pretoria as well as an honour's and a master's degree in criminal justice from the University of Cape Town.

WOUTER WERNER is Professor of Public International Law at VU University, Amsterdam, the Netherlands. His main fields of interest are international legal theory, the interplay between international law and international politics, and the international legal regime on the use of force. Recent publications concern the politics of legal cosmopolitanism, the concept of humanity across international law, and the political implications of the International Criminal Court. Recently, Werner has started a project researching documentaries on international criminal law. He is director of the graduate school at VU University and co-founder of the Centre for the Politics of Transnational Law, www.ceptl.org.

Acknowledgments

My largest debt of thanks is to the scholars who agreed to participate in this project. In conceiving of the project, I sought to gather together some of the best recent work on security undertaken by researchers in several disciplines.

When I invited the authors to participate in this multidisciplinary book on security, I threw four challenges at them. First, I asked them each to act as the sole representative of his or her respective discipline. Everyone will agree that in and of itself this is daunting task for any scholar. Second, I asked them to write their chapters with an interdisciplinary audience in mind, laying out clearly how their particular discipline approaches security, while considering how a multidisciplinary dialogue could stimulate and enrich the understanding of security that prevails in their field. Third, I strongly invited each scholar to produce a chapter that served as both a state-of-the-art overview and a thought-provoking piece of argumentation that would push other disciplines to reflect on his or her conceptualizations of security. Fourth, to ensure the book's coherency and to induce interdisciplinary dialogue, I asked each author to engage, directly and without detour, with four questions concerning security: (1) What are the questions orienting the research on security in your discipline? (2) Are there dominant theories of security in your discipline? (3) How is the concept of security studies in your discipline? and (4) What are the biggest strengths and limits of your discipline in the way security is studied and theorized? As the reader will soon realize, each of this volume's contributors has risen to these challenges with undisputable brio, professionalism, and command.

A workshop was held with the contributors in Namur, Belgium, in the spring of 2014. I am indebted to the Department of Political Science, Sociology, and Communication at the University of Namur, the Tocqueville Chair in Security Policies at the University of Namur, to the Department of Political Science at the Free University of

Brussels, and to the Belgium Fonds national de la recherche scientifique for organizational and financial support of this workshop. I thoroughly enjoyed our discussions from the workshop and from the numerous e-mails I exchanged with each contributor, and I thank all the participants for their willingness to have their understanding of security shaken and subjected to debate. Being challenged by a colleague from your own discipline on a particular aspect of security is one thing; being invited to rethink your disciplinary foundations by a scholar from another discipline is another thing altogether.

I am grateful to the efficient team at Cambridge University Press and, in particular, to John Haslam, a great editor. I also want to acknowledge two anonymous reviewers at Cambridge University Press for their stimulating and constructive comments. Finally, I want to thank colleagues in the Department of Politics and International Studies at the University of Cambridge for welcoming this project and for their input and discussion on issues presented in this book.

1 | A multidisciplinary dialogue on security

PHILIPPE BOURBEAU

Security is omnipresent in our daily lives.* From apparent trivialities, such as locking the front door, wearing a helmet to cycle with the kids on a bright Sunday afternoon, or remembering an increasing number of passwords, to more significant issues like dealing with domestic violence, monitoring nuclear proliferation, and limiting ethnic conflicts, security, it seems, is everywhere.

Likewise, the ubiquity of security in almost all social sciences disciplines is undisputable. Groundbreaking work by prominent criminologists has placed the concept of security at the centre of criminological scholarship for many years to come (Loader and Walker 2007; Shearing and Wood 2007; Wood and Dupont 2006; Zedner 2009). In Anthropology, security is an emerging research area that has recently gained substantial traction (Goldstein 2010, 2012; Hamilton and Placas 2011; Holbaard and Pedersen 2013). Geographers have been active in highlighting the ways in which biopolitics, territoriality and resources deeply influence security considerations and vice versa (Dalby 2009; Ingram and Dodds 2009; Le Billon 2012). Security has been one of the paramount research themes in International Relations scholarship for a long time, but only recently has this focus of this framework shifted, permitting previously marginalized perspectives to be increasingly embraced (Abrahamsen and Williams 2011; Adler and Pouliot 2011; Buzan and Hansen 2009). In sum, scholars from all manner of social sciences are turning their attention to the study of this complex concept.

Despite this demonstrated interest in security studies within a host of academic fields, scholars rarely communicate their findings across disciplines. Students of security do not approach the study of security

---

* I would like to thank Keith Krause, Vincent Pouliot, Richard Price, Juha Vuori, and colleagues in the Department of Politics and International Studies at the University of Cambridge for input and discussion on issues presented in this introduction, as well as their helpful comments on previous drafts.

from a shared paradigm, but from a variety of theoretical and conceptual viewpoints fragmented across disciplines. In some cases, these various theoretical viewpoints are seen as competing against each other; in most cases, however, these viewpoints are simply expressed and developed in near total disciplinary isolation. Within any given discipline, work done in the other social sciences on security is at best briefly mentioned, at worse, politely ignored.

This book attempts to bridge these disciplinary canyons. The aim is not to provide a comprehensive theory of security applicable across disciplines, cases, and areas. We do not intend to offer a unique paradigm within which to conduct research on security, nor do we want to propose a unified or orthodox view of the concept. Rather, in revisiting security from an interdisciplinary perspective, the book makes two critical contributions. First, it proposes to take seriously the prospect of a multidisciplinary approach to security. Such an approach is both propitious and timely. The rise in electronic surveillance, the prominence given to immigration as a security threat in Western countries, the concern over climate change and environmental degradation, the recent international interventions (or absence of intervention), and the tension between liberty and security arising from terrorist attacks, have mobilized security scholars to analyse the role and the impact of security in our contemporary social world. These issues, and many others, transcend disciplinary boundaries and create the need for a multidisciplinary analysis of how, why, when, and by whom security is deployed, constructed, institutionalized, and structured. Likewise, studying the strategies and processes by which security is challenged and disputed also entails a multidisciplinary approach. To understand how individual, local, national, and international securitization is produced, reproduced, and transformed, as well as how actors are differentially involved in these processes, requires a consideration of different disciplinary expressions of security. If this book gently shakes the relative disciplinary isolation of security scholars and starts to move the conversation in the direction of a multidisciplinary study of security, it will have achieved its objective.

The cross-disciplinary approach advocated in the present volume offers several advantages for students of security. It liberates scholars from pre-emptive rebuttal of their work as being *only* an importation of work done in another discipline. Scholars are sometimes held dismissively to be borrowers or importers, as if these scholars took the "easy road" by "simply" translating work done in another discipline and tailoring it to their own research theme. International Relations has been (and still is) particularly vulnerable in this regard. Take, for example, the constructivist approach in International Relations – an approach that stresses the social construction of world politics and that is the current dominant perspective among International Relations scholars (even in the United States), according to a recent survey (Maliniak *et al.* 2012). Not so long ago, most constructivists were regarded with contempt as merely translators of work done in sociology (in fact, some would argue that such an attitude still persists in certain sub-fields). Constructivists have gone to great lengths to justify the merits of their approach in its own right, without turning their backs on the fact that that approach has been deeply influenced by sociologists. Acknowledging a multidisciplinary perspective in the study of security invites scholars to move away from the binary distinction of importers/exporters by legitimising and reinforcing cross-disciplinary dialogue. The approach also encourages the consideration of how the different disciplinary understandings of security interact and relate to one another. To be sure, some canyons might still seem too wide to be bridged. Yet, unless we begin the process of opening up cross-disciplinary dialogues on security, scholars might find themselves endlessly trapped in their narrow, discipline-specific fields of inquiry, reinventing the wheel again and again. A multidisciplinary approach encourages scholars to seek external correctives to their own literature gaps and go beyond in-field analytical stalemates.

This is not to suggest that anthropologists should become philosophers or that geographers should become psychologists. I do not wish to "discipline" scholars into embarking on interdisciplinary research projects. It is not the case that all research projects must – or should – be interdisciplinary. Nor do I want to suggest that interdisciplinarity is always, by essence, enlightening. It is not. Work done in an interdisciplinary space has both a dark and a bright side; it is not inherently beneficial. Interdisciplinarity can, for example, be instrumentalized as a disguise to justify a (often hidden) hierarchical understanding of the relationships between disciplines: that is, to produce a unidisciplinary study with "interdisciplinary sugar" on it. Translation problems can also arise, in which scholars import a partial and incomplete set of elements from a discipline to address a given issue, but leave aside the more nuanced understandings of this discipline that have been developed over the years in the literature. Although a parsimonious shortcut might thus be obtained, it is gained at the great expense of exactitude, richness, and complexity.

While acknowledging the importance of these issues, I argue that multidisciplinary studies can offer a unique and insightful approach to an issue, provided that they are structured in a way that allows different disciplines to actually engage in a meaningful debate around a set of mutual concerns. The contributors to this volume certainly demonstrate that a healthy dose of willingness to communicate across disciplines can go a long way toward enhancing, deepening, and strengthening our understanding of the multifaceted expressions of security.

The second contribution of this book is that it offers a rich and unparalleled understanding of how security is understood, studied, and theorized within the social sciences. The contributions included in this volume bring together essays by leading scholars in Anthropology, Criminology, International Political Economy, Geography, Law, Philosophy, Political Science/International Relations, Psychology, and Sociology.[1] Acknowledging that each discipline has its preferred way of framing a research question, of searching for hypotheses, and of conducting research, the contributors were asked to discuss and assess the following four points:

1. **Research questions**
What are the fundamental questions orienting the research on security in your discipline? Is there a large consensus about the benefits of organising the scholarship around these central questions?

2. **Theoretical perspectives**
Are there dominant theories of security in your discipline? Which perspectives are considered marginal? Is the primary objective of the research to propose nomothetic theory building or idiographic explanation?

3. **Research methods**
How is the concept of security studied in your discipline? Is there a dominant research method? Do we observe a clear demarcation between qualitative and quantitative scholarship?

---

[1] The limitation of the present discussion to scholars from these particular disciplines is not intended to imply that other disciplines have nothing meaningful to say about security. They do. Sadly, however, a selection had to be made for feasibility and length purposes.

4. Strengths and limits

What are the biggest strengths and limits of your discipline in the way security is studied and theorized? Would a more interdisciplinary approach to the concept of security help in reducing the identified limits of your discipline?

Although the discussion centres around these questions, the contributors were strongly invited to go beyond a traditional literature review to seize on the prime opportunity to push other disciplines' boundaries and encourage them to seriously evaluate the way they study and theorize security. The results are insightful, commanding, and challenging.

In this chapter, I introduce five unifying conceptual elements and areas of common ground that a multidisciplinary approach to security provides: (i) the referent objects of security are multiples; (ii) the processual nature of security; (iii) the objective and subjective dimensions of security; (iv) the instrumentalization of security as a tool for some other purposes; and (v) the importance of methodological pluralism to a compelling and thorough analysis of security. The first section of this chapter discusses each of these unifying elements in more detail. The second section presents the contributions of each chapter, focusing on the substantive research and analytical tools that each discipline offers, while intertwining and situating these contributions within a multidisciplinary study of security.

Toward a multidisciplinary study of security

While there has been a tendency in the literature on security to consolidate the research into particular disciplines, a need is emerging to zoom in on commonalities rather than differences. The time has come to recognize and harness the strengths of each discipline, and to identify fruitful commonalities that contribute to our understanding of security. One of the objectives is to bolster current research on security by moving the conversation away from disciplinary isolation; sophisticated theoretical and empirical studies do demonstrate the veracity and usefulness of elements of each discipline, an observation that calls implicitly for further investigation into the complementarity of disciplines. Focusing on the factors that unite security scholars, rather than those which separate them, can help us to consolidate security scholarship, allow us to better connect our research with contemporary social world, and open new avenues of collaborative research that have only been tackled in isolation in the past. As the contributions assembled in this volume demonstrate, five unifying conceptual elements of security can be identified. In the next few pages, I turn my attention to each one of them.

Security has multiple referent objects

In the past two decades, scholars from a variety of disciplines have broken wide open the box of the referent object – i.e., the question of what needs to be securitized. The diversification of the referent objects of security in all disciplines is striking. Whereas the state has been for a long time almost the sole referent object of security studies in Geography and International Relations, other referent objects have gained (and are still gaining) increasing attention of late. As Le Billon points out, while some geographers still consider geography as a discipline at the service of statecraft and be deeply connected with state security interests, others have engaged with broader security agendas, including global warming, population displacement, food and health insecurity, and disaster prevention. In a similar vein, while "national security" was one of the signature concepts of International Relations scholarship in the years following World War II, this field of research has witnessed an explosion of referent objects of security. Security scholars in International Relations have increasingly turned their attention to the environment, ethnic relations, immigration, cyberspace, identity, and gender issues, to name just a few.

While Geography and International Relations have increasingly moved away from a sole focus on state security in recent years, Anthropology has moved somewhat in the other direction. Some anthropologists have lately begun to discuss security in the terms established by the state. For instance, in the context of the United States' "war on terror," some anthropologists have offered their expertize on "enemy culture" in the hope of helping the United States to wage counter-insurgency campaigns more effectively (the Human Terrain System program). This approach, which represents the mainstream perspective that has lost its hegemony in Geography and International Relations, is considered marginal in Anthropology. Yet, the mere existence and influence of this approach in a discipline such as Anthropology is revealing of the increasing diversification of referent objects of security in social sciences. In other words, while the diversification of security referent objects has caused a shift away from national security in the disciplines of geography and International Relations, it has led in Anthropology to a renewed focus on the state's defined security imperatives.

Not everyone sees the explosion of referent objects in positive terms, however. In Geography, scholars have argued for the need for a closer engagement with issues of war and peace. For some, the vitality and relevance of Geography "is sustained by engaging relevant topics and other disciplines: the key, real world issue is war and peace, and peace studies is the relevant body of literature" (Flint 2003, 166). Flint's exhortation suggests that, rather than casting itself as a vector for the diversification of security referent objects, one of the biggest contributions that Geography can make to the study of security is precisely not to deviate from its focus on war.

The most vocal resistance to a wider understanding of security referent objects has come from International Relations. Scholars have argued that an "excessive" expansion of security studies threatens its intellectual coherence. According to "orthodox" or "traditional" security scholars, any field of study – even such a massive one as security studies in International Relations – cannot and should not be too elastic. Even though they are sometimes artificial, biased, and restrictive, boundaries are nonetheless a fundamental axiom of a field of research (Miller 2010). Advocates of this standpoint have forcefully argued that to study security is to study "the conditions that make the use of [military] force more likely, the ways that the use of force affects individuals, states, and societies, and the specific policies that states adopt in order to prepare for, prevent, or engage in war" (Walt 1991, 212, see also Wohlforth 2009). For most critical-theory-attuned security scholars, this call exemplified the narrow and obtuse nature of the orthodox strand of security studies; for orthodox security scholars, however, it represented a much-needed attempt to provide the field with coherence and delimitation.

In many respects, these calls for understanding security only in military terms are not only strikingly unidisciplinary in nature but also seem to speak to what security studies should be rather than offering an analysis of current expressions of security. Clearly, other issues than war have entered the realm of security in the past decades, and defining security as (only) the study of the role of military forces in war does not sit well with the vast majority of the literature discussed in this book. Equally, it makes very little sense to exclude the use of military force from security studies – an argument rarely heard in some critical security studies journals. Instead of searching for what security scholars should be studying, which incidentally increases the likelihood of proliferating calls for scholarly closure, the central questions that all contributors to this volume underscore are: why do some issues get securitized and not others?; do all the referent objects of security possess the same significance?; does the interaction of referent objects, and consequently security itself, express itself in scalar terms, or not?

Security is processual

Security is not a fixed attribute or a dispositional quality, but a dynamic and complex process. It is constantly in flux and it does not express itself in a flat, stable or variation-free way. Security, then, does not imply finality, as the process can never be fully completed; security needs to be produced and reproduced all the time. This understanding of security dislodges the scholarship from a research programme that seeks to capture the essence of security, and it consolidates studies on how, when, why, and to what effects an issue becomes securitized.

Several disciplines explicitly recognize that security is processual. Critical anthropologists understand security not as a reality immanent in the public arena but as a process that is produced, reproduced, and transformed through cultural and political forces at work in contemporary societies. In International Law, the process of security is often put in place and then invoked to justify measures that deviate from rules that would otherwise apply. Geographers have recently focused much of their attention on how particular issues are framed within security narratives and practices. Starting from the premise that framing a phenomenon as a security issue is both a performative event and a social process, geographers have focused much of their attention on underscoring the descriptive, prescriptive, and reflexive aspects of the processes of securitization. Equally, many criminologists understand security as a process founded in ambiguity, uncertainty, and incompleteness. As Jan Froestad, Clifford Shearing, and Melani van der Merve points out, multiple calls have been made by criminologists to embrace the study of security rather than to fight it, precisely because security does not breed certainty.

A similar situation is arising in Sociology, where an increasing number of scholars are advocating for a break from the traditional focus on attributes and vectors of economic security or food security to a study of the institutional, discursive, and 'practice' processes by which certain phenomena get to be classified as security issues. In International Relations, one of the most dynamic strands in security studies of late has been research on the process of integrating an issue into security frameworks. Debates persist as to whether the process follows the logic of exception, which holds that speech acts labelling an issue as an existential security threat best explain the securitization process, or the logic of routine, which contends that issues become securitized through the routinized practices of particular social agents (Bourbeau 2014a). Yet, scholars on both sides of the fence share the consensus that security is processual.

In a related way, if security is a process that is constructed, reconstructed and transformed time and time again, then surely the study of security invites analysis of other social mechanisms occurring prior, concurrently, and subsequently to security. For instance, Werner, inspired by the work of Judith Shklar (1986), juxtaposes the logic of security with the logic of legalism in order to highlight and to illustrate why lawyers find it increasingly difficult to accept that international law in fact contain provisions that prioritize the logic of security over the logic of legalism. Such lawyers have, consequently, sought to contain, limit, and fight the logic of security by subjecting it to international legal standards and accepted canons of interpretations. Whereas the politicization process seem to remain within the disciplinary boundaries of International Relations and has been hypothesized as a process that leads to security on some occasions (Williams 2011; Zürn *et al.* 2012), desecuritization (broadly defined as the unmaking of the securitization process) is studied in both Geography and in International Relations. Geographers, such as Hyndman (2007), have argued for the need for desecuritization, on the grounds that security practices create uneven contemporary regimes of power, while heated debates are currently unfolding in International Relations concerning the ethics of desecuritization (Browning and McDonald 2013; Floyd 2014; Hansen 2012; Vuori 2011). Resilience is another social mechanisms interacting with the process of security in Psychology, Geography, and International Relations, where it is interpreted, respectively, as the capacity of an individual to bounce back following a threatening event, the ability of an ecosystem to adapt and regain its equilibrium after a disturbance, and the pattern of adjustments adopted by a society or an individual in the face of endogenous/exogenous shocks (Berkes *et al.* 2003; Bourbeau 2013; Luthar 2003). Elsewhere, I have argued that the process of securitizing an issue is the disturbance in the face of which a resilient strategy is deployed in order to challenge, counter, and debunk the dominant security-attuned reading of the issue at hand. The collective strategy is not to take the issue out of the security realm (i.e., to de-securitize it) but rather to build social and community resilience in the face of an increasingly securitized world (Bourbeau 2014b, 2015).

Objectivity, subjectivity, intersubjectivities, and security

A central theme in several disciplines is the distinction between objective and subjective dimensions of security. In Philosophy, the objective/subjective dichotomy juxtaposes the idea, points out Jonathan Herington, that security is the actual protection against basic forms of violence with the idea that security is constituted by freedom from the fear of violence. This debate exhibits striking parallels with the much-talked about concept of ontological security (Giddens 1991; Kinnvall 2004; Mitzen 2006; Noble 2005; Steele 2008).

While the objective/subjective differentiation finds its way into Criminology literature, it is at the heart of the scholarship in Sociology. As Lisa Stampnitsky and Greggor Mattson note, sociological studies on security are divided into two strands. One sees security as an "objective, real state of affairs" and seeks "to measure the realities of security" in fields of research including economic security, social security, and family security. The other strand of literature emphasizes the subjective, socially constructed dimension of security, including how individuals perceive security dangers and the production of knowledge associated with discourses about security.

In International Relations, the objective/subjective dichotomy goes back to one of the founding texts of the discipline. In the early 1950s, Arnold Wolfers (1952, 485) argued that "security, in an objective sense, measures the absence of threats to acquired values, in subjective sense, the absence of fear that such values will be attacked." From 1950 to the mid 1980s, the focus was decidedly on the objective components, with the military agenda of security questions surrounding nuclear weapons and their proliferations omnipresent in the literature. In the late 1980s, with the end of the Cold War, the pendulum swung to the other side, helped by poststructuralist and critical scholars who argued that security is self-referential and does not refer to objective threat; security is thus open to interpretation.

Psychologists offer a unique spin on the debate. Studies of intergroup conflicts distinguish between realistic threat and symbolic threat. The former refers to the perception by one group that its security and very existence are imperilled by another group, while the latter refers to the perception by one group that its way of life or value system is endangered by the presence of an outgroup. Drawing a distinction between types of threats is important, argue psychologists, because it can have profound consequences on intergroup relations and their potential conflict.

A good example of the diversity and disciplinary interconnectedness of security studies can be found in the realm of human security. Indeed, human security is a concern that transcends disciplinary isolation, with anthropologists, geographers, psychologists, and scholars of Law and International Relations actively participating in the debate (Eriksen *et al.* 2010; Matthew *et al.* 2009; Owen and Martin 2014). Leaving aside both the exhilaration and the lambasting which have arisen concerning human security, the fact remains that the emergence of human security as one of the most important referent objects of security studies has put the objective/subjective divide at the forefront of the scholarship. Caroline Thomas (2000), on the one hand, regards human security as describing an indivisible "condition of existence," while Roland Paris (2001, 2004) and Kyle Grayson (2008), on the other hand, contend, respectively, that the numerous definitions of human security illustrate the inherent subjectivity and asymmetrical power relations of the concept. Analysing the ways in which the objective/subjective security divide is connected with the diversification of referent objects of security should capture a good deal of scholarly (and interdisciplinary) attention in the near future.

Scholars have recently tried to reconcile the objective/subjective divide by proposing a middle-ground position that accepts the existence and the complementarity of both objective and subjective security threats. In laying out the foundations for her analysis of the link between security and justice, Rita Floyd (2011) argues that while one can accept that threats become security threats by virtue of social and political construction, some threats are real and objectively present whether or not anyone has even taken note of them. Although Herington disagrees with such a dualist position, he nonetheless acknowledges that some philosophers have also started to move in that direction as well (e.g., Waldron 2006).

Building on the objective/subjective debate, the idea of intersubjectivities has gained momentum of late in several disciplines. In Geography, this discussion takes place under the rubric of space. On the one hand, mainstream security geography understands space as a set of "facts" guiding the elaboration of security policies. Using Geographical Information Systems (GIS), for example, scholars can describe the spatial pathways by which security threats are diffused. On the other hand, reflexive geographers have proposed a wider understanding of space that underscores the importance of intersubjectivities, social dimensions, and the contingent historical particularities of spatial "facts."

Intersubjectivities are a focal point as well in International Relations, although most of the discussion in this discipline centres on the role of political communities. Scholars have argued that, rather than focusing on objective security threats (and their measurements) from which all communities must seek to protect themselves, we might more fruitfully focus on security as an intersubjective process. Different communities identify some issues as security issues and not others, diachronically and synchronically. Most scholars would not reject the idea that some issues have nearly universal security implications or that some security situations have less interpretation "space" than others. However, proponents of an intersubjective approach to security point out that, by examining how a given community interprets and potentially securitizes an issue, we gain insight into how security is expressed, conveyed, experienced, and dealt with.

This standpoint dovetails neatly with recent psychological research on security, although the latter focuses on groups rather than political communities. This scholarship has indeed been arguing for some time now that examining how different groups perceive and react to security threats provides fertile grounds for theorizing intergroup conflicts. A much-discussed hypothesis in the literature (which for some is now an accepted and confirmed proposition due to the weight of favourable evidence accumulated over the years) holds that greater perceived threat is typically accompanied by greater xenophobia and greater support for violent policies against outgroups.

Security is instrumentalized

The instrumentalization of security – the idea that security, rather than being regarded in absolute terms or as an objective to aspired to, should be seen as an instrument or a tool for some other purposes – can take several forms. The use of security, and in particular of national security, for political purposes is well documented, whether in the form of authoritarian regimes instrumentalising security to legitimize their positions of power, or in the form of a democratic leader invoking security to legitimize particular policy viewpoints on a given issue.

Werner offers a unique perspective on the instrumentalization of security. He argues that, in international law, security often works as a "trump card" allowing agents to present in an acceptable way the deviation from – or the annulment of – rules that would otherwise apply. Readers attuned to Securitization Theory as developed by Buzan *et al.* (1998) will find his discussion particularly insightful.

In broader terms, security is also seen, on some occasions, as a neoliberal tool for governance. Strands of the literature in several disciplines understand security, and the production of security discourses, as representing regimes of power that produce vast inequalities. The omnipresence of security and its ever-expanding jurisdiction serve in part to reproduce and to legitimize time and time again a particular neoliberal mode of governance. To be sure, most scholars go at great lengths to contextualize and relativise this claim. They don't argue that security is *by nature* a neoliberal strategy for higher social controls across time, areas, and cultures. While this claim constitutes the mainstream approach to security in some disciplines (Anthropology), it is a marginal one in others (Criminology, Psychology), and a much-discussed alternative in others (Geography, International Relations, and Sociology). Yet, in all disciplines, there is the notion that the omnipresent, ever-expanding umbrella of security serves in parts to reproduce and to legitimize neoliberal forms of governance.

Ronen Palan and Hannah Petersen show that a large section of the International Political Economy literature understands security as a social process at the service of the (re)production of a particular type of governance by a dominant class. Taken in this context, security represents the language of power and of domination by the ruling class; in short, security is nothing less than a form of violence.

Many anthropologists see security as a set of power-infused discourses and practices that fully participate in neoliberal processes of creating, consolidating, and advancing a particular socio-political order. Promoting a "critical anthropology of security," these scholars seek to demonstrate that the process of securitization is coloured by and maintained through the relation of power within a given historical (and neoliberal) context. Geographers have also highlighted the instrumentalization of security as a neoliberal component of global governance. Scholars have talked about a neoliberal nexus between security and biopolitics, or about security as an effect of neoliberalization. The instrumentalization of security has also been a key research theme in Criminology. Some scholars have criticized mainstream criminology for viewing only the bright side of security, and ignoring the fact that security is in fact a mode of governance that shapes societies around a specific ideology of order. In this sense, security is seen as a discursive practice allowing governmental authority to neutralize political resistance and thus legitimize the institutional violence on which the contemporary social-political order is built.

Yet, it would be a mistake to reduce security to a neoliberal product at the service of state domination. Although security may be in some instances a neoliberal device for governance, it has a wider range of meanings as well – a point to which the numerous chapters of this volume unequivocally testify to. The relationship between security and contemporary global governance is multifaceted, and one of the fruitful ways to tackle the complexity of the relationship might be to combine insights from one discipline with expertise of another discipline. For instance, International Relations scholar Rita Floyd (2011) has proposed to take seriously the morality of the process of securitising an issue. Inspired by the "Just war" theory developed in Philosophy (McMahan 2002; Orend 2013; Walzer 2006), she argues that, if there is an objective existential threat endangering a morally legitimate referent object to which a security response is seen as appropriate, then and only then will the securitising process be morally right and justifiable. Floyd's approach is one path among many. As the reader will discover, the contributors to this volume offers numerous, equally strong propositions including among many others a combination of Geography-attuned idea of the Anthropocene to Criminology to push criminologists toward developing a security focus in their field, or a suggestion to blend Psychological and Sociology's work on symbols and symbolic security representations. Such an multifaceted approach to security not only enhances our understanding of the possibility that a multidisciplinary approach offers, but also provides further incentive for taking a broad approach in analysing the complexity of the relationship between security and contemporary local, national, and global governance.

Security invites methodological pluralism

Although each discipline has its preferred ways to frame research questions that relate to security and, thus, to organize a research design, a willingness to study security with methodological pluralism is hard to miss upon reading the contributions included in this book. The pluralism implies the transdisciplinarity of methods; methods usually associated with one particular discipline are increasingly employed in other disciplines. Take, for example, the experimental method, which is closely associated with Psychology. A particular strength of experimental research design, as O'Brien and Tropp remind us, is that it demonstrates causal relationships between variables while controlling for a range of variables that might influence relationships among those variables. Yet, scholars in Geography, Anthropology, and International Relations have capitalized on the strength of this method – without disregarding the numerous concerns that have been raised about the generalizability of applying experiments to real-world situations – and have employed experimental research design in their own studies on security (Gartner 2008; Johnson *et al.* 2014; Levy 1997; Mercer 2010, Mintz *et al.* 2006; Tucker 2012).

Another example of methodological transdisciplinarity is the use of ethnography, which represents the main research method in Anthropology. As Goldstein notes, ethnography grounds anthropologists' "interpretations in the observed realities of life actually lived." At the same time, ethnography has also been employed in International Relations and Geography, and has made a significant contribution to the study of security in these disciplines (Ackerly *et al.* 2006; Cohn 2012; Hyndman 2004; Megoran 2006; Tickner 1997; Wilkinson 2011). Experimentation and ethnography are not alone; discourse analysis, process tracing, content analysis, and statistical analysis are methods found across the broad range of disciplines covered in this book.

There is another facet to this pluralism: increasingly, scholars use a combination of research methods when studying security. Of course, these scholars would not necessarily label their work as the "mixed–method" described by Johnson, Onwuegbuzie, and Turner (2007). Nor do all such scholars subscribe to James Fearon's and David Laitin's (Fearon and Laitin 2008; Laitin 2002) provocative argument that a research design should involve a combination of qualitative research methods, formal theory, and statistics. Yet, a consensus is emerging that one of the most useful ways to understand the multifaceted process of security is by drawing evidence from several research methods. The process of combining methods can take three forms: first, an intra-qualitative (or quantitative) combination in which several qualitative methods (such as interviews, content analysis, ethnography, genealogy, and so on) are employed; second, a sequential use allowing evidence obtained through qualitative research method to be contrasted with – or enriched by – findings obtained through quantitative (or formalization) research method (or vice versa); third, a concurrent use where qualitative and quantitative data are collected simultaneously in order to provide the most comprehensive analysis of a particular securitized issue. As the contributions assembled in this book show, Geography, International Relations, Psychology, and Sociology all use sequential and/or concurrent methodological combinations. Overall, the incorporation of a multiplicity of research methods into our quest to better understand security is both immensely valuable and desirable.

The question of whether security should be understood in binary terms is an important one to be raised in the context of methodological pluralism. By and large, scholars have studied whether an issue is securitized or not. The question of *level, intensity,* or *variation* of security is, by contrast, rather underdeveloped and under-theorized in all disciplines included in this book. Scholars distinguish between un-securitized and securitized issues, but once an issue enters the security realm, no further distinction is made. In other words, security is largely seen as a one-size-fits-all concept.

This tendency calls into question the issue of how to distinguish, label, describe, and measure variation in security. Variation can be problematized across cases, across time, and across issues. This is not a disguised attempt to squeeze post-positivist scholars within the confines of a single and dominant model of understanding variation in security. The study of the level or intensity of security need not and should not be limited to one particular epistemology. The main point is that not all interpretations of a phenomenon are equal, not all dangers are equal, and not all securitized issues are equal. It certainly seems important for scholars to consider whether, for example, security practices that relate to migration are more or less prevalent in one country vs. another, and in one time period vs. another. It also seems relevant to be able to determine whether migration is securitized to the same extent as, say, nuclear weapons. And if a given issue is "more" securitized than another issue, it also seems rather pertinent to be able to pinpoint the knowledge mechanisms through which we have arrived at this conclusion.

This speaks to the issue of generalization. While some security scholars aim to present an understanding/explanation of security that is applicable across cases and times, others bristle at the idea of generalizing their set of arguments beyond the specifics of their particular study. While it is hard to dispute the (generalizing) claim that throughout history, humans have sought security for themselves and their loved ones, it is equally difficult to disregard the argument that security has expressed itself quite differently across spaces and times. Similarly, accepting the possibility of generalization within and across the social sciences does not necessarily mean searching for all-inclusive, comprehensive, or law-like generalizations. There are reasons to believe that circumscribed, confined or contextualized generalizations not only exist, but are relevant and welcome in the social sciences. Surely, then, investigating the generalizability of security might include problematizing the variation in security.

Several disciplines are participating in this effort. Philosophers draw a distinction between "thick" and "thin" security. While the former captures the idea that security is an inescapable component of an individual's state of being, the latter conveys the notion that security is a mode of enjoying other goods. In Geography, one of the foci has been to interrogate and to compare the spatialities of security issues in terms of whether they were global, regional, or local (Ingram and Dodds 2009). In International Relations, I have proposed to distinguish between weak and strong securitization in my comparative analysis of legal documents, policy statements, and security practices that relates to the securitization of migration in Canada and France between 1989 and 2005 (Bourbeau 2011). Undoubtedly, initiating a dialogue among these ways of understanding security in scalar terms will significantly enhance our comprehension of contemporary and multifaceted expressions of security.

Organization of the volume

In Chapter 2, Jonathan Herington traces with unquestionable clarity the philosophical evolution of the concept of security from the Romans and the Epicureans to the contemporary usage, demonstrating that a major shift occurred in the Enlightenment era. Whereas security was understood in the pre-Enlightenment period as a sense of internal-psychological calm attained through a detachment from religious or political commitments, it came to be interpreted in the Enlightenment as physical safety in the inescapable condition of war that can only be guaranteed by a political authority. The work of Thomas Hobbes was pivotal in this regard, argues Herington. Noting that contemporary philosophers have treated security with relative neglect, he nonetheless explores with great insight the current engagements of philosophy with security, notably the metaphor of a balance between security and liberty, that security is an "essentially contested concept," and the proliferation of untargeted surveillance of private communications and public spaces.

Daniel Goldstein, in Chapter 3, explores the complex engagement of Anthropology with security by arguing that in some ways Anthropology has always been concerned with security. To do so, he draws a distinction between "security anthropologists" and "critical anthropologists of security." The former engage with security in terms determined by the state, while the latter advance an understanding of security as a set of discourses and practices producing particular social realities and social differentiations. Goldstein underscores that anthropologists are not "strict disciplinarians" but "omnivorous" and deeply interdisciplinary scholars when it comes to the study of security. Anthropology is thus superbly positioned, argues Goldstein, to make sense of contemporary expressions of security and of insecurity, which have become so complex that a single disciplinary approach is bound to offer only a partial understanding. Among the strengths of Goldstein's analysis is his illustration of the insights that critical anthropologists of security bring to the study of the securitization of migration in the United States. He contends that ethnographic approaches can not only reveal the repressive practices of both state and local governments, but can also uncover the strategies employed by migrants themselves to contest these security practices.

Philippe Le Billon splendidly makes the case for taking a critical stance on security in Geography in Chapter 4. Wanting to move beyond the traditional understanding of Geography as a discipline in the service of statecraft (particularly with issues involving national security), he shows that geographers have engaged with broader security agendas, including human security and environmental security. Le Billon convincingly demonstrates that geographers have also been particularly interested in sites of desecuritization where, on the one hand, the impact of spatial security representations, discourses and practices on social power relations is exposed, and, on the other hand, alternative narratives are proposed.

Lisa Stampnitzky and Greggor Mattson, in Chapter 5, explore how Sociology theorizes and studies security. They argue that the study of security within Sociology is bifurcated, with a small but robust tradition that studies political security alongside other disciplines, while the disciplinary core has focused on social, economic, or interpersonal insecurity. In comparing these two sociological conceptualizations, the authors suggest that scholars should distinguish between political security as an explicit object of discourse and practice, and security as a broader category of cultural understandings of safety and disorder. They conclude with a univocal and compelling message: one of Sociology's unique contributions to a multidisciplinary study of security is to provide tools to examine the relationships among these different kinds of (in)security – connections that are lost when research focuses solely on external threats to the nation at the expense of internal, domestic processes.

In Chapter 6, Philippe Bourbeau, Thierry Balzacq, and Myriam Dunn Cavelty celebrate the eclectic dynamism of security studies in International Relations. They discuss three preconceptions or myths that seem to be persisting: (i) that security's typical referent object is still national security, (ii) that American scholars produce mainstream security studies while European scholars are the gatekeepers of critical security studies, and (iii) that critical approaches to security are incompatible with methods generally associated with a positivist epistemology, whereas orthodox or traditional approaches to security cannot work with anything other than a positivist epistemology. They highlight works that cut across traditional divides and that shift the discussion towards the factors that unite security scholars rather than those that divide them to argue, ultimately, that International Relations is in a superb position to embrace and champion a multidisciplinary approach to security.

Thomas O'Brien and Linda Troop, in Chapter 7, examine how the discipline of Psychology tackles the issue of security and insecurity. Starting from the assumption that insecurity is an undesirable psychological state that people feel motivated to act upon and diminish, they analyse the psychological factors that typically predict feeling of security between groups. Focusing on intergroup relations, they underscore the many factors that can induce (in)security on a phenomenological level, such as an individual's threat perceptions, emotional responses to conflict, and identity as a member of various social groups. Studying these factors is central is gaining a better understanding of situations in which a group seeks a renewed sense of security through in-group protective measures, contend O'Brien and Tropp. They conclude with a strong and coherent set of strategies to enhance feelings of security, including the deconstruction and reconstruction of boundaries between groups toward superordinate group identity and dual identities.

In Chapter 8, Ronen Palan and Hannah Petersen examine the deep interconnections between International Political Economy and security. Their main claim is that, contrary to common perceptions, all major theories of International Political Economy assume a connection between economy, stability, and security. They raise the stakes by arguing that attempts to ignore this intimate connection are bound to lead to analytical failure. In urging scholars not to consider political economy and security in isolation, Palan and Petersen expose the roots and influence of various strands of political economy paradigms in the study of security.

Jan Froestad, Clifford Shearing, and Melani Van der Merwe, in Chapter 9, describe how strands of criminology have started to move beyond the traditional focus on crime and crime management to embrace the notion of security and of security governance. This is a road littered with hurdles, however; the authors underscore the relatively high level of resistance with which this strand of scholarship is received by some fellow criminologists. Nonetheless, they argue that if criminology wants to embrace the notion of security, the discipline

A multidisciplinary dialogue on security

will have to abandon its reliance on a Hobbesian understanding of the management of human-to-human relationships as the foundational order of security, as well as its reliance on the criminal justice system as a set of responses to security threats. Readers will find their analysis challenging and penetrating.

Finally, Wouter Werner, in Chapter 10, argues for a more methodologically informed study of security in the field of international law. His main claim is twofold. He first demonstrates that, although methods seems generally left unconsidered, the literature is structured by a well-developed set of assumptions that allow certain forms of argumentative practices and exclude others, notably the widely shared assumption that "international law is ultimately rooted in the consent and practices of states." Werner also shows that the logic of legalism and the logic of securitization are very much in competition. Using the case of the United Nations Security Council, he shows that the Security Council is empowered to use security as a trump card that allows deviation from rules that would otherwise apply. The fact that security provisions prioritize the logic of securitization over the logic of legalism in the highest political organ of the UN has profound methodological and theoretical consequences for international lawyers, superbly contends Werner.

2 | *Philosophy*
The concepts of security, fear, liberty, and the state

JONATHAN HERINGTON

Security language is opaque. When we hear or read the word "security" we are often left to guess at its precise meaning: at the epistemic and evaluative claims that are being made by the author or speaker. In part, the opacity of the word "security" is the result of a complex etymological history and a corresponding proliferation in contemporary definitions of what it means to be secure. Philosophical engagement with security promises to make clear the structure, content, hidden value commitments, and (potential) incoherence of the concept as it is used in other disciplines. From an explanatory perspective, precise definitions of security give scholars a standard to assess descriptive claims about the presence or absence of security and forge explanatory linkages between security and other concepts (such as power, domination, and justice). Normatively, philosophical engagement with security can help structure critiques of security policy, identifying the precise values at stake and the hidden moral commitments of particular policy approaches. Yet, by and large, this promise has gone unfulfilled. While security seems central to many moral and political problems, sustained examination of the concept by contemporary philosophers is rare.

In this chapter I seek to reignite philosophical interest in security by uncovering some of the ways in which the concept has been both understood and misunderstood. I begin by exploring the scarce historical understandings of security within the Western philosophical canon, from the Epicureans through Hobbes and on to contemporary political philosophy, identifying the key themes that arise within the literature. I then provide an account of the structure of the concept of security, which lays bare its relationship to contemporary debates on the distinction between "natural" and "social" threats, on the political significance of fear, and on the nature of rights. Finally, I identify four key problems in moral and political philosophy – the balance between state and individual security, between liberty and security; the status of moral principles during emergencies; and the trade-off between privacy and public safety – where a finer grained understanding of security can benefit normative theorizing.

I. The history of "security"

Contemporary usage of the term "security" includes an incredible diversity of meaning.[1] It can denote a type of financial instrument, a psychological condition, systems of defense, a physical state of being, and much more besides. While much of this contemporary diversity appeared only in the twentieth century, it is the product of a long and complex etymological history. In what follows I lay out a roughly chronological history of the word "security," highlighting the major shifts in meaning and emphasis from its etymological antecedents in Greek and Latin through to the twentieth century.

The ancients and ataraxia

The direct etymological antecedent of "security" is the Latin *securitas*, which literally translates as "freedom from care" (from the phrase *sine cura*: without care) (*Oxford Latin Dictionary* 1982). While there are some important ambiguities, Roman and medieval usage of *securitas* referred primarily to a serene state of mind (see Arends 2008, 269). This state of mind was, in the pre-Christian era at least, intimately connected with a quiet and reflective life disconnected from the baser pursuits of politics, business, and society. In this sense, *securitas* and the reflective life that accompanied it were not only seen as valuable but were so virtuous as to be the "object of supreme desire" (Cicero quoted in Rothschild 1995, 61).

This close connection between the early Roman usage of *securitas* and a serene disposition is a product of its association with the Greek concept of 'ἀταραξία' (*ataraxia*), which refers to an "impassiveness (or) calmness" (Liddell and Scott 1940). This concept is associated predominantly with the Epicurean tradition, which viewed the possession of a serene disposition as one of the prerequisites for *eudaimonia* ("flourishing") (Striker 1990). The Epicureans viewed the attainment

---

[1] At least 20 different definitions of the noun "security," a further 21 definitions of the adjective/adverb "secure," and 28 of the verb "secure" can be found in the 2nd edition of the *Oxford English Dictionary*.

of *ataraxia* as a purely internal project, not only unbound from the concrete facts of an individual's circumstance, but hindered by too great a participation in civic life. *Ataraxia*, rather than something that could be furthered by living within a functioning political community, was to be found in detaching oneself from religious and political commitments and pursuing a life of quiet reflection.

The notion that the Roman concept of *securitas* is synonymous with the Greek concept of *ataraxia* is attractive, but there are two important caveats to this simple story. First, *securitas* was not solely associated with a state of mind, but also with the concrete circumstances that made the attainment of that state of mind possible. While in early Latin *securitas* may have straightforwardly referred to an inner calm, in later Roman usage (c. first–third century CE) *securitas* became associated with the Pax Romana, which assured the physical safety and political liberty of Roman citizens (Arends 2008, 270). The printing of coins declaring *securitas publica* and *securitas perpetua* during the tumultuous reign of Gallienus typifies this shift, insofar as the coins formed part of a propaganda effort to remind citizens of the empire that underwrote their comparatively serene and carefree lives (Hammond 1963; Mathew 1943). The Epicurean notion that *securitas* was a purely internal project was thus replaced by an acknowledgment that concrete circumstances could undermine the attainment of tranquility.

Second, *securitas* was not always viewed as a valuable trait. The literal Latin meaning of "freedom from care" imbues the term with an ambiguous value: sometimes denoting an admirable quality of calm wisdom, sometimes denoting foolhardy self-assuredness or carelessness (Arends 2008, 269). As the meaning of *securitas* shifted to encompass the external circumstances that underpinned an individual's carefree state of mind, it further reinforced that an individual could be unjustifiably carefree. Indeed, early Christian usage of *securitas* referred to a sinful kind of certitude, and this meaning carried over into early English usage of the word.[2] Thus, as the connection between *securitas* and the external world began to strengthen, so did the term acquire a negative connotation.

While these points complicate the picture, the meaning of *securitas* is dominated during the pre-Enlightenment period by an association with

---

[2] See the use in *Macbeth*: "security; Is mortals' chiefest enemy" (Shakespeare 1988, act 3, scene 5, line 31).

a sense of internal calm and freedom from fear. The classic association between *ataraxia* and *securitas* inaugurates the connection between the concept of security and freedom from fear. This is security as a psychological disposition – manifested as a defeasibly valuable state of mind that individuals hold largely without reference, or in opposition, to their external circumstances. Some of this sense remains in standard usage throughout the Latinate languages. In modern French, *sécurité* principally denotes the feeling of being safe, and the Spanish, *seguridad*, also holds a similar sense. Since the great works of Enlightenment political philosophy, however, the English language concept has lost much of this meaning. We now turn to consider this shift.

The Enlightenment and asphaleia

Although pre-Enlightenment usage of *securitas* is profoundly influenced by the concept of *ataraxia*, during the Enlightenment, *securitas* (and in English "security") came to be associated with an entirely different Greek concept: ἀσφαλεία (*asphaleia*). In the Greek, *asphaleia* is a negation of *sphallô*, which is a term associated with ancient wrestling, meaning "make to fall, overthrow, (properly) by tripping up" (Liddell and Scott 1940). Ancient Greek usage of *asphaleia* mostly implied the physical stability of an individual or object, but, as Arends (2008, 265) notes, it was also used to denote the stability of city-states and empires. The most prominent example of such usage is found in Thucydides' *History of the Peloponnesian Wars*. In the famous dialogue between the Athenians and the Melians, *asphaleia* is repeatedly used by Thucydides to denote the stability of the Athenian Empire (see, in particular, book V, chap. 91–99). The preoccupation of the Athenians is to prevent the bloody collapse of their empire and ultimately the "overthrow" (here, a version of *sphallô*) of their city-state by its former colonies in violent war. *Asphaleia*, in this sense, bears a striking resemblance to the modern concept of national security.

The association between "security" and *asphaleia* owes much to the peculiar intellectual trajectory of Thomas Hobbes, and the profound influence of his thought on later political philosophers. Hobbes's first substantial work, written well before his influential political philosophy, was his 1628 translation of *The History* into English. In this formative work, Hobbes translated *asphaleia* as, variously: "assurance," "protection," "safety," and "security" (Thucydides 1843). The preoccupation with stability and protection within Thucydides' work, particularly from physical violence and war, infused the later Hobbes's work and his usage of the word "security" (see Schlatter 1945). In his first substantial original work, *The Elements of Law* (1640), we see the emergence of a political philosophy preoccupied with physical safety, which he equates with security:

> The end for which one man giveth up, and relinquisheth to another, or others, the right of protecting and defending himself by his own power, is the security which he expecteth thereby, of protection and defence from those to whom he doth so relinquish it. And a man may then account himself in the estate of security, when he can foresee no violence to be done unto him. (Hobbes 1994, chap. 20)

Thus, writing *Leviathan* in 1651, he supposes that the "end of common-wealth" is "security," by which he meant the mechanism by which citizens get "themselves out from that miserable condition of war" (Hobbes 1996, chap. 17, §1). Furthermore, in Hobbes's subsequent Latin translation of *Leviathan* (published in 1668), he uses *securitas* to refer to just the same concept of physical safety. Hobbes's use of "security" and *securitas* to denote physical safety is an important milestone in the history of the word and highlights that for Hobbes "security" (and *securitas*) refers to the Thucydidean concept rather than the Epicurean affect.

Hobbes's interpretation of security not only firmly establishes the primacy of the concrete over the psychological in the concept of security; it also inaugurates the Enlightenment belief that security can only be *guaranteed* by a political authority. For Hobbes, the legitimacy of the state is dependent on its ability to protect its citizens "from the invasion of foreigners, and the injuries of one another" (Hobbes 1996, chap. 18, §13). Hobbes famously contends that citizens seeking security can only achieve that end by subordinating their natural right to self-defense to the state.[3] Writing in a similar vein, Locke, in 1690, considers that the tie that binds men and women in political community is one that "secure(s) them from injury and violence" (Locke 1690, book II, chap. 2, §8). Later figures, such as Condorcet, Paine, and Rousseau, likewise saw security as a guarantee, given by the state, that

---

[3] For a commentary on the moral basis of Hobbes's political theory, see Sorell (2007).

citizens would be protected from violence against their person and property (Rothschild 1995, 63–65). This is stated in even starker terms by Leibniz, who *defines* the state "a great society of which the object is *la seureté commune* (the common security)."[4] The motif, running throughout Enlightenment political philosophy, is that a citizen should not merely be free from moment to moment from violence: She should be *assured* that she will be safe. The association between "security" and a guarantee is noted later by Bentham:

> Man is not like the brutes, limited to the present time, either in enjoyment or suffering, but that he is susceptible of pleasure and pain by anticipation, and that it is not enough to guard him against an actual loss, but also to guarantee to him, as much as possible, his possessions against future losses. The idea of his security must be prolonged to him throughout the whole vista that his imagination can measure. (Bentham 1843, chap. 7)

By grasping the sense of security as an assurance or a guarantee from one entity to another, Bentham illustrates another important connection: that between security and the domain of rights. Indeed, in many Enlightenment and industrial era accounts, security is enshrined as a right that is one of the preconditions for the enjoyment of all other rights. As Condorcet characterizes it: The "natural rights of humanity" begin with "the security of one's person, a security which includes the assurance that one will not be troubled by violence, either within one's family or in the use of one's faculties" (Condorcet, quoted in Rothschild 1995, 67). For Mill, it was the case that security was "the most vital of all interests" since

> on (security) we depend for all our immunity from evil, and for the whole value of all and every good, beyond the passing moment; since nothing but the gratification of the instant could be of any worth to us, if we could be deprived of anything the next instant by whoever was momentarily stronger than ourselves. (Mill 1991, 190)

The French Revolution, echoing this concern for the necessity of security, enshrined the rights to "*la liberté, la propriété, la sûreté et*

---

[4] Leibniz, writing in French, employs *sûreté* to denote an objective state of being safe, rather than the psychological feeling of being safe denoted by *sécurité*: 'Ma définition de l'Estat, ou de ce que chez les Latins est appellé *Respublica* est: que c'est une grande societé don't le but est la seureté commune' (My definition of the State, or of what the Latins call Respublica is: that it is a great society of which the end is common security) (Leibniz 1864, 143).

la résistance à l'oppression" (*Déclaration des droits de l'homme et du citoyen* 1789, para. 2). Whereas the state guaranteed each individual's interest in *sûreté*, the wider freedom from anxiety denoted by *sécurité* was the preserve and responsibility of each individual (Rothschild 1995, 63). For political philosophers of this era, security is thus a fundamental objective of all individuals that can only be gained through the state. Rational actors seeking protection from the violence of others form the state to safeguard this fundamental interest. More importantly, the state is seen as *necessary* for the maintenance of security, in stark contrast to the inner calm of Roman *securitas*, to which it is at best irrelevant or, at worst, an impediment. The necessity of the state to security thus becomes enshrined within the concept itself.

Contemporary work

Given this rich intellectual history, we might expect a great deal of contemporary philosophical work on security. Yet while the concepts of justice, liberty, and equality have all been thoroughly interrogated and interpreted by contemporary political philosophers (see, for instance, Anderson 1999; Pettit 1996; Rawls 1985), literature explicitly targeting the concept of security is sparse.[5] Analysis of the concept of security has largely been the domain of scholars in international relations (and particularly the subfield of "critical security studies"): producing reinterpretations of national security, human security, and the process of securitization. This is not to say, however, that contemporary political philosophy has no contribution to make to the study of security. First, philosophy is uniquely placed to help clear the conceptual thicket that has accumulated around security, identifying the conflicts and complementarities among the various conceptions of security. Second, the content of the concept of security can be informed by parallel debates within political philosophy on the status of natural and social threats, objective and subjective harms, and the nature of rights. Finally, long-standing debates within moral and political philosophy on the status of torture, privacy, and emergency powers may help inform discussions on the normative status of "security

[5] The only contemporary analyses of security I am aware of within the Anglo-American philosophical literature are Herington (2012), Waldron (2006), and John (2011). This can be contrasted with the deep interest in the concept among scholars in the Continental political tradition (see Foucault 2004; Gros 2012).

policies" within other disciplines. Philosophical engagement with the concept of security therefore ought to be a foundational component of the interdisciplinary conversation.

II. A conceptual structure

Given the diversity of historical and contemporary understandings of security (many of which are explored in other chapters within this volume), it is unsurprising that security is often described as an "essentially contested concept" (Buzan 1983, 6; Smith 2005, 27–28). A concept (x) is *contested* when there are many conceptions of $x(x_1, x_2, \ldots x_n)$, each vying to be the proper definition of x (Swanton 1985, 811). While each conception may implicitly or explicitly agree to the concepts' "common core," and there may be agreement that some conceptions are clearly ill-fitting, no consensus exists on which of the reasonable conceptions is uniquely fitting. This contest over the concept becomes *essential* when x is an evaluative concept (e.g., liberty, beauty, goodness, right), potentially constituted by a complex set of internal parts, which requires each conception to make a judgment on the relative contribution of each part to the concept's overall evaluative character.[6] The heavy emphasis on value commitments within these conditions has lead most commentators to suggest that a concept is essentially contested, rather than merely contingently contested, when "rival uses of it express conflicting moral and political commitments between which reason cannot arbitrate" (Gray 1977, 334). On a straightforward reading of essential contestability, it therefore seems as though we have good reason to suppose that security is an essentially contested concept. It signifies something valued,[7] it is internally complex, and its constituent parts are held to contribute to its value in a diverse set of ways. Indeed, definitions of security are seen as "derivative" of conflicting visions of the "character and purpose of politics" (Booth 2007, 109).

Properly understood, however, "security" does not refer to a single essentially contested concept. Rather, we can distinguish at least three

---

[6] This characterization is derived from the work of Gallie (1955, 171–172), Gray (1977), and Swanton (1985).

[7] Cf. Baldwin (1997, 10–12), who suggests that security cannot be evaluative because it is not the sole or primary goal of states. This seems to me a misreading of "essential contestability," since something can obviously be valued even if it is not lexically prior to all other values or is sometimes traded for some other value.

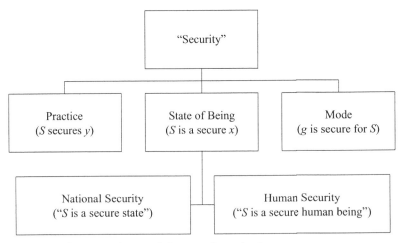

Figure 2.1 Conceptual map of the term "security."

distinct concepts to which the word "security" refers (see Figure 2.1).[8] First, security can denote a kind of *social and political practice*. This view of security, predominant in the self-avowedly critical corners of disciplines such as international relations, criminology, and geography, defines security via reference to a set of social and political processes (e.g., of control or exclusion) and practices (e.g., emergency measures, "threat-defense" logics).

Second, we might view security as a particular *mode* of enjoying a good. It is common to suggest that a person's job (or property, or civil rights) is secure, such that the term adopts an "adjectival" meaning – wherein it is understood to be "a mode of enjoying other goods" rather than a good in and of itself (Waldron 2006, 318). This strand of theorizing on security is small, but it attempts to capture the sense in which

"security" is not something we can have more of or less of, because it is not a thing at all. It is ... the name we use for a temporally extended state of affairs characterized by the calculability and predictability of the future. (Valverde 2001, 85)

On this view, security is a "thin" property that does not entail any claims about what kinds of things are valuable, nor their contribution

---

[8] This typology expands upon the account given in Herington (2012).

to a referent's overall state of affairs,[9] but simply denotes a particular kind of relationship between a referent (e.g., John) and a particular good (e.g., access to water). Importantly, secure enjoyment of a good is both a tensed and a modal relation. In particular, it is future-focused, such that whether or not an entity enjoys a good securely in the present is determined by facts about the future, and subjunctive, such that whether or not an entity enjoys a good securely is determined, not just by whether or not the entity *actually* enjoys the good, but by whether the entity enjoys it in a range of possible futures.[10]

Third, security can be thought of as a *state of being*. On this view, it is a "thick" property of particular entities – states, human individuals, communities – that is constituted by an evaluative judgment about a subset of the entity's overall state of affairs. This is, historically, the concept that has received the most attention from political theory and international relations. While we sometime speak as if there is an account of what it means to be secure *simpliciter*, in reality, accounts of being secure are always accounts of what it means to be secure as a particular type of entity. For instance, accounts of "national security" should be viewed as accounts of what it means to be secure as a state, while accounts of "human security" are accounts of what it means to be secure as an individual human being. Thus, for any class of entities, x, we might imagine an account of what it means to be secure as an entity of that kind. We might therefore have different accounts of what it means to be a secure human being, a secure prisoner, or a secure state, without a fully determinate account of being secure *simpliciter*. In this sense, this conceptualization of security can be broken down into a number of different instances of security as a state of being – that is, national

---

[9] The distinction between "thin" and "thick" concepts is controversial within moral philosophy (see Gibbard and Blackburn 1992; Williams 1981, 140–142) but is a useful heuristic for our purposes. Roughly, thin concepts (e.g., hot, cold, tall, bald) do not entail judgments about the goodness of particular properties, whereas thick concepts (e.g., justice, liberty, virtue) do entail such evaluative judgments, often because the property that the concept describes is thought to be valuable (or, at least *pro tanto* valuable).

[10] In this sense, security is an alethic modal property (similar to probability, possibility, and necessity), which tells us about the truth of a proposition, not just in the actual world, but within some subset of possible worlds (in this case, the set of worlds that are possible futures of the present).

security, individual security. Much like the concepts of brotherly and romantic love, these concepts need not be seen as in contest with one another, but simply as particular instances of what it means to be secure as a particular kind of entity. We might therefore say that an individual referent object, i, may or may not be secure as a type of entity, x_1, and may or may not be secure as a different type of entity, x_2, with no holistic sense in which that referent is secure.

Keeping these concepts distinct has inordinate benefits, insofar as we can coherently discuss whether security practices (such as the subversion of democratic processes) secure the kinds of goods that are morally valuable. Likewise, we can analyze the connection between individual security and national security, without claiming that one is totally constituted by the other. Finally, this conceptual structure has benefits for interactions between disciplines, insofar as the study of the causes and consequences of security as a state of being (e.g., by psychology, law, or development studies) can be used to explain and critique the deployment of particular security practices (e.g., by anthropology, international relations, or geography), and vice versa.

Security as a state of being

Of the three concepts that "security" can refer to, perhaps the most historically important is security as a state of being. Use of the term "security" – from the Roman *securitas* to national security and human security – is dominated by references to what it means to *be* secure. Typically, such conceptions identify a set of goods that a referent (the individual, the state, etc.) must enjoy in order to be secure as an entity of that type. An account of human security might, for instance, suggest that an individual must enjoy access to adequate food, shelter, and freedom from violence in order to qualify as a secure human being.[11] Likewise, an account of national security might suggest that a state must enjoy territorial integrity and freedom from domination and provide a basic level of welfare to its citizenry in order to qualify as a secure state (Buzan 1983, 19; Lasswell 1950, 51;

[11] The content of human security is heavily contested; in broad strokes it can be seen as involving the protection of "the vital core" or basic needs of a human life (see Alkire 2003, 2; King and Murray 2001; Owen 2004; United Nations Development Program 1994, 23).

Morgenthau 1965, 562; Ullman 1983, 133). Each thickly described conception of security differentiates itself through the goods that it suggests must be enjoyed by the referent in order for it to be secure in the relevant way.

Importantly, however, it is not just that the referent must enjoy those goods; he or she must enjoy them securely. An individual is secure not merely because he is free from violence today, but because he can be reasonably assured of being free from violence tomorrow, the next day, and so on. Indeed, it seems that part of what is distinctive about thickly described security, as opposed to well-being or flourishing, is that it connotes an assurance, or guarantee, that certain goods will be reliably accessible to the entity.[12] This suggests three major points about the proper specification of the relationship between security as a state of being and security as a mode of enjoying a good.

First, the conditions for being secure as a particular entity can be thought of as propositions of the form "i enjoys g," where g is a good and i is a referent that could hold or enjoy that good.[13] The truth of the proposition in the actual world tells us whether the referent will enjoy the good, whereas the security of the proposition tells us whether the referent will enjoy the good in a particular class of possible futures. Second, it is important to note that not much hinges on the idea of enjoying a good. I am not claiming, for instance, that a referent must actually value the good in order to enjoy it, nor that the referent must even be aware of her relation to the good.[14] The point is merely that the referent must in some sense "have" the good in question – whether that requires legally possessing it, having access to it, or possessing the capability to use it is a consideration that can be packed

---

[12] This was recognized in the original UNDP report on human security, which made a clear distinction between development and security: "Human development is ... a process of widening the range of people's choices ... (whereas) ... human security means that people can exercise these choices safely and freely- and that they can be relatively confident that the opportunities they have today are not totally lost tomorrow" (United Nations Development Program 1994, 23).

[13] In what follows, I will sometimes simplify the relation of enjoyment between a referent and a good such that it is expressed as a proposition, p. However, where I discuss the security of p one should typically assume that I am talking about propositions of the form "i enjoys g."

[14] For an account of enjoying goods that does associate enjoyment with valuation, see Kagan (2009).

into the specification of the good itself.[15] Finally, a great many different things can act as goods within the proposition, but they must be well specified. Speaking very generally, a good is just a thing or class of things that individuals could have reason to value.[16] Goods can be concrete objects (e.g., a car), abstract objects (e.g., transportation), social phenomena (e.g., diversity, cultural tradition), particular relations (e.g., friendship), events (e.g., a sunny day), and expectations (e.g., anticipated utility). Any of these things can substitute for *y*, with the only requirement being that it is felicitously specified. What counts as a felicitous specification will, of course, be heavily contingent on the good. In general, however, the specification of the good should include consideration of the following questions:

1. Is the good a simple object (e.g., apples) or a quantity of some object (e.g., five apples)?
2. Is the good an exact quantity (e.g., exactly five apples) or merely the satisficing of some threshold (e.g., *at least* five apples)?
3. Is the good enjoyed in a particular mode (e.g., *access* to apples)?
4. Are there temporal components to the good (e.g., an apple *a day*)?

Getting the specification of a good right is important since it will affect both the degree to which the good is secure and the degree to which its security is valuable. For instance, our *basic* liberties will, in general, be more secure than our liberty per se, and the security of enjoying those basic liberties will, in general, be more valuable than the security of enjoying all our liberties.

Given our discussion of the structure of the concept, we can now provide an account of the common core of conceptions of being secure:

An individual referent, i, may be secure as a type of entity, x, if and only if i enjoys a set of relevant goods, $(g_1, g_2, \ldots g_n)$ securely.

This is just a preliminary account of the structure of conceptions of being secure, and there may well be many more specific ways of capturing the relationship between the concepts of being secure and the mode of security. For instance, one way of cashing out the sense in which an individual is a secure human being may be via reference to her secure

---

[15] For instance, an individual may, variously, enjoy "access to shelter," "legal possession of shelter," and/or "the capability to find shelter when required."

[16] I remain neutral between objectivist and subjectivist accounts of value. For a comprehensive account of these different accounts, see Griffin (1986).

enjoyment of the set of *necessary conditions* for being a human.[17] Likewise, one might seek to restrict the relevant goods to only those that are not strictly necessary but are, in some sense, the "core" goods for the particular kind of entity (see Alkire 2003; McDonald 2008). Regardless of the ultimately correct formulation, this structure provides a framework for systematizing claims about what it means to be secure as a particular kind of entity.

This analysis of the concept of security has two important implications for work in other disciplines. First, conceptions of being secure require several different kinds of value judgment: including on the kinds of goods that constitute security as a state of being, on the degree to which each of these goods must be enjoyed securely, and on the relative importance of the secure enjoyment of each good to the security of the entity as a whole. Second, this analysis suggests that while each instance of the concept of being secure might be essentially contestable, this neither prevents us from analyzing the concept, nor from tracing the connections among different instances of security (state security, human security, etc.).

We can conclude, therefore, that though there is no contest over the meaning of the word "security" per se, there are numerous contests over what it means to be secure as a particular kind of entity. Furthermore, these instances of being secure are essentially contested by virtue of the large number of value judgments required to constitute each conception. The "common core" of each instance of being secure is the model framework we established, and in particular, its reliance on the notion of secure enjoyment. This establishes a clear framework for thinking about how the notion of secure enjoyment is crucial to accounts of what it means to be secure, and how each of these accounts relates to the others.

III. Philosophical themes

While explicit engagement with the concept of security is almost non-existent within contemporary Anglo-American political philosophy, there are three philosophical debates relevant to the study of security in other disciplines: the status of natural and social threats, fear and security, and whether security is a good or a right.

---

[17] This formulation was suggested to me by David Wiens.

Natural and social threats

The first debate is between those who prioritize protection from other agents and those who make no distinction between "natural" threats and those from other agents. In some respect this debate will resonate with those disciplines familiar with the broad and narrow conceptions of human security, since it seems to pivot on the extent to which security should emphasize the UN goal of universal "freedom from fear" or "freedom from want." Proponents of a narrow perspective on the set of goods advocate limiting human security to physical violence against the individual (Thomas and Tow 2002). Proponents of a broad perspective are concerned with expanding the set of goods beyond physical violence to include the social, political, and economic goods they view as necessary for human flourishing (Ogata and Sen 2003).

The debate also applies, however, to the concept of "secure enjoyment" insofar as what it means to enjoy a good securely may involve claims about protection from all kinds of risks or merely those arising from human agency. If there is a unifying theme to traditional accounts of national and individual security, it is that they are concerned with freedom from harms (whatever those harms consist in) that are intentionally inflicted by other agents. For individuals, security is protection from assault and murder; for the state this is protection from military conflict and the violation of its territorial integrity. The intentionality that characterizes these threats is crucial to the traditional account of security and is commonly held to ground a sharp distinction between safety and security.

> Safety is a more general concern than security because safety requires prudent protection from all probable dangers, whereas *security* is protection from dangers arising from the illegal aggression of others. (Zack 2009, 91)

One way of systematizing this view is described by Pettit (1999), who suggests that his distinction between freedom as nondomination and freedom as noninterference can be understood, to a certain extent, as different ways that noninterference can be secured.

> To try to secure non-interference in the protection sense is to try and reduce interference in those possible worlds where other people take against you or you are not so cunning or whatever; and to do this regardless of the probability of those worlds. To try to secure non-interference in the promotional sense is to try and reduce interference in various possible worlds, but

in a way that takes account of how probable it is that those worlds are ways the actual world may be. (Pettit 1999, 74, fn. 7)

While Pettit is concerned only with the secure enjoyment of noninterference, the two conceptions of security he describes may be generalizable to the enjoyment of other goods. Roughly speaking, on the promotional conception, the degree to which a good is enjoyed securely is solely the chance of that good obtaining. Yet securing noninterference in the promotional sense, Pettit suggests, can be accomplished simply by ingratiating oneself with the powerful or duping them into believing you are choosing according to their preferences and thus may involve leaving control of the good in the hands of another (Pettit 1999, 74). This kind of obsequiousness may lower the likelihood of losing the good, but, in an important sense, it does not seem to protect the agent's enjoyment of the good in a stable way. What is required is to secure noninterference in the protective sense: to reduce the probability of interference regardless of the different dispositions that powerful agents may have toward you.[18]

Fear and security

The second debate is over the relative importance of subjective and objective security. On the one hand, we might think that security is constituted by actual protection from violence (or hunger, or political oppression). On this view, security is important insofar as these goods are considerations that matter gravely to our future selves, and current protection of them is therefore essential to our future well-being. On the other hand, we might think security is constituted by freedom from the fear of violence and is important insofar as that fear itself is currently debilitating – endangering our present (as well as future) well-being (Goodin and Jackson 2007; John 2011, 70). Or we might think, following Waldron, that security consists in some amalgam of these two considerations, such that it

---

[18] In later work, Pettit has clarified that this only renders certain domains nonprobabilistically relevant to the analysis of freedom: the domain in which "the endangered agent's choice-dispositions vary" and the domain in which "there is variation in the interference-dispositions of endangering agents." It is, in this sense, not equivalent to securing noninterference across *all* possibilities (Pettit, 2008, 218).

comprises protection against harm to one's basic mode of life and economic values, as well as reasonable protection against fear and terror, and the presence of a positive assurance that these values will continue to be maintained into the future. (Waldron 2006, 320)

The debate over the subjective and objective dimensions of security rages, not only in political philosophy but across political science, criminology, and sociology.[19]

I would suggest, however, that the simple distinction between objective and subjective security is misleading and obscures more than it illuminates. Rather than thinking of subjective/objective security as a single distinction, we ought to think of it as encompassing two sets of distinctions. The first distinction is between the kinds of goods that constitute thick accounts of security. On the one hand, we might think being secure consists in possessing certain concrete or material goods, such as freedom from violence, access to water, adequate nutrition, and shelter. On the other, we might think that being secure consists in possessing a certain affect of assuredness, tranquility, and calm.

The second distinction is between the different perspectives from which we might assess the secure enjoyment of these goods. On the face of it, we can assess the secure enjoyment of a good relative to the facts, the available evidence, or an agent's actual beliefs (Parfit 2011, 150–153). We can think of fact-relative security as the degree to which a good is secure given the actual facts, evidence-relative security as the degree to which an individual would be *warranted* in believing that a good is secure given the evidence available, and belief-relative security as the degree to which a good is secure given an individual's actual beliefs about the world (which, of course, may or may not be warranted). Thus, an individual whose evidence about her security is obtained from crime reports in the local newspaper might be warranted in believing she has a 1/100 chance of being robbed this year. She may, however, believe that the newspaper and police are colluding to hide crime and so hold the erroneous belief that she has a 1/10 chance of being robbed this year. Likewise, the newspaper reports, though diligent and normally reliable, may be at odds with the actual (objective) 1/10,000 chance of being robbed.

---

[19] See, for instance, the concept of "ontological security" in Giddens (1991).

There appear to be two major benefits to this more nuanced account of the connection between security and fear. The first is a richer explanatory toolkit for exploring the connection between fact-relative security and the affect of security, such that the disciplines of psychology, criminology, and political science can investigate the relative importance of concrete, rational, and nonrational means of reducing fear of insecurity. Second, the value of fact-relative, evidence-relative, and belief-relative security may come apart, such that the precise way in which security is important to flourishing can be identified and our political ends modified in suitable ways.

A good or a right?

The third contemporary debate concerns whether or not security is best conceived as a fundamental right to be honored or as a good to be promoted (Pettit 1991, 231). The view that security is a right is most prominent in conceptions of human rights, where it is taken to signify a right to freedom from violence by other agents (i.e., a thick, agential account of security) (Griffin 2008, 32–33; Shue 1980, 30). On this account, security is a *moral* right insofar as all other agents possess a corresponding duty to refrain from violating the bodily integrity of the individual. Moreover, security is a *political* right in the sense that political authorities (i.e., the state) have a positive duty to protect each individual under their authority from a range of "standard threats" (Shue 1980, 32).[20] The protection of this right is commonly held to be an either/or proposition, such that a failure to provide a sufficient degree of protection is a failure to provide any security at all. Moreover, the right to security is often held to have special status over and above that which attaches to broader civil and political rights such as the right to freedom of speech or democratic participation. Henry Shue, for instance, claims that security is one of four "basic rights" upon which all other rights depend, and that protecting this right (along with the other basic rights) is necessary for our enjoyment of all other rights (Shue 1980). In this sense, we might think that the state has a strict and nonnegotiable obligation to

---

[20] The idea of a "standard threat" is notoriously vague, but it identifies something important, which is that it is not a failure of security if we fail to protect individuals against highly extraordinary circumstances (Waldron 2009, 10).

protect all citizens from the full range of standard threats to their persons, regardless of what this implies for nonbasic or nonfundamental rights.

Contrast this account with the view that security is a good, like any other, that can be promoted and distributed in a number of ways. One such view of security is given by King and Murray, who define an individual's security as "his or her expectation of years of life without experiencing the state of generalized poverty" (King and Murray 2001, 592). Though philosophers have not typically discussed human security in these terms, this view has important parallels with work on measures of poverty (Alkire 2003), and the notion of basic needs (Brock 2009; Reader 2006). On these accounts we can make interpersonal comparisons between individuals regarding the degree of security they enjoy, summarize the degree of security within a population (i.e., by simple aggregation), and investigate various distributions of security within and between communities. This view of security is undoubtedly behind the common refrain that we can "balance" the provision of security against the protection of our liberties. Precisely whether this balancing metaphor makes sense, and what it elides with respect to maximizing the security of the many at the expense of the liberty (or security) of others, is a key pivot point for those who hold this view of security (Waldron 2003).

IV. Security, liberty, privacy, and emergency

These debates have implications not only for theoretical work within political philosophy, but also for work on the normative implications of security practices in other disciplines. In particular, there appear to be four debates – including the use of torture, restrictions on liberty, intrusions into privacy, and the use of emergency powers – that may benefit from a more fine-grained analysis of security. I briefly discuss each of these in turn.

The first debate concerns the tension between the security of the state and the security of individuals. This is a central concern of scholars investigating the normative status of national security policies (in international relations, anthropology, and law) and would benefit from far greater attention from political philosophers. It has long been recognized that securing the basic conditions that maintain a political order (authoritarian or democratic, legitimate or illegitimate) may involve diminishing the security of some individuals (both citizens and noncitizens). What is not typically recognized is that this tension can often be redescribed as a tension entailed by promoting the security of a great many individuals at the cost of violating the right to security of some. This is most readily apparent in the literature on the use of torture to prevent harm from terrorism. Walzer (2000, 40), for instance, argues that in cases of "supreme emergency," the normal constraints against using torture lose their force, and "a certain kind of utilitarianism reimposes itself," (see also, Allhoff 2012; Dershowitz 2004). Others argue that seeking to legitimize acts of torture fails on utilitarian grounds (since it ignores the downstream effects of weakening the norm on torture), and that the "ticking-time bomb" methodology used to justify the supreme emergency exemption is so implausible and extreme that our intuitions are unreliable (Brecher 2007). Regardless of the position taken, however, the dispute is one over the proper *distribution* of individual security rather than a question of whether state security has moral worth independent of its instrumental role in ensuring individual security.

The second debate concerns the tension between liberty and security. In a seminal paper, Waldron discusses the common idea that there is an optimal balance between security and liberty, such that just as we are willing to place limits on our freedom to do as we please to maintain security, we are willing to live with some degree of insecurity for the sake of our liberties (Waldron 2003, 193–194). One of the problems with the balancing metaphor, however, is that it may obscure a more complex set of trade-offs between securing the enjoyment of our basic liberties and maximizing our enjoyment of liberty per se. We can envisage a case in which collectively maximizing the scope and scale of our liberties (i.e., by perhaps being able to bargain away our labor rights or to enter into exploitative contracts) involves the risk that the powerful among us may be able violate our basic liberties. Indeed, this is precisely the concern that appears to motivate Enlightenment philosophers, particularly Locke, for whom securing freedom from the interference of the powerful in the pursuit of our basic preferences (not to be murdered, robbed, enslaved, or coerced) legitimizes the forfeiture of some of our more peripheral freedoms. In this sense, while a tension between security (as a state of being) and liberty is evident, we should guard against the view that security and liberty are "two sides of the same coin" (Booth 1991, 319). Critical work in criminology and human rights law may be advanced by considering whether limits on the scope of our freedoms by security practices are justified by the extra robustness of our basic freedoms that those policies may bestow (see List 2006, 217).

The third dilemma is the tension between privacy and security. Of particular interest, to critically minded criminologists, for example, is the extent to which protecting individual security justifies state (or corporate) surveillance of individuals. Surveillance can take many forms (e.g., close-circuit cameras, e-mail snooping), be covert or overt, be targeted in different ways (e.g., at suspects, particular ethnic groups, or totally untargeted), and be aimed at public (e.g., parks, streets) or putatively private acts (e.g., homes, private electronic communications). Of these types of surveillance, perhaps the most relevant to security policy is untargeted surveillance of private communications and public spaces, about which two major concerns are raised. The first is that such surveillance is inherently wrong: either because it treats all individuals as suspicious without evidence for that suspicion (Hadjimatheou 2014), or because it involves showing disrespect for their dignity as autonomous individuals (Rubel 2007, 146). Such arguments are popular, but insofar as they show that any and all untargeted surveillance by groups (be they the authorities, individuals, or civil society) violates an individual's dignity, they are too strong. While many recognize the value of privacy (Bruin 2010; Nissenbaum 1998), some proportionate intrusions into privacy (such as metal detectors) seem necessary in order to protect individual security (Rubel 2007, 141), and when in the hands of actors other than the state, to protect other valuable ends such as democratic accountability (i.e., such as when police officers are filmed by protestors). The second concern is that, regardless of whether or not surveillance is intrinsically wrong, it is often a necessary enabler of some further wrong: such as racial profiling, voyeurism by operators, and blackmail (Hadjimatheou 2014, 188). This argument has power, however, only insofar as we think the introduction of untargeted surveillance raises the risk of such wrongs occurring and that safeguards to prevent such wrongs (such as outlawing of racial profiling, strict penalties for misuse by those in authority, and democratic oversight) are likely to fail. In this respect, the balance metaphor seems appropriate in the case of surveillance, insofar as intrusions into privacy in order to protect security may be made acceptable by enforcing principles of proportionality, nondiscrimination, and accountability.

Finally, we might be interested in the moral legitimacy of "securitizing" issues outside the normal security agenda (Agamben 2005). The securitization literature views "security" as social and political practice, whereby the use of "emergency measures" is required in order to protect some valued referent (Buzan *et al.* 1998, 25). In general, the practice of security is viewed as normatively undesirable (Burke 2007; see Neocleous 2008; Waever 1995), but there is a small literature that seeks to identify conditions in which the use of emergency measures is justified (Elbe 2006; Floyd 2011; Selgelid and Enemark 2008). What is noticeable, however, is that this literature has so far neglected the connection between the justifiability of security practices and the protection of individual security (as a state of being). Given a more complex conceptual structure, however, we can see that conflict between the concept of security as practice and security as a state of being is not necessary, and that the value of the latter may provide a ground for the justifiability of the former.

Conclusion

In this chapter I hope to have provided some taste of the ways in which philosophy can demystify and deepen our discussion of the concept of security. In particular, by applying the tools of conceptual analysis to the term, and investigating its genealogical history, we can begin to untangle the *aporia* of security. By making distinctions among multiple senses of security and showing how these are compatible, philosophers facilitate the exceptional empirical and theoretical work being done in international relations, anthropology, criminology, and elsewhere. Likewise, other disciplines can inform and constrain the work of political philosophy. Psychology and cognitive science can provide important insights into the relationship between evidence-relative and belief-relative security, as well as the relationship between the affect of security and our beliefs about security. Work in the disciplines of anthropology, geography, and criminology can inform questions on the feasibility of particular security policies. Insights from international and domestic law can likewise identify the dangers of instituting emergency powers and licensing the legitimacy of violating legal rights in "special circumstances." In this respect, there is much philosophical work left to do with respect to the concept of security, and much to be learned through dialogue with other disciplines.

3 | *Anthropology/ies: Moving beyond disciplinary approaches to security*

DANIEL M. GOLDSTEIN

As an analytical construct, "security" is either something entirely new to anthropology or a basic element of its disciplinary foundation.* Anthropology has in some ways always been concerned with security, understood broadly as the production and maintenance of social order and the management of threats to the general social good. Some of anthropology's earliest disciplinary innovations were framed in terms of social structures and the functions they served, providing for humans' basic needs while enabling them to deal with uncertainty (in both the natural and supernatural realms) and to ensure the ongoing continuity of their societies (particularly famous ethnographic examples include Evans-Pritchard 1937; Malinowski 1922). Once understood as a consensual, homeostatic mechanism for facilitating human survival amid perpetual challenges, the anthropological concept of "culture" could be seen as one of the earliest interventions in a field that would later be called "security studies." From this perspective, as Pedersen and Holbraad (2013, 4) observe, "the history of anthropology itself could be rewritten as a story about security."

On the other hand, anthropological studies of security have only recently begun to proliferate as anthropology, like other disciplines, has ridden the wave of interest in security that emerged in the wake of 9/11. Deploying a contemporary understanding of culture as contested and contingent, and grounded in a historicized, politicized, global perspective, many anthropologists today regard "security" with a critical eye. These anthropologists approach security, as they do other social constructs, with characteristic mistrust. They consider security

---

* My thanks to Philippe Bourbeau for the invitation to participate in this project, for hosting the workshop in Namur, and for his helpful suggestions on an earlier draft of this chapter. Thanks to Philippe Le Billon for his discussant comments at the Namur workshop; to Carolina Alonso for research assistance; and to Robyn Rodriguez for some early collaborative work on the securitization of immigration.

as part of a larger process of neoliberal social transformation in which states and societies worldwide are engaged. Security is understood as a discourse, a way of perceiving, acting in, and talking about social reality that is not innocent but infused with power and mobilized to serve particular interests. I count myself among those who advance what I have termed a "critical anthropology of security" (Goldstein 2010a), scholars whose ethnographies examine the role that security – as a set of discourses and practices – plays in producing particular kinds of political and legal order in societies around the world.

This chapter explores the diverse and complicated engagement of anthropology with security and its deeply wedded counterpart, insecurity. It examines the elements of anthropology's characteristic approach that have proven to be especially productive for understanding the "cultures of insecurity" (Weldes *et al.* 1999) that have emerged in recent years, in different societies around the world. In particular, the chapter explores one area of research to which anthropologists have been productive contributors – the securitization of immigration – to demonstrate the kinds of insights that a critical, ethnographically driven approach to security can bring to contemporary political and social issues.

Anthropology offers a unique take on security and insecurity in contemporary society, grounded in a theoretical framework that is processual, transnational, and decolonializing. Having long ago abandoned older theories of functionalism and structuralism, and having thoroughly internalized the critiques of postmodernism and poststructuralism, anthropology today draws on theory from sources as diverse as interpretivism, phenomenology, and Marxism to understand its subject. Beholden to no dominant theoretical framework, anthropologists of security draw on concerns widely shared across the discipline. These include anthropology's orientation toward understanding culture not as product but as process, its tendency to view all of human life as colored by politics and contestations over power and resources, and its insistence that non-Western and frequently marginalized perspectives on global issues be consistently addressed. Many anthropologists of security also employ a critical approach to the state, drawing on the work of such political theorists as Antonio Gramsci, Giorgio Agamben, and Michel Foucault, among many others, to understand the workings of power both within and without institutional structures of state authority and administration. This tendency to look beyond formal institutions while not losing sight of the role of state power in contemporary society is a critical element of anthropological theories of security (see, e.g., Fassin 2013). Additionally, many anthropologists of security today are concerned with questions of social justice and equality. Breaking with older tendencies that insist on an objectivist distancing from their study subjects, many anthropologists now take an "engaged" or "activist" approach, specifically seeking to put their knowledge, skills, and findings to work in the service of those whose situations they study (for more, see Hale 2008; Lamphere 2003; Skidmore 2008). This is not a universally agreed upon approach, however, and represents an area of contention within the discipline today (see Low and Merry 2010).

In what follows, then, I point to the ways in which the topic of security is almost inescapably interdisciplinary. As the preceding description suggests, anthropology does not manifest one single theory of security or deploy one characteristic analytical framework for understanding security and insecurity in contemporary society. Nevertheless, given the importance of security concerns within pervasive and enduring frameworks of cultural reproduction, security should be understood as a significant concern of anthropologists working across an array of topics and locations (Maguire, Frois, and Zurawski 2014). Anthropologists, the chapter shows, are not strict disciplinarians but omnivorous consumers of conceptual models that enable them to interpret effectively the situations they encounter in the field. While they remain committed to an ethnographic methodology that grounds their interpretations in the observed realities of life actually lived, anthropologists look beyond the confines of their own discipline to make sense of the complexities that they encounter in their fieldwork. The anthropology of security, I think, is typical in this regard. The diverse perspectives that anthropologists employ in the study of security allow us to speak productively of the *anthropologies* of security, which partake of a rich field of conceptual insights and include practitioners from a wide range of disciplines. Given the overarching themes of the present volume, such a conclusion demonstrates both the need to move beyond any sort of strictly disciplinary analysis of security and insecurity and the contributions that an anthropological approach, broadly understand, can make to an interdisciplinary understanding of security.

Anthropologies of security

As the aforementioned example of "security anthropology" suggests, the relationship between security and anthropology should be understood as complex and multistranded. This can be seen in the diverse sets of issues that these anthropologies of security address. Anthropology engages a broad range of topics that other disciplinary scholars might not choose to analyze through a "security" lens, both expanding the range of what can be considered security issues in contemporary societies and broadening the relevance of a security-oriented approach to culture. Anthropological work has examined such diverse themes as "food security" (Benyshek and Watson 2006; Pottier 2000), "biosecurity" and public health (Collier, Lakoff, and Rabinow 2004; Lakoff 2007, 2008; Lakoff and Collier 2008), and "cybersecurity" (Dubartell 2006; Kelty 2005). Anthropological studies of security have defined their sites both narrowly and broadly, ranging from individual bodies and psychologies (Caduff 2012; Metz 2010; Owczarzak 2009; Zeiderman 2013) to nations (Caton and Zacka 2010; Lutz 2001; Masco 2006) to transnational corporations (Welker 2009) to global communities (Feldman 2010; Stepputat 2012; Wilson 2005). Anthropological work in these domains has considered the emergence of "cultures of (in)security" and their formative impacts on the people living within them.

Indeed, it is through the concept of "culture" – historically anthropology's signature concept, though one that in recent years has seen waning usage by anthropologists themselves, even as it has been taken up widely by others – that anthropologists offer a characteristic take on security. From this point of view, security and its counterpart, insecurity, are not a priori realities immanent in the public realm. Rather, many anthropologists are concerned with the *production* of security and insecurity, the ways in which these are generated, imagined, and maintained through cultural and political forces at work in contemporary societies. This is the case even when the issue in question is national security itself. Fosher, for example, in an ethnography of the daily work of those charged with making national security in the post-9/11 United States, describes "U.S. homeland security as practice, as something that is not monolithic but constructed, not impenetrable but accessible to field research and analysis" (Fosher 2009, xiv). An ethnographic perspective on security makes real what is too often mystified by more "top-down" perspectives, illustrated by Fosher's descriptions of policy makers and frontline staff, their perspectives and practices, as they assume responsibility for the production of homeland security.

Anthropologies of security are also dialectical. The discourse of security, as Bubandt (2005, 280) has argued, is inherently tied to its alter, insecurity; security entails the "constant manufacture of uncertainty" and insecurity, without which security would lose all meaning, and the political project upon which the modern state depends would deflate (see also Beck 1992). A dialectical approach, of course, is characteristic of anthropology across a range of issues that have no relation to security,[1] but it bears particularly well on efforts to understand the many entailments of security in modern nations and communities. For example, anthropologists have examined the production of a "security culture" in the United States, providing insightful analyses of the ways in which national structures of security shape daily lives – including domestic architectures and the behaviors that occur within them – while offering a critique of the official ideologies that support such structures (Gusterson and Besteman 2009; Low 2003). Other anthropologists have taken a similar approach to understanding the worldwide trend toward fortifying urban spaces (Caldeira 1996; Low 1997) and the production of public fear (Ochs 2011; O'Neill and Thomas 2013; Skidmore 2003), which can include the criminalization of racialized and sexualized populations deemed to be "dangerous" (Valverde and Cirak 2002; Waterston 1997). These approaches evidence a concern with what the anthropologist Michael Taussig (1984) called a "culture of terror," or what the sociologist Barry Glassner (2010) has identified as the "culture of fear." People's sometimes violent responses to terror and insecurity (including the emergence of "extralegal" security apparatuses) are also the objects of anthropological analysis (Burrell 2010; Deal 2010; Goldstein 2003, 2004; Jaffe 2012). Other scholars in anthropology, geography, and related disciplines have explored the material and technological dimensions of securitization, in border zones (Sundberg 2011),

---

[1] The kind of anthropology I identify here has its roots in a Marxian approach to social life, especially with its emphasis on production. But, I would argue, this is a fair characterization of the mainstream of contemporary anthropology, one that joins the semiotic with the material in an effort to understand their mutual construction.

airports (Maguire 2009, 2014), and urban spaces of surveillance (Frois 2013). These studies, again as in other subfields of anthropology, also offer richly historicized discussions of the security cultures they analyze, grounding contemporary neoliberal structures of security and insecurity in a diachronic framework (Gambetti and Godoy-Anativia 2013).

In all of these cases, security and insecurity are understood as processes, rather than products, within contemporary societies. Security is constantly unfolding, subject to negotiation and contestation, saturated with power and capable of producing powerful effects. From this perspective, the well-known "Copenhagen school" (e.g., Buzan, Waever, and de Wilde 1998) of security studies provides a ready complement to the anthropology of security. "Securitization" – the process by which some phenomena come to be identified publicly as security threats, understood as existential challenges to "our" collective survival – is constructivist, processual, and symbolic, and so a fundamentally anthropological concept that accords well with the kinds of ethnographic approaches to security that most anthropologists take. Anthropological work on security contributes to the call to "broaden" scholarly understandings of security, to look beyond military- and state-based accounts to include domains more commonly understand as part of civil society or the economy (Collins 2013). The interdisciplinary field of security studies pushes anthropology to look beyond local contexts, to relate specific ethnographic findings to larger analyses of what is unavoidably a global regime of security and securitization. Moving beyond the localities in which their studies are grounded, anthropologists of security today situate their ethnographic understandings in broader political and economic frameworks that are historically the domain of political scientists, sociologists, or social psychologists. This growing engagement of anthropology and security studies speaks to the utility of an interdisciplinary conversation on security, a point to which I will return.

But whereas much of the corpus of security studies focuses on Western societies, the anthropology of security introduces an international and cross-cultural dimension. Some of the most interesting recent work in the anthropology of security employs what we might call an "ethnological" approach, one that examines local understandings of security and insecurity comparatively and in non-Western contexts and cultures. This research is critical for broadening our understanding of what security entails, and for recognizing the neocolonial project embedded within some Western scholars' approach to security (Hönke and Müller 2012). Kent's (2006) work in Cambodia, for example, explores the culturally and historically specific ideas that Khmer people have about "security," contrasting these with more hegemonic Western notions that these people associate with democratization and economic liberalization. Kent argues that a situated understanding of security helps us to realize that "notions and practices of security are ultimately cultural and embedded in deeply cherished and often unquestioned value systems"; to apply universally any particular definition of security, she contends, "though it may appear to be a neutral, analytical tool, may actually perform as a kind of cultural colonialism" (2006, 344). Similarly, Bubandt (2005, 276) observes:

When the global concept of security is contextualized in terms of local political histories, it becomes apparent that "security" as a political problem is neither unchanging nor semantically homogenous. Complex processes of accommodation, rejection and reformulation take place in the interstices between global, national and local representations of the problem of security. These processes, in turn, are related to the political history of the local ontological ways in which danger, risk and (in)security are defined.

Another approach to anthropology and security, rather distinct from those described previously though sharing some common elements, is advocated by a group of self-described "security anthropologists" who lend their expertise to the US government in fighting its "war on terror." Rather than adopting a critical approach, these anthropologists engage security largely in the terms established by the state (McFate 2005; Selmeski 2007). In an effort that has received much public and media attention, these anthropologists seek to understand "enemy culture" so as to wage counterinsurgency campaigns more effectively, supposedly enhancing the security of local societies and in the United States. This perspective on the relationship between anthropology and security has been widely criticized (see, e.g., Goldstein 2010b; González 2007; Gusterson 2005; Price 2011) but is revealing nonetheless. As other anthropologists have noted, however, the engagement of anthropology and the security apparatus of the state should not be reduced to its most public and problematic element, the Human Terrain System (HTS). As these authors point out (e.g., Albro *et al.* 2011; McNamara and Rubinstein 2011), there are many other ways in which anthropologists and ethnographers can work in the field of "security anthropology" that differ from the sometimes stereotypical conceptions elaborated by its critics. The debate here again points to the different conceptual orientations toward security that exist within the discipline, and the different ways in which anthropologists' engagement with security and security-making institutions may be understood. It illustrates the ways in which ethnography and security can be joined in the service of quite divergent political objectives, both to bolster the national security endeavors of states as well as to oppose them.

My own recent writing on Bolivia provides another example of how security and related concepts can be differently configured "on the ground" in a particular sociocultural context (Goldstein 2012a). I examine the circumstances facing the indigenous residents of the marginal urban neighborhoods of Cochabamba, Bolivia, where people feel themselves to be abandoned to face crime and violence without the protection of the democratic state and its rule of law. In response to the absence of official legal guarantees operative in their communities, many local people have themselves turned to violence, including the vigilante lynching of criminal suspects, in an effort to create "security" for themselves and their families. Ironically, even as they violate the due process rights of their victims and demand harsher laws (including the death penalty) to punish the accused, many lynch mob participants assert their own "right to security" as the paramount right that trumps all others and that justifies violence to attain. Indeed, even as transnational conceptions of rights have provided the fuel that recently put indigenous social movements (and their leader, President Evo Morales) in power in Bolivia, many indigenous residents of the marginal neighborhoods regard "human rights" as a foreign imposition, an alien concept that privileges the perpetrators of crime against its victims and so contributes to the greater insecurity of their communities. My writing on these topics explores the conjuncture of two powerful transnational discourses – security and human rights – examining their deployments and transformations in daily social practice to reveal the ways in which "security" ultimately can work to defeat "rights," as violent local actors operate within and against national and transnational formations of politics and law.

My research, like other work on the anthropology of security, is grounded in an ethnographic methodology, but draws on insights from history, geography, sociology, economics, political science, international relations, and legal studies to inform its interpretations of local Bolivian reality. Similar intersections characterize the interdisciplinary study of immigration and security, a field to which my own attention has recently turned. A close examination of the broad theoretical framework in which the "securitization of immigration" is conceptualized demonstrates the utility of an ethnographic and comparative approach to the study of lived security and securitization processes in contemporary society, both in the West and elsewhere. It also reveals the various interdisciplinary borrowings and intersections that the anthropological study of security characteristically employs – while I cite many of the most prominent anthropological scholars of this topic, I also invoke the findings of other social scientists whose work has been influential for anthropologists studying this topic.

The securitization of immigration

During the last decade, migration to the United States has again come to be seen as a threat to national security by both policy makers and ordinary citizens. In the immediate aftermath of the terror attacks of September 11, 2001, the US government introduced new laws intended to prevent foreigners from entering the country, and to increase the surveillance of migrants residing in the United States, regardless of their immigration status (Cornelius 2004).[2] Tellingly, the administration in charge of managing national security domestically (the Department of Homeland Security) in the wake of 9/11 was also tasked with the enforcement of immigration law. More recently, the Latino day laborer – perceived as a threat to American jobs, the health of domestic populations, and the stability of "our way of life" – has emerged as a new kind of archetypal security menace (joining the stereotypical "Islamic terrorist" in the popular and official imaginations). In this context the "securitization of immigration" (Bourbeau 2011) – the public rendering, in discourse and law, of immigration as a security problem – has shifted public attention from the nation's borders to the various localities within those borders where immigrants

---

[2] However, as Brotherton and Kretsedemas (2008) have observed, we should be careful not to overemphasize the significance of 9/11 in the control of immigration: Many of the policies pertaining to immigrant securitization have their roots in histories that well predate that event.

work and reside.[3] New sets of highly restrictive immigration laws have emerged in various US states and municipalities, many of them aiming to criminalize the very presence of undocumented Latinos on US soil. Municipal, county, and state governments have passed ordinances restricting undocumented immigrants' mobility and limiting their access to housing and employment. At the federal level, the Obama administration has deported record numbers of undocumented immigrants under its policy of "Secure Communities" (Khimm 2012). The very name of this policy approach to immigration frames the phenomenon as a security threat.

In this environment, marked by an increasingly securitized framework of law and public opinion, US immigration policy today represents a new approach to national security. It reconceptualizes security as the "collective management of subnational or transnational threats and the policing of borders and the internal realm, rather than just the defense of territory against external attack" (Faist 2002, 9). This concept of the "securitization of immigration" – developed largely by scholars in a range of disciplines studying the European context (Bigo 2002; Buonfino 2004; Feldman 2011; Huysmans 2006) – has been fruitful for those studying immigration and the "anthropology of removal" in the United States (Peutz 2006; see also Walters 2002, 2004; Zilberg 2011). The anthropologist Nicholas De Genova (2007), for example, has called attention to what he has termed "the Homeland Security State" and the placement of migrant noncitizens as its particular objects of regulation and control. De Genova's work explores the conflation of immigrants with a generic terrorist threat; he describes the current immigration policy regime in the United States as predicated on a "metaphysics of antiterrorism" (2007, 437) that justifies the abrogation of basic human and political rights of detainees and the deployment of increasingly restrictive forms of surveillance and control of all populations, documented and undocumented alike, who are seen as posing a possible threat to the "homeland."

De Genova's work (see also 2002, 2005) also points to the racialized dimensions of this securitization process, and the ways in which fear – as is the case in so many other security scenarios (e.g., Larchanché

---

[3] The US/Mexico border, however, continues to be an important focus of national efforts to securitize immigration, and so the site of ongoing anthropological study. See, e.g., the essays in Donnan and Wilson (2010).

2012) – provides a fundamental basis for its elaboration. The criminalization of immigrants who have not in fact committed any crimes is in part a response to what Leo Chavez (2008) calls the "Latino threat," in which the Latino day laborer emerges as a particularly alarming social type. Linda Newton (2008, 30) explains that the perception of immigrant deviance derives from the very fact of a transgressive border crossing associated with "illegal" immigration: "The border, now more than a geo-political boundary, looms large in contemporary immigration discourse, and its pathologies (real and imagined) follow the people associated with its transgression." Such perceived pathologies (drug trafficking, violence, pollution, etc.) nourish a fear that conflates the distinction between those suspected of being (or suspected of having the capacity to be) "terrorists" and those suspected of being unauthorized migrants; people racialized as "Muslim-looking" can become targets for detention (Ahmad 2002; Cainkar 2004). In this context, legality becomes a fungible concept, such that even those who have papers can be swept up and detained as part of the generalized "illegalization" of Latino migrants. The rightlessness that derives from illegalization relies on what Giorgio Agamben (2005) has identified as the state of exception – an influential paradigm in recent anthropology of the state (Goldstein 2007) – within which the protections against detention or expulsion that legal status provides become precarious or endangered, their suspension justified by the exceptional threat that such liberties supposedly pose to society and the state. These insights are not far from those articulated by the Copenhagen school and other securitization scholars.

Of course, the danger posed by immigrants is always balanced against the need for their labor in the host nation's economy (Gomberg-Muñoz and Nussbaum-Barberena 2011; Mize and Swords 2010). Even while it preaches securitized immigration, the US federal government has not historically worked to eliminate undocumented immigration completely and continues to entertain the possibility of immigration reform. Kretsedemas (2008, building on Ong's [1999] theorization of governance under conditions of neoliberal globalization) attributes the simultaneous enabling and restricting of immigration to a "graduated" form of state sovereignty; he argues that a fragmented and discontinuous terrain of governance has emerged in the United States, wherein the state alternatively tightens and eases its restrictions on immigrant populations to meet neoliberal free market imperatives. The state, in other words, has an interest in maintaining flows of immigrant workers into the country, even as it generates a politics of rule through their securitization. The United States' immigration laws – inconsistently applied and often internally contradictory – have their foundation in this overarching set of political and economic considerations.

Significantly for anthropology, the effects of this management of immigration are unfolding most consistently at the local level. As the federal government debates (or, at the time of this writing, refuses to debate) comprehensive immigration reform, governments at the state and municipal levels are actively engaged in developing new forms for the regulation and enforcement of their own securitized immigration policies. In the states of exception that new forms of graduated sovereignty have enabled, officials at the most local of levels have found a position from which to set the terms of belonging within their particular jurisdictions. Ethnographic research in these local contexts can provide a better understanding of the impacts of contemporary immigration policies on immigrant communities – a perspective unavailable to studies that consider only national law and state policy-making processes (see Glick Schiller and Caglar 2010). Ethnographic methodologies are particularly well suited to exploring both the official processes and the local impacts they have on populations of documented and undocumented immigrants, and on the nonimmigrant populations who share their spaces of residence, work, and sociality.

Research on the securitization of immigration at the local level can also consider immigrant subjectivity as a new terrain of official regulation. Local laws intended to regulate the minutiae of individual and group behaviors – how people move through space, for example, or the details of their residence patterns – reveal the extent to which migrant self-conception, consciousness, and identity have emerged as battlegrounds in the war against undocumented immigrants. These laws reflect the neoliberal focus on individual self-governance, emphasized as the only rational response to diminishing public resources and reduced public services, such that even noncitizens may be induced to comply with the normativizing order of the state. Such policies further condition the outward behaviors and internal lives of noncitizens through their regulatory regimes, which make any action that draws attention to one's self potentially risky, such that driving a car or looking for work on the street become dangerous, putting one at risk of detention and deportation. In response, many undocumented migrants may adopt behaviors that limit their exposure to such risk, effectively internalizing the laws that would keep them out of sight and out of mind (Bosniak 1998; De Genova 2002).

Anthropologists and others writing about the law's impacts on migrant populations in the United States have remarked extensively on the contradictory legal position of undocumented communities (Bosniak 2006; Calavita 2005; Coutin 1999, 2000). Previous research by scholars in a range of disciplines has revealed the ways in which undocumented people are subject to the many strictures of US immigration law, even as they are denied the rights of citizens guaranteed under the constitution (Coutin 2003; Wishnie 2003). The victimization of unauthorized migrants under a legal regime that limits their mobility, residence, and ability to work as it targets them for detention and deportation has been extensively documented in migration scholarship (see, e.g., Davis and Erez 1998; Gleeson 2009; Varsanyi 2006). Complementary to these findings are other studies that have explored the ways in which migrants more actively engage the law. In approaching the study of undocumented immigrants and their relationship with the US legal system, some scholars have turned their attention to the legal alternatives offered to those deemed "illegal." For example, research has considered the constitutional rights of undocumented migrants under the First Amendment (Wishnie 2003), the implications of legal rulings against undocumented workers' ability to demand back pay (Baldwin 2003; O'Donovan 2005), and the availability of workers' compensation benefits for undocumented people (Purcell 2008). Academic work, both in the United States and internationally, has commented on the various ways in which unauthorized immigrants navigate the legal system in an effort to obtain refugee status and to "regularize" their immigration situation. Coutin (1995, 2003, 2007), for example, has done important ethnographic work on undocumented Salvadorans' and Guatemalans' legalization strategies in California and Arizona (see also Menjívar 2006); while Bloch et al. (2011), Nyers (2003, 2010), and Ticktin (2011) have written about the legal maneuvers of undocumented asylum seekers in the United Kingdom, Canada, and France, respectively.

Ethnographic approaches to the securitization of immigration, therefore, hold the potential to document not only the repressive practices of state and local law, but the responses of migrants themselves to these repressive regimes. Scholars such as Gordon (2007) and Honig (2001) have pointed to undocumented immigrant workers' collective political participation in campaigning and protesting as positive illustrations of democratic citizenship. De Genova (2009, 2010) has analyzed the Immigrant Workers Freedom Ride of 2003, as well as the unprecedented mobilizations of migrants throughout the United States in 2006 in a mass proclamation of collective defiance ("¡*Aquí Estamos y No Nos Vamos!*" [We Are Here and We're Not Leaving!]), to argue that migrant workers assert their autonomy and prerogatives through insubordinate acts calling attention to the mere corporeal fact of their deportable presence. Similar research has been done on undocumented migrants' collective protests and human rights advocacy in Israel (Kemp *et al.* 2010; Rosenhek 1999) and France (McNevin 2006). Community-based organizations represent another space of legal agency for undocumented people in the United States and function as institutions to which immigrants turn as they strive to build vibrant communities and attain economic and political rights (Varsanyi 2006). Rocco's (1999) ethnographic research on undocumented workers in Los Angeles; Martin, Morales, and Theodore's (2007) study of migrant worker centers in Chicago; and Fine's (2006) ethnography of various worker collectives across the United States all describe how community organizations enable undocumented people to gain access to social services, advocate for their own civil and human rights, and organize to improve wages, working conditions, neighborhoods, and public schools.

Other anthropological work examines the ways in which undocumented people can themselves deploy the US legal system to resist the vulnerability that being undocumented imposes on them. My own current research (see, e.g., Goldstein 2012b) explores the extensive use of the US legal system by undocumented Latino migrants in the United States. Using an ethnographic research methodology, the project studies the ways in which the undocumented – in addition to being subject to and living in avoidance of the increasing penalty of anti-immigrant sentiment and law – are themselves active users of the US legal system. I consider how the legal system, which in some moments serves to restrict migrants' rights, in other moments provides them with resources to defend and expand those rights and to counter the difficulties that they experience in their daily lives. Additionally, in contrast to the ways in which undocumented migrants are typically depicted in the United States – that is, either as criminals and security threats or as hapless victims of injustice – my research proposes that the undocumented are active agents who use the law and the courts to advance their interests, demand their rights, and seek redress of grievances.

Conclusion

This chapter details the kinds of insights that an anthropological approach to security and securitization – in the case explored most extensively here, the securitization of immigration – can offer. Such *anthropologies of security* – as I call them, because of the diversity of topics they engage and theoretical frameworks they deploy – can make significant contributions to the interdisciplinary study of security more broadly. Anthropologies of security consider a broad range of topics, many of which are not typically understood within a security framework by other disciplinary scholars. Calling attention to such topics and rendering them as security concerns – in this essay I have referred to issues of religion, health, and the regulation of urban space, among others, and the list goes on – can broaden the scope and relevance of security studies more generally, by exploring the varied and diverse domains that have become objects of security practice in recent times. Furthermore, by considering these topics in a range of societies around the world, anthropology broadens security studies geographically, pushing beyond the occidentalist tendencies within the field and bringing other, non-Western perspectives to bear on the conceptualization of security. Anthropologies of security move beyond the macrolevel processes of states and institutions to consider the daily practices and lived experiences of those whose lives are shaped by them, and who must negotiate the challenges that they impose. Anthropologies of security also take us inside the state and its institutions, to consider the daily processes by which states and state agents do their work of making and enforcing policy and law, revealing the ideologies and discourses entailed in their production and implementation. Anthropology also takes us beyond the state, to see how state policies and practices impact the different populations subject to them. Here we discover additional diversity and come to see the objects of securitization as more than the passive victims of often oppressive policies, but as active individuals and communities who respond to, appropriate, resist, and absorb the strictures that security, its rhetorics and its policies, imposes.

Ethnography, I have suggested, is a key dimension of the anthropological approach generally and of the anthropological study of security specifically, and represents another vital contribution to interdisciplinary security studies. Ethnography brings to life the often static representations of securitization and social life, putting into motion those processes that otherwise might be misunderstood as structures. The ethnographic method places anthropologists face to face with the lived realities of security and insecurity that their research subjects encounter on a daily basis. Perhaps for that reason, ethnographic methodologies (sometimes referred to as "qualitative research") are becoming increasingly popular among scholars across a range of disciplines and represent an important contribution of anthropology to an interdisciplinary study of security, among other topics. There are challenges and dangers associated with ethnographic work, however, especially in insecure places, and scholars of all disciplines are advised to seek training in their effective use and potential risks (for a review of the literature on staying safe while conducting qualitative research, see Goldstein 2014).

Such proximity offers unparalleled insight into these contemporary realities. It also imposes special obligations, however, which can lead to disagreement among practitioners. As I mentioned briefly in the introduction, some anthropologists understand their work as having implications and potential effects beyond the academy and take an explicitly "engaged" or "activist" approach to their scholarship by making their work accessible to nonacademic readers and/or using their knowledge and status to advocate for the causes to which their research subjects are committed. Not all anthropologists agree that this engaged approach is appropriate, however, with some suggesting that it undermines the discipline's objectivity and scientific potential (see the discussion in Goldstein 2012a). Others worry about the political implications of anthropological advocacy, expressing concern that the work of "security anthropologists" in support of US military operations overseas could induce the perceptions that non-Western people have of anthropologists as employees of the state. Nevertheless, given the significance of security concerns in the lives of the people whom many anthropologists study, the question of how, or whether, to direct anthropological research to the public's benefit remains open in the discipline.

Anthropologies of security, as I have tried to make clear, are unavoidably interdisciplinary. Anthropologists of security and insecurity share a basic set of orientations. Their work is grounded in ethnography; they situate that ethnography, historicizing local culture in a broader framework to understand its antecedents and development, and in a wider social field seen both from the "top down" and the "bottom up"; they look cross-culturally and privilege the perspectives of those whose voices are often muted or absent in public debate; and they broaden what is often considered to be the proper domain of security studies. But their work draws on a variety of different concepts and categories, many of them developed by practitioners of other disciplines, to ground and develop their analyses of the situations they observe. What is more, the utility of the ethnographic approach has been widely recognized, and ethnography is being deployed by other disciplinary researchers in pursuit of their own scholarly objectives. These facts make it difficult to define a single "anthropology of security," or to limit the practice of anthropology to those who publicly self-identify as anthropologists. Better to welcome the inherent multivocality and interdisciplinarity of the approach, and to appreciate the unique insights that these anthropologies can offer to a study of security and securitization in contemporary societies.

# 4 | *Geography*
Securing places and spaces of securitization
PHILIPPE LE BILLON

With disciplinary roots in imperialism and the military, geography has long engaged with security issues. As the French geographer Yves Lacoste (1976) famously stated, "La géographie ça sert d'abord à faire la guerre" (Geography serves, first and foremost, to wage war). Mainstream geography grounded in materialist positivism provides spatial information to identify and address a broad range of security risks, including crime and terrorism but also natural disasters, diseases, pollutants, or chronic poverty. In contrast, critical geography drawing from anarchism, feminism, and postmodernism mostly seeks to demonstrate how insecurity is often paradoxically generated by dominant security discourses and practices, while striving to bring about progressive alternatives. Geography is thus not only a discipline deploying spatial analysis to achieve greater security, but also one concerned with the consequences of "securitization" and with emancipatory possibilities for a less vulnerable world. This chapter provides a survey of geography's engagement with concepts of security, charting some of the main questions, theoretical approaches, and methodologies of this broad discipline before discussing some of its strengths and limitations.

Geography has been and remains deeply connected with "official" security agendas (Mamadouh 2004; O'Loughlin and Heske 1991). Tasked with the mission of "knowing the world" and helping to pinpoint the location and movements of threats, geography and geographers have been mobilized in the production of military maps, atlases, and systems of geosurveillance ranging from CCTV to drones and satellites. Indeed, many professional geographers have served, and continue to serve, "national security" agendas – some in the direct employ of the military (Woodward 2005). My own alma mater department at Oxford was the first academic home of Professor Halford Mackinder (of "geographical pivot of history" fame); during the Second World War, the department also played an active role in the British war effort, assembling an odd mix of spatial information – from geological surveys to tourism leaflets – to produce British operational maps. The department, anecdotally, was also said to be a place for MI6 to recruit undergraduates. Geography, from this perspective, is partially a discipline in the service of statecraft – a necessary instrument of spatial analysis in the toolbox of security practices, as seen in the context of 9/11 and the "War on Terror" (Cutter et al. 2003; Flint 2003). Yet geography is also a discipline engaging more broadly with "security."

As Philo (2012, 1) states, the broad concern of geographers is to understand "how worldly geographies are implicated in achieving or compromising the security (safety and sustainability) of environments, peoples, and communities." Reflecting such extensive definition of "security," geographers have deployed geographical knowledge and approaches beyond the "classical" realm of narrowly defined state security interests, examining broader threats and spaces of (in)security. Disaster prevention, famine relief, and health service provision, to name a few, have all benefited from geographical perspectives and inputs to increase the security of individuals and communities (Meade 2012; Wisner et al. 2004). It is no surprise, therefore that some geographers have expressed an interest in broader and more progressive conceptualization of security, such as "human security," and that, in turn, the field of human security has drawn from geography – most notably in terms of spatial analyses of insecurity at individual and community scales (Owen 2008).

Geographers have also provided a critique of *securitization* (i.e., the framing of particular issues within security narratives and practices). Such framing is a performative *event* in the sense of constructing an existential threat supposedly necessitating securitization, often at the expense of other perspectives and more accurate and/or nuanced portrayals – with Dalby (1988, 415) demonstrating how US cold war–era "security discourses ... ideologically construct[ed] the Soviet Union as a dangerous 'Other.'" Framing also consists of a social *process* that legitimates "urgent and exceptional measures" and suspends usual political processes; see Buzan and de Wilde (1998). Moreover, securitization often enables the "hardening" of disciplinary processes to address the supposed threat, notably through deploying physical violence and suspending rights. Yet, in this respect, geographers tend to use instead the terms "militarization," or the imposition of military-like order or force, and "militarism," or the (in)direct "extension of military influence [and ideology] into civilian political, social and cultural spheres" (see Barnes and Farish 2006; Gregory and Graham 2009, 464–465).

As this chapter seeks to demonstrate, many geographers have taken a critical stance on "security" – as both a key signifier within public discourse and a set of often-repressive practices, and some have pursued a scholarly agenda of "desecuritization," focusing in particular on biased security discourses and practices that entrench uneven power relations and enhance the security of privileged populations at the expense of the most vulnerable (Hyndman 2007). Both feminist geography and so-called critical geopolitics – and their hybrid approaches and variants – have been at the forefront of this agenda, which seeks to expose spatial representations and discourses of "endangerment" but also provides alternative narratives and modes of collective action (Tuathail 2000; Koopman 2011). As summed up by Dalby (2002, 163), one of the founders of the subfield of "critical geopolitics": "Security ... is about control, certainty, and predictability in an uncertain world, and in attempting to forestall chance and change, it is frequently a violent practice." Critical geography scholars have denounced the violence of security practices, and most notably its spatial structures often constitutive of traditional security practices (Till *et al.* 2013), and other spatial forms of exclusion and subordination involved in the uneven distribution of security among individuals and communities (Hyndman 2004; O'Tuathail 1996).

Providing an overview of geography's engagement with security-related concepts, this chapter focuses on critical studies of securitization processes, social injustice, and power inequities. In a broad range of subdisciplines – from economic geography and urban studies to political geography and disaster studies – geographers place questions about human welfare and dignity, indigenous rights, and environmental protection at the core of their research. Security, from this perspective, is both a stated objective (e.g., addressing threats to human dignity and well-being) and, given its frequent partiality and uneven consequences, a threat to this objective (e.g., securitization processes protecting some people, yet endangering others and the environment). In the remainder of this chapter, I explore these issues by presenting some of the central research questions in the discipline before examining the main theoretical perspectives and methodological approaches in various subdisciplines. I then discuss strengths and limitations of some of the analytical approaches adopted across the discipline of geography before concluding.

Beyond geographical trivia: questioning security from a spatial perspective

The etymology of the word "geography" reveals something of its intellectual origins: "writing about the earth" or "writing of space." Such activity requires an interdisciplinary approach seeking to bridge the "natural" and "social" sciences in the study of human interactions with landscapes, settlements, and socioenvironmental processes – with ideas of separation and relation between the "natural" and the "social" varying significantly across cultures and periods (Latour 2013). At the core of the discipline is, of course, space. It is thus important to understand how the discipline conceptualizes space before turning to specific security-related questions engaged by geographers.

Space, geography, and security

Geography is often thought of as a set of "facts," such as the location of mountains or rivers, the size of countries, the length of borders, the location of capital cities, or the concentration of ethnic minorities. This is particularly the case in political science and international relations studies seeking to account for "geographical context" variables (Buhaug and Gates 2002; Collier and Hoeffler 2002). Arguably, the collection and analytical integration of these geographical variables constitute a foundation of classical geography. Such classical geography is still prevalent in mainstream security-related studies, with spatial variables informing statistical analyses on security risks. Space, in this view, corresponds to a "container" within which geographical facts influence security-related processes (for a critique, see Agnew 1994). Based in material positivism and generally following an inductive approach, this conventional approach mostly combines predictive models, spatially referenced data collection, and statistical analysis using Geographical Information Systems (GIS). Classical disciplinary concepts – such as concentration, diffusion, networks, and scales – are used to describe, for example, spatial clusters of (in)security or the geographical pathways involved in the diffusion of threats. Much of this research, especially when related to "national security" risks, is currently conducted by intelligence agencies and subcontractors, as with geospatial analyses of risks to US "homeland security"; see Baker *et al.* (2004).

Much of contemporary academic geography, however, criticizes this approach. To start with, such an approach is generally deterministic, attributing particular properties and effects to a broad category of "geographical facts," such as borders. If statistical patterns can inform understandings of the effects of such "facts," they do so at the risk of erasing the diversity within each category (e.g., not all borders are the same), the historical processes and contingencies involved (e.g., how borders came to be constituted and thereby express preexisting power relations), and the social dimensions of these "facts" (e.g., how borders become constitutive of "national" identities).

From a critical perspective, and as mentioned previously, space is not a "container" within which a bundle of geographical facts are physically located or even a neutral "stage" on which social processes are played out (e.g., a "resource area" to be fought over). Rather, as Massey (1992, 70) argues, space is deeply relational and "far from being the realm of stasis, space and the spatial are also implicated ... in the production of history and thus, potentially, in politics."[1] Space, from this perspective, is both socially constructed and socially constructing. Geographers thus do not simply "map" the spatial *outcomes* of social processes, thereby supposedly leaving the understanding of these processes to other disciplines, but rather expose the many spatial *dimensions* of social processes.

In relation to security, this means that space is at the same time the way security is performed and the way securitized space becomes performative in relation to security-related actors and objects. Space is thus itself a political object constituted by, and constitutive of, security discourses and praxis. The logics of securitization are expressed in space (e.g., the reinforcement of borders and the transformation of neighboring

---

[1] For an analytical framework on space, see Harvey (2006). Harvey distinguishes between, on the one hand, absolute space (space as a "thing in itself," e.g., a space in which objects are located), relative space (space existing through objects being relative to each other, e.g., space between two objects), and relational space (space existing through mutual relationships between objects, e.g., objects defined by contrast to another); and, on the other hand, between material or experienced space, representations of (or conceptualized) space, and spaces of representation or lived spaces.

landscapes), and, in turn, the logics of "security spaces" inform social and environmental processes (e.g., how the spatiality of borders and borderlands modifies social behaviors and influences both the patterns of, and perspectives on, criminal activities, local environments, and the identities of residents and migrants). If geography is about the "writing of space" and is centrally engaged with the question of how "space matters" (Massey 2005), then geographies of security are, by analogy, about the writing of "secure(d) space" and how such "spaces of security/securitization" are causally effective on political processes.

In his brief discussion of "geographies of security," Philo (2012, 4–5) identifies three principal spaces examined by the discipline from critical perspectives. The first consists of *carceral spaces*: "spaces set aside for 'securing' – detaining, locking up/away – problematic populations of one kind or another." Mainly examining prisons but also asylums and camps, carceral geographies focus on physical and symbolic dimensions of boundaries serving to *keep in* inmates (in contrast to most spaces of security, which seek to keep threats out – although boundaries and "bordering" practices play multiple roles in relation to opposing flows; see Diener and Hagen 2009); for instance, the Berlin Wall was officially constructed to prevent the infiltration of Western imperialists but also served symbolically and physically to sever and retain a population seeking refuge in the West. The second is *spaces and landscapes of defense*, which Gold and Revill (2000, 2–3) define as "landscapes shaped or otherwise materially affected by formal or informal strategies designed to reduce the risk of crime, or deter intrusion, or cope with actual or perceived threats to the security of the area's occupants." This includes studies of the spatialization of threats and defense strategies at a variety of scales but also inquiries into the securitization of fears, by which a security logic privileging some options, such as policing, over others frames or reinforces legitimate or fabricated anxieties. The third consists of *scripted geopolitical spaces of (in)security*; with most notably "critical geopolitics" seeking to deconstruct the "establishment" security discourses of security officials, strategic think tanks, and leading media (see later discussion).

Approaches to security issues

Conventional geographical approaches to security have centered on the question of – usually military – control of spaces and territories. Historically, this conventional approach has analyzed various aspects of spatial distribution, including location and differentiation across space and scales. Akin to the materialism of realist international relations perspectives, these conventional approaches have mostly sought to document the "facts on the ground" (e.g., through the US National Geospatial-Intelligence Agency, focusing on satellite imagery) by documenting the Euclidian spatiality of landscapes, populations, resources, and infrastructures (especially transport networks and urban areas). This information is then used in spatial analysis – quantitative approaches mostly relying on georeferenced statistical analysis – in order to operationalize risk and vulnerability assessments to feed into predictive models. There has also been a revival of "regional geography," which combines geospatial data collection with socioeconomic, environmental, and cultural analysis in search of greater legibility and internal consistency within a defined area. In the most elaborate manifestations, the idea of relational spaces and dialectical relationships between security and "local" social-environmental processes constituting the new "battlescapes" of the War on Terror have included some degree of reflexivity – albeit often within the ultimate goal of implementing "official" security agendas. More critical analyses have tended to take an ethnographic approach, drawing parallels between conventional geopolitical perspectives and urban security, especially in terms of ideas of secured territory and "zero-tolerance" policies (Herbert 1996; Graham 2011).

To some extent – parallel to the renewed interest in, and pressure on, "area studies" in the post-9/11 era – conventional geography has seen some tools and practitioners being put at the service of the US-military 'Human Terrain System,' for example, for the war in Afghanistan (Crampton *et al.* 2014; Shami and Godoy-Anativia 2007). Renewed interest in "facts on the ground" and the celebration of classical geopolitical insights ("what the map tells us," e.g., classical geographic features) are also part of this trend (Kaplan 2012). Geography has not experienced the depth of debates that characterized the controversial mobilization of anthropology/ists by the US army and intelligence agencies to improve understanding of the "human terrain" of "battlescapes." Yet, critics have questioned, documented, and denounced the (profitable) complicities of conventional geographies, long at work in previous colonial aggressions (Bryan 2010; Crampton *et al.* 2014; Flint 2003).

There is also a growing interest in better understanding how spatial representations influence security discourses. For example, critical geopolitics scholars have demonstrated the importance of simplistic and biased spatial representations to bolster security discourses. Denominations such as "rogue states," "unstable regions," "porous borderlands," or "dangerous neighbourhoods" are constructed and mobilized to render invisible many of the characteristics of these areas (and their inhabitants), thereby allowing for a hegemonic perspective on how these places and people are to be dealt with through security measures (Gregory 2004). In this regard, questions about the spatialization of fears and securitization processes are central to recent geographical inquiries into security issues (Gregory and Pred 2007; Klinkenberg 2007; Sparke 2007).

Although many of the discipline's fundamental questions relate to space, it is not geographers' only "referent object" in research on security. Indeed, much of what are conventionally considered geographical approaches are undertaken in the field of security studies – *outside* the bounds of geography as a discipline.[2] For example, the aim of much of geography's geopolitics subdiscipline – in contrast to political science and, in particular, "security studies" – is to expose and deconstruct geopolitical discourses seeking to justify official security objectives, rather than contribute to them (Dalby and Tuathail 2002). Even if not exclusively focusing on the spatial dimensions of security, most geographers do emphasize spatial (and historical) contingency rather than look for "universal laws" – thereby arguing for "place-specific" understandings of security issues.

From a research purpose perspective, three main types of inquiries can be distinguished: *descriptive*, *prescriptive*, and *reflexive*. While most "professional" geographers work on the first two, many "academic" geographers are now focusing on the third set of reflexive questions – partly in the hope that such critical engagement will prevent further harm to populations and environments targeted by securitization processes. In this sense, the order of these three types of inquiries explored later can be understood as sequential and progressive (though historically contiguous when considering some of the early "radical" geographers).

---

[2] For a detailed discussion of political science approaches to security and space, see Brauch (2008).

Questions associated with *descriptive* inquiries seek, in essence, to determine the geography of risk and (in)security, mostly by describing where threats are originating and which areas or communities are most vulnerable or insecure and assessing their main causes. Epitomized by military geography seeking to understand better the "terrain" of operations, this type of descriptive geography is also applied in disaster, water, and food security studies as well as in criminology to find likely "hotspots" of insecurity (Bakker 2012; Herbert 1982; Woodward 2005). The second set of inquiries is primarily *prescriptive*: aimed at determining where preemptive or reactive measures might be most efficiently deployed (for example, responding to flood risks through land use planning, famine through food aid, or threats of violence through police deployment). Both descriptive and prescriptive sets of inquiries draw from spatial analysis and emphasize interactions between human and physical geography (Burton *et al.* 1978; Klinkenberg 2007; Wisner *et al.* 2004). Together, they constitute much of the praxis of conventional and "professional" (rather than academic) geography.

The third set of inquiries can be described as *reflexive* in the sense of seeking to understand critically processes of securitization through which security narratives and practices are not only deployed to render (in)secure but also to pursue other objectives (such as entrenching uneven power relations). Here the aim is to grasp better how the pursuit of securitization makes some spaces and people (more) insecure. More broadly, the aim is also to identify the "nexus of security and the social" (Cowen and Smith 2009, 32) whereby securitization strategies do not simply emanate from security apparatus but also pervade a society organizing itself around the production of (violent) security (Bernazzoli and Flint 2009). The main questions are thus about who is made (in) secure where, how, why, and with what consequences.

Some of these inquiries are also *self-reflective* in the sense that they reflect upon the effect of their own critiques on the object of study, one observation here being that critiques tend unintentionally to reinforce security narratives by reproducing them and failing to provide alternative conceptualizations and processes (Sharp 2000).

Main themes

Thematically, political geography has engaged with a large number of referent objects, from the state and geopolitical orders to populations and the environment. In the following, I discuss some of the more specific referent objects within geographical studies of security.

State, territory, and sovereignty

The most prominent "referent object" within political geography is the state and the associated interstate system. Chief concerns falling under the broad rubric of state or national security are questions of political stability and sovereignty and their territorial dimensions. Territory was, and remains, the traditional object of security for mainstream geopolitics. Reflections about state security and its territorial dimensions can be found as early as in the studies of Aristotle and Strabo on the stability of city-states and empires and in some of the foundational works of "modern" political geography, including those of Friedrich Ratzel.[3] In recent years, concerns have turned to querying "national security" discourses naturalizing nation-states as a "security container" and identifying existential threats that range from competing or failed states to terrorist groups and illegal migrants (the latter two being at times merged). The subdiscipline of "critical geopolitics" mostly seeks to understand the power/knowledge dimensions of geopolitical representations, their entanglement with militarism, and their relations with "national" identity (O'Tuathail 1996): How do practitioners of statecraft and "security studies" construct ideas about people and places through the essentializing lens of geopolitical representation (e.g., East/West); how do these representations "influence political behaviors and policy choices" (e.g., humanitarian interventions); how in turn do these ideas and representations affect understanding of people, places, and politics (Fouberg *et al.* 2012, 535); and how do "national" security discourses contribute to the construction of national identity and with what consequences?

---

[3] A foundational element of political geography, itself indirectly tied to some forms of environmental determinism in the application of social Darwinism to the evolution of states as "organisms." Initially largely concerned with nationalist concerns, "classical" political geographers such as Rudolf Kjellen (Sweden), Friedrich Razel (Germany), Halford Mackinder (England), and Isaiah Bowman (United States) were strongly partisan – and nationalistic – in their views on empire yet at times critical. For an introduction to political geography, see Painter (2008). For a recent revisiting of foundational works and the role of Friedrich Litz, see Palacio (2013).

In one of the earliest works to address these questions, Sharp (1993) examines the role of public media in reproducing geopolitical fears, deconstructing the *Reader's Digest* to understand national identity construction among the US public better. Similarly, Campbell (1998, x) explores "American" subjectivities associated with US foreign policy largely driven by "national" security concerns and seeks to identify how the "moral spaces made possible by the ethical borders of identity as much as the territorial boundaries of states are constituted through the writing of a threat." In a recent study, Irene Vélez-Torres (2014) exposes the ways through which the Colombian government is recasting a militarization of rural areas that protects the "rights" of foreign extractive companies over those of local communities through a discourse of "democratic securitization." This governmentality regime first claims that "terrorism" (armed insurrection) is the antithesis of democracy and thus "outside the national project," thereby necessitating annihilation; second, it impels society as a whole to participate in the project of securitization, following in the footsteps of the military and the state; third, it promises the ensuing "rule of law" to be the guarantor of development and economic prosperity.

Issues of territorial infringements and losses have long constituted the major security threat to the *geobody* of the nation – the geographically bounded imagination of a "people" crystallized through the spatial contours of the "country" (Thongchai 1994) – while territorial acquisitions constituted the core of colonial ventures. Strategies for securing territory may seem both passé and acutely *current*. Such territorial concerns and strategies seem passé in the sense of a supposed move toward largely "deterritorialized" forms of (in)security within an international context in which networked forms of threats (e.g., Al Qaeda) and geoeconomical logics and practices of dominance (i.e., wealth accumulation through market control) seem to have overtaken geopolitical ones (i.e., dominance through territorial control). In this perspective, as Cowen and Smith (2009) argue, territorial control and acquisition remain mostly a "tactical option rather than a strategic necessity." Yet, territorial concerns continue to be relevant – from discourses and practices of indigenous land rights to "homeland security." The main issue is thus how *current* territorial logics work – one most notably explored within the context of the "War on Terror"; see Ingram and Dodds (2012). In much-noted studies, Elden (2009) demonstrates the relevance of territorial sovereignty, or lack thereof, and violations of territorial integrity – whether in Al Qaeda's territorial objectives and operations or those of US military interventions – while Gregory (2004) exposes the many geographical dimensions of the "colonial present" in Afghanistan, Palestine, and Iraq. Geographical inquiries into the spatialities of the US military base in Guantanamo Bay, Cuba, have probed into the "security-sovereignty-territory" nexus, enabling a discussion of Agamben's concept of "spaces of exception" (Gregory 2006; Reid-Henry 2007).

Questioning US "homeland security" discourses and praxis, Sparke (2006) highlights the security dilemmas and tensions in US management of the flows of goods and people across borders within a neoliberal framework. For example, it is within this context that the institutionalization of securitization policies is translated into "thickening" spatial contexts, which are expressed in the harder materialities of boundaries, the larger waiting rooms at airports and the ever more complex instruments of surveillance and "visibility" (Konrad and Nicol 2011). As such, the state and the interstate system have been among the main referent objects of geography research on security and will likely continue to be so; however, as discussed later, this has merged with or given way to other referent objects and research themes.

Geopolitical (dis)orders and transitions

So-called geopolitical orders and transitions in-between also constitute referent objects. The most prominent ones within geography are the "end of the Cold War" and the move to the "War on Terror" – in part the result of their coincidence with renewed disciplinary interest in geopolitics and security themes. Such transitions are for many societies part and parcel of the reframing of various scales of security – from international stability to the domain of the intimate. Here again questions about identity arise: How do security discourses evolve, for example, in the context of post–Cold War transition and possible European integration for Eastern European states, and how does such evolution play out in relation to "national identities"? Examining the case of Estonia, Kuus (2002, 91) finds that "both pro- and contra-EU arguments pivot particularly on claims about geopolitical and cultural threats. On the one hand, international integration is constructed as a security measure against the Russian threat. On the other hand, insofar as supranational institutions pressure Estonia to naturalize its

Russian-speaking residents, who are construed as representatives of the Russian threat, international integration is also depicted as dangerous to Estonian identity." More broadly, how is sovereignty renegotiated from a security perspective in the context of regionalization and globalization? Kuus (2002) argues that political debates frame international integration in terms of trade-offs between national security (resting on notions of independence from previous tutelage) and autonomy (from the interference of current ones – such as the institutions and rules of the European Union).

Transitions also constitute the result of, or at least introduce hope for subaltern/alternative security perspectives and approaches. Among the questions here is how such departures can gain traction. As further discussed later, feminism and postcolonial studies contribute to critical perspectives on and alternatives to "national" security. Postcolonial studies have drawn attention to subaltern discourses, with feminism further helping to embody and scale down analysis while promoting a progressive agenda. Not only seeking a denunciation of dominant realist security discourses, these perspectives have also pursued effective resistance and alternative options. For Koopman (2011), "other securities" are not only possible; they are happening. These alternatives include "antigeopolitics" – efforts by groups to refute and reject hegemonic geopolitics and essentialized identities of securitization discourses; see Routledge (2003) – as well as "altergeopolitics" – projects through which local communities seek actively to construct their own peace through spaces of nonviolence; see Koopman (2011). Using the example of Tanzania, Sharp (2013) seeks to call greater attention to "subaltern geopolitics" in an effort to improve understanding of what she terms "postcolonial security" in the context of both the War on Terror and Nyerere's "Third Way" geopolitical project of nonalignment and unity for Africa. Such inquiries help in understanding not only how realist security narratives, such as the War on Terror, play out in "subaltern" settings, notably though the public media, but also how postcolonial security projects – in the sense of both a postindependence context and awareness of the "colonial present" – come to fruition or not.

Populations and biopolitics

Populations have also become an important referent object of geographical study of security (Legg 2005). Rather than situating territories as their main referent object, security regimes focus in this case on populations. Here inquiries deal with the governance of life, most notably by the state, and the biological features of human populations as a referent object of securitization strategies. Considerations for the spatial dimensions of the biopolitical include attention to the geobody of the state and the biobody of the nation and associated perspectives on sovereignty, such as from territorial forms of sovereignty to social forms of sovereignty preoccupied with the life and biological characteristics of populations.[4] This theme is now mostly approached through Foucault's concepts of biopower and biopolitics, which he developed in a series of lectures including "Society Must Be Defended" (Rutherford and Rutherford 2013a,b). Critical studies mostly examine securitized subjectivities – seeking to answer questions about securitization processes turning *subjects* into *objects* of security, such as in relation to the value of life through Agamben's notion of "bare life" (Sylvester 2006) or in reference to life and labor through Polanyi's concept of "fictitious commodities" (Rossi 2013).

These studies have mostly engaged with two populations, which – at the risk of constructing gross binaries – consist of a national one in need of security and a subaltern one to be made secure. The first population is the nation's population, or "biobody," and the need to secure it from threats. This population with "national characteristics" becomes a politically contested arena of governance. For example, "undocumented immigration" (discussed later) is cast as a major threat, but also racist policies constructing threats to the biobody from within the geobody of the state – through, for example, ethnonationalist discourses motivating and legitimating state-led genocides (Coleman and Grove 2009; Tyner 2012). Scaling down biobodies to the self, Holmes (2008, 375) investigates agoraphobia and the notion of a "secure base" in relation to private and public spaces, while Katz (2008) exposes what she calls the "parental hypervigilance" in the age of the "Security State," pointing at the increasing use of "nanny cams" (video cameras to spy on child care workers), child ID kits including DNA samples, and child electronic chipping and GPS tracking.

---

[4] Rudolf Kjellen, who coined the term "geopolitics," considered these dimensions through the concept of *phylopolitics* (form of society) and *biopolitics* (life of society); see Haggman (1998).

The second population (which also includes but extends beyond the national population) consists of people variously represented as "threatened" as a result of their "vulnerable," "marginalized," or "subaltern" status but is also portrayed as "threatening" to themselves and to more privileged populations and thus in need of securitization. Among such populations are those who are essentialized as "migrants," "refugees," "squatters," and "the poor" in general (Nally 2008). Again, spatial questions related to the construction of these identities are prominent and explored notably through studies of the "spaces of refugees" such as "refugee camps" (Hyndman 2000; Ramadan 2013) as well as informal urban dwellings (Sanyal 2012). Springer (2008), for example, decries the consequences of authoritarian neoliberalism and the associated discourses of "security through economic growth" that have renewed processes of dispossession and the creation of spaces of exception targeting urban "squatters" in particular.

Overlaps between these two populations provide fertile ground for analyses of securitization processes. This is notably demonstrated by Hyndman (2007) in her study of the securitization of fear in "post-Tsunami" Sri Lanka, where she looks at the interplay of aid donors and "recipients" and the ways in which "fear is produced and framed to justify violence, exclusion, and hatred" – including through international aid provision that lacks conflict sensitivity and is driven by perceptions of vulnerability "at home" from future refugees. In part related to biopolitics and the security of "idealized" nations, migration has also become an important theme because of its strong security overtones in many countries. This theme is particularly prominent in geography because of its many spatial dimensions, including flows, borders, and territorialized identities. Among the many questions associated with this theme are the changing identities of migrants, the interactions between movement and order, the tensions between the economic need for "open borders" and fears of Others closing up borders, and the causes of securitization. Bourbeau (2011) compares strong versus weak securitization in France and Canada, respectively, stressing the importance of cultural factors especially in the domestic audience. Finally, the security dimensions of population health and, in particular, the threat of pandemics have also attracted the attention of geographers (Brown 2011). Ingram (2008) examines the spatialization of fear, questioning the scaling up of health threats to the "global" level, the (re)location of causes to external agents and contexts, and the consolidation of hegemonic interests through the pursuit of "global health security."

Urban spaces, surveillance, and militarized policing

Urban spaces have unsurprisingly become the focus of security-related studies within geography (Graham 2008; Gregory 2003; Smith 2010). Not only are cities constituted in part by violent uprooting processes resulting from the securitization of rural spaces – often with dual objectives of accumulation through dispossession and counterinsurgency (e.g., on land enclosures, see Wolf 1999, and on forested landscapes, see Peluso and Vandergeest 2011). Cities are also "targeted by terrorist groups, and these threats are used in turn to legitimate widespread efforts to securitize cities through installing checkpoints, defensive urban and landscape designs, and systems of intensified electronic surveillance" as well as militarized police (Graham and Gregory 2009).

Elaborating on the securitizing of urban spaces, Crang and Graham (2007, 789) reflect on the politics of "sentient cities" – urban space shaped by the omnipresence and embeddedness of information processes, "where we not only think of cities but cities think of us, where the environment reflexively monitors our behavior." Whether applied to "homeland" cities or "war-zone" cities, "the key dynamic centres on attempts at rendering complex urban flows and structures permanently transparent to tracking and surveillance systems" (Crang and Graham 2007, 799). To this end, new spatial scales and temporalities of surveillance are needed – beyond instant CCTV, drones, and satellite imagery to tracking individuals over extended periods, algorithmic deciphering of suspicious behaviors, identification of potential threats, and validation of likely targets. Pervasive biometric sensors, ubiquitous identity tagging, and constant big data mining have come to constitute the new "panopticon" of twenty-first century urban space, feeding "dreams of securitized urban omniscience surrounding the 'war on terror'" (Crang and Graham 2007, 794).

Cyberspace is also an object of inquiry by geographers. Early examples include studies of the "constant and reciprocal connections between cyberspace and other social spaces" to counter hegemonic discourses, such as the Zapatistas' challenge to the Mexican government's neoliberal securitization discourse (Froehling 1997, 291) and more recently discussions of Wikileaks' denunciation of US security practices (Springer *et al.* 2012). Another aspect is the extension of securitization and militarization through, and because of, cyberspace. Resulting in part from changes in military doctrine, 9/11, and new information technologies, cyberspace becomes the object of securitization processes to protect critical infrastructures and to identify potential terrorists and militarization to conduct disabling attacks on targets. From this perspective, cyberspace extends an "everywhere war" supposedly required to address the "differentially distributed but widely dispersed" vulnerabilities resulting from (para)military and terrorist violence (Gregory 2011).

Geographers have as well inquired into the securitization of space through policing modes of governance. Most have given particular attention to the hardening of policing in the regulation of urban space, with studies examining the broadening of policing functions to a whole array of actors and institutions including "state, private and voluntary actors" (Yarwood 2007, 447). In contrast to studies of the hardening of policing through the merger of military and police actors and functions, Paasche (2013) points at the "softening of security," whereby policing functions of social services are imposed on the urban poor. These services complement a policing network of public police, private security, and neighborhood watches within a broader governance framework of control and under the guise of "assistance", for example to "street people" in certain neighborhoods of Cape Town. Much of the policing literature in geography thus points at discourses and practices of policing that result in the exclusion of certain people from particular spaces under securitization modes of governance that extend the idea of threatened and secured space to everyday spaces of circulation, including downtown areas, buses, and malls (Beckett and Herbert 2009).

Resources and environmental security

Another theme is that of environmental security and, more broadly, referent objects such as the environment, natural resources, or populations (Barnett 2001; Dalby 2002; Le Billon 2012; Peluso and Watts 2001).[5] These objects are now frequently set within the context

---

[5] These concerns derive first from (critiques of) classic environmental determinist perspectives that characterized some of the discipline, at least until the 1930s,

of a general shift to the "Anthropocene," this new geological era defined by the vast extent of anthropogenic impacts on the planet; this concept further widens the purview of environmental security both spatially and temporally (Brauch 2008; Dalby 2009). Much of the "practical" geography on environmental security remains geared toward descriptive and prescriptive purposes, mobilizing geographical knowledge to mitigate or adapt to environmental risks (e.g., flooding) and resource scarcity (e.g., in relation to ecosystems' carrying capacity). Yet, critical geography perspectives, as best demonstrated by Dalby (2009), seek to determine who is made (in)secure through the securitization of environmental or resource issues and what forms of violence come to be exercised on the environment and communities. Much work, for example, has focused on the security aspects of climate change, such as food insecurity and broad human security risks (Barnett and Adger 2007; Bohle *et al.* 1994), the risk of climate-related armed conflicts (Raleigh and Urdal 2007), or the regressive consequences of prominent climate security discourses and policies (McDonald 2013). Several geographers have also inquired about the coercive dimensions of "securing" resources and the environment through biodiversity conservation (Peluso 1993; Neumann 2004), counterinsurgency-based forestry regulations (Peluso and Vandergeest 2011), and food security regimes (Sommerville *et al.* 2014).

Summary

If the core concern of the discipline has been about the spatial dimensions of security and securitization processes, the breadth and scope of questions and areas of inquiries are vast – ranging across questions of environmental security, classical geopolitical concerns about nation-states and the international system, and preoccupations with social cohesion related to identity construction and everyday forms of socio-economic vulnerability. The perspectives taken on framing these questions have also varied considerably. While geographic praxis is generally tied to the pursuit of "official" security agendas, many geographers have taken a critical stance, which is reflected in their attention

but also "environmental possibilism" – a more nuanced but still divisive relational approach between social and natural systems (Sprout and Sprout 1957). In contrast, recent concepts, such as "socionature," have been seeking to remove boundaries between the social and the natural (Swyngedouw 1999).

to uneven power relations and the biased effects of securitization processes.[6] Some geographers have followed suit, particularly from the 1970s onward, focusing on the discriminating character of security discourses and repressive character of securitization processes as well as their spatial dimensions. As discussed later, the theoretical grounding of "critical geography" in poststructuralism, feminism, and postcolonial theory has contributed much to such alternative perspectives. What is at stake now is a more thorough combination of the three main approaches outlined previously – descriptive, prescriptive, and (self-)reflexive – so that geographical studies of security extend beyond spatial tool or pure critique to advance a progressive conception and praxis of security rejecting the discriminatory logic of securitization and the many forms of violence involved in security practices. Such goals may appear as naïve and utopic when considering many of the concerns and routines of "security." Yet, it is precisely those goals that are needed to bring about inclusive and progressive forms of security that reduce the various forms of violence and the most respect for difference.

Theoretical perspectives and methodological approaches

Emerging as a "modern" discipline in the nineteenth century in Western countries, geography's theoretical engagements with security evolved over time and drew from several fields including political economy, sociology, and the history of sciences. Such engagements with new theory followed not only from scholarly innovations in other fields but also from self-reflexivity within the discipline in the face of broader ethical concerns about deep-seated inequalities and the complex interplay of superstructure and agency within capitalism (and later, neoliberalism). In short, there was a sense among a few geographers, such as David Harvey, that the discipline needed to move beyond the environmental determinism, descriptive regionalism, and universalism of the 1950s "quantitative revolution" prevalent in most

---

[6] Such critical stances can be found in the work of late nineteenth century anarchist geographers, such as Reclus and Kropotkin, who pursued alternative paths to a more broadly defined "security." Denouncing the inequities of capitalist economies and rejecting oppressive forms of state-led governance (including communism), these geographers advocated alternative forms of security, such as "mutual aid," in the case of Kropotkin (Springer 2012).

of mainstream geography at the time. From the early 1970s to the early 1990s, a number of shifts occurred within geography, including feminist theory and postmodernism (Johnston 2010).

Geography and critical theory

The main theory objectives of contemporary geographers have been to explain how an issue came to be included in the security realm and to explore its normative and embodied implications. From the early 1990s onward, much of geography joined the "critical turn" in security studies – most notably through the emergence of the subfield of "critical geopolitics." Critical geographical studies of security thus became about the writing of space through security as a concept: how secure or insecure spaces, and the means to render people (in)secure, are constructed and performed. Such studies mostly draw from poststructuralism in seeking to disrupt established meanings and narratives and expose power relations that sustain the "truth effects" of spatial categorizations. Building from Foucault's concept of "power/knowledge," a focus on discourse and deconstruction of meanings offers opportunities to understand better why some issues are framed in security terms, and how. Drawing from postcolonial theory and most notably the works of Edward Said, critical geographers have been especially attentive to the "colonial vocabularies within which geopolitical thought in general, and security discourse in particular, remain enmeshed" (Dalby 2002, 184; Gregory 2004).

A major contribution, in this respect, results from the deconstruction of endangerment narratives. Through maps, texts, and discourses more generally, "geographical imaginations" shape understandings of safe areas, danger zones, "Us" versus "Them" perceptions, and the like. Imagined geographies are performed perhaps most visibly by state officials, security advisers, and public media commentators but also by popular discourses such as those conveyed by movies, video games, and social media (Dittmer and Dodds 2008). Imaginative geographies of (in)security take on material dimensions, which in turn shape security narratives and practices. Through reiterative and referential practices, the performance of these discourses achieves concrete outcomes, whereby understandings of certain places as inherently (in)secure become "naturalized." As Bialasiewicz *et al.* (2007, 406) note, "understanding discourse as involving both the ideal and the material, the linguistic and the non-linguistic, means that discourses are performative ... [and] constitute the objects of which they speak." Attention to the performativity of discourses moves analyses "away from a reliance on the idea of (social) construction towards materialization, whereby discourse 'stabilizes over time to produce the effect of boundary, fixity and surface'" (Butler 1993, 9, 12, cited in Bialasiewicz, Campbell *et al.* 2007, 407). As Butler (2011, xii) argues, through reiteration and citation, a "discourse produces the effects that it names." From this perspective, discourses of endangerment produce the very dangers that they (falsely) construct in the first place. Bialasiewicz *et al.* (2007, 405) survey "how geographers have documented the performative nature of US security strategies, and identified key mechanisms through which geographical knowledge has been wielded to support specific political agendas." The "security-entertainment complex" (Sterling 2009) now increasingly shapes agendas and modes of being – constituting what Thrift (2011) defines as an era in which the "co-extensive sectors" of security and entertainment see the former "boosted by the replacement of the binary of war and peace by a generalised state of conflict" and the latter as "a quotidian element of life, found in all of its interstices amongst all age groups." This permanence and intimacy shape relational spaces of being – spaces in which securitization is pervasive and militarism rampant.

Feminist theory also influences contemporary studies of security within geography through attention to scale and embodiment. Yet whereas conventional geographers are generally interested in scale in terms of a threat's intensity and reach, feminist geographers are attentive to scales at which threats play out in different yet connected ways. Feminist geopolitics is particularly discerning vis-à-vis the scalar dimensions of securitization processes. Its contribution is not simply to challenge the "scales of geopolitics and refocus on the mundane, everyday reproductions of geopolitical power" (Massaro and Williams 2013) and thereby call attention to the "micro"; rather, its main contribution is "to argue that the intimate and global are intertwined and co-constitutive – and it looks at security not across but as it threads through those entangled scales."[7] Feminist geopolitics do empirically focus on the everyday – but one in which the "international is personal," and vice versa (Dowler and Sharp 2001; Enloe 2000). In doing so, feminist approaches seek to build new theoretical insights

---

[7] Personal communication, Sarah Koopman, February 4, 2014.

into transscalar processes of securitization between the "global" and the "intimate" (Fluri 2011). In her study of intimate partner violence policing in the United States, Cuomo (2013, 856) argues that "policing practices are situated within narrow conceptions of masculinist security that often fail to address victims' multiple security need ... [and that] can create additional and different embodied fears and insecurities for victims." "Feminist geopolitics" is used here to identify the limitations of masculinist security and reimagine security "to consider the emotional security needs and fears of those being protected" (ibid.).

Embodiment and relationality are key to theorizing everyday experiences of (in)security, as Hyndman and De Alwis (2004) demonstrate in their account of gendered and spatially differentiated security in Sri Lanka during the civil war and as Clark (2013) shows in her study of migrant women and gendered violence in southeastern Turkey. By questioning the separations often made between the "exceptional/political sphere," on one hand, and the "everyday/domestic" sphere, on the other, feminist geopolitics thus not only pursues a downscaled and embodied geopolitics (O'Tuathail 1996) that is attentive to emotions (Pain and Smith 2012), but also reflects back on "macrolevel" securitization processes.

Methodological approaches

Methodological approaches by geographers reflect their theoretical perspectives, with a predilection for deductive and qualitative approaches among critical studies of security while most "practical geography" studies rely on quantitative approaches, either deductive or inductive. If there is a relatively clear demarcation between qualitative and quantitative scholarship, an increasing number of geographers bridge the divide via mixed methods.

Quantitative approaches

Large-N studies dominate some types of security-related geographical inquiries, such as studies of patterns of armed conflicts, crime, and natural disasters as well as food and health insecurities. The shift to quantitative "spatial analysis" – or the so-called quantitative revolution of the 1950s – represented a theoretical move, notably toward econometrics, and a methodological innovation, through the use of formal models, large-N statistics, and Geographical Information Systems (GIS). Born of the US World War II regime and deeply connected to the cold war military-industrial complex, this quantitative shift pursued universality through the empirical use of spatial analysis (Barnes 2008). Concerned with finding statistically demonstrable patterns of (in)security, GIS and quantitative approaches have been extended to many domains of inquiry (Klinkenberg 2007). With spatial disaggregation becoming an important requirement of large-N studies of armed conflicts in the last decade, many researchers have scaled down data to administrative units, grid units, or the specific coordinates of individual events. In this respect, several new data sets have been built up, most notably that of ACLED (Raleigh and Hegre 2009). The methodological objective here is to disaggregate insecurity more accurately spatially and to decipher causal linkages through correlation with other variables. Beyond the prescriptive elements often attached to these descriptive findings, there is nevertheless a reflexive element in the ways practitioners reflect upon the spatial categorizations that their studies create or reproduce. Formal models have remained largely absent from critical geography, though geospatial analysis is making a comeback (in part due to "critical spatial analysis" – a subfield focusing on the critique and critical use of GIS; see Schuurman 2006).

Qualitative methods

Most qualitative research methods rely on textual analysis, interviews, field observation, and ethnographies. Critical geopolitics has long used discourse analyses of security-related texts and "expert interviews" – and has received criticism for doing so; feminist geographers in particular have pointed out that such methods produce disembodied "critical geopolitics" accounts and reproduce dominant patriarchal narratives (Sharp 2000). Feminist qualitative methods aim to provide more nuanced contextualization, account for a diversity of voices and perspectives, enable embodied encounters, account for emotional dimensions, and provide opportunities for conducting research "in solidarity" with the victims of securitization processes (Mountz and Hyndman 2006). Some studies rely on long-term ethnographic approaches with researchers maintaining a regular presence in particular places for a decade or more (for example, the US–Mexican border).

Wright (2013) has documented over the past fifteen years the justice struggles of working women and their families in downtown Ciudad Juarez within a broader context of securitization and neoliberal gentrification. Seeking to restore materialism to critical geopolitical accounts through repeated detailed fieldwork along the most remote parts of the US–Mexican border, Sundberg (2011, 318) demonstrates "how deserts, rivers, Tamaulipan Thornscrub, and cats inflect, disrupt, and obstruct the daily practices of boundary enforcement, leading state actors to call for more funding, infrastructure, boots on the ground, and surveillance technology"; her serious engagement with "nonhumans" as actors in securitization practices "alter[s] explanations for the escalation of US enforcement strategies." Increasingly, critical geographers rely on mixed qualitative methods, and even occasionally include quantitative approaches (albeit mostly based on data collected through survey questionnaires and community mapping).

Strengths and limits: How (in)secure is geography?

Geographical engagements with security take many forms and follow diverse approaches. If the discipline classically imposes a positivist materialism on identifying the spatial distribution of threats and the geographical options to address them, more critical engagements take a poststructuralist approach examining spatial representations associated with security and demonstrate the performative importance of (in)secure(d) space. A strength of geography is thus its ability to contribute to other disciplines through such diversity of perspectives and approaches – though one should note that this diversity is not so much harnessed within the field itself, as discussed later.

Another strength of the discipline is to provide more complex geographical concepts such as space and scale and key referent objects such as territory. Space, for example, is not simply a container for security threats and practices or even the socially constructed "imaginative geography" of a supposed existential threat; rather, it is a constitutive element of securitization processes through its performed and performative dimensions. Similarly, the conceptualization of scale as well as the use of multiscalar analysis constitute important contributions from the discipline, notably through feminist perspective emphasizing embodiment. Finally, a major strength of the discipline is its engagement with the field and the use of direct observation, even if long-term ethnographies remain rare. In this respect, a "new materialism" – keen on engagement with matter (Bakker and Bridge 2006) and "posthumanism" – is further enriching reflections about the "grounding" of security practices, notably around borderlands (Sundberg 2011). Overall, geography's greatest potential strengths include its diversity, its openness to new theories, its relative acceptance of multiple methodologies, and its widespread commitment to critical inquiries and progressive goals.

The discipline's main limit is a still-weak theoretical engagement with the concept of security (at least outside the spatial dimensions of securitization). There does not seem to have been a serious conceptual debate around ideas of "strong/weak security" (akin, for example, to the one about "strong/weak sustainability"). Geographers have discussed the relative intensity of security but more in the senses of the extent of securitization processes (i.e., their emergence and pervasiveness) and of the relative hardening of security practices (i.e., militarization). Such relative intensity is notably described through everyday experiences of anxiety, the "hard" rhetoric of securitization discourses, the thinning or thickening of spaces of security, the radical "verticality" of the security gaze – for example, on Arab cities (Graham 2011; Gregory 2011) and the multidimensionality of the securitized terrain (Elden 2013). More generally, critical geographers have both called for and pointed at emancipatory conceptions of security, but they have not deeply engaged with other disciplines – especially political philosophy – to define how such alternative conceptions would look and how they would differ, for example, from conventional liberal theorizing on basic needs and antidominative politics (see Herington, this volume).

Another limit is geography's tendency to move rapidly to new topics and approaches rather than take a more incremental approach to refine methods, data, and findings. More specifically, the number of geographers directly engaging with the concept of security remains low overall despite increased attention to the topic resulting from US securitization policies, notably in the wake of 9/11. Critical geographers therefore tend to play an "intermediary" role: exploring new theories often borrowed from other disciplines through a limited number of case studies and refining their spatial dimensions but rarely "testing" them more systematically. As a result, many studies consist of critical discussions illustrated by discourse analysis and insights from field observation. While this may represent a justifiable antipositivist stance, it often leaves the field of "hard data" – and the associated "legitimacy" in the eyes of policy makers – to strategic think tanks and geospatial analysis contractors, who are rarely paid or ideologically motivated to demonstrate the empirical validity of critical arguments denouncing securitization policies. Collaborative work is also still relatively limited, with single-authored writing as the norm rather than the exception in critical studies. Research funding's move toward larger and collaborative grants, deepening cross-fertilization across disciplines and partnerships with researchers based in or originating from "fieldwork countries" may help move geography further toward greater interdisciplinarity and more diverse perspectives. Collaboration between quantitatively oriented academics and critical geographers may be difficult to achieve but should probably be encouraged, when applicable.

Limited policy engagement on security issues is another relative weakness of the discipline. Though frequently immersed in security policy material, critical geographers rarely engage *through* policy. This can be explained in part by a desire to change the system from outside, rather than from within – which, in turn, relates to the discipline's historical legacy of complicity in imperial projects and ongoing instrumentalization in "practical aspects" of militarism and security apparatuses. Some geographers had noticeable policy impacts until the 1950s, especially in the United Kingdom and United States – notably Alford Mackinder and Isaiah Bowman (Smith 2003) – as well as in Nazi Germany (Barnes and Minca 2013; Heske 1987). Many of these historical figures were driven by state security or imperial objectives, often at the expense of "non-national" populations (though some did play a role in emancipatory movements). Much applied research does directly seek to contribute to the implementation of security policies (Bryan 2010). If many critical geographers (and in particular those within "critical geopolitics") generally remain in the intellectual realm of academic critique, others (especially among feminist geographers) seek to work "in solidarity" with people made more vulnerable through securitization policies (including through protests, advocacy, and support). In his review of human security and food security, two areas well suited to geographical approaches, Huish (2008, 1386) stresses that "social justice theorization must maintain the audacity to envision radical improvements to the human condition, albeit pursuing working definitions for policy-makers." By maintaining a radical edge, rather than "tinkering" with prevailing policies, geography may remain at the margins of the established security establishment – yet thereby keep alive an imaginary of alternatives, a much needed task within a policy world under "neoliberal" hegemony.

Conclusion

For Alan Ingram, studying geographies of security is about considering "how security is enacted across a range of sites and scales; the drivers and effects of security practices; and the ways in which they are experienced, questioned and contested."[8] As geographers, scholars do not simply seek to explain how conditions differ across space and why – that is, spatial differentiation – but rather "how certain spatial categorizations work, what enactments they are performing and what relations they are creating" (Tyler 2008, 2). Interested in spatial representations of endangerment and in the spatial tropes mobilized in discourses of security and securitization, geographers ask how some particular spaces are discursively perceived, represented, and materially constructed as (in)secure, and how processes of securitization unfold spatially. This reflexive approach to the interpretative tools of the discipline means that many geographers take on a "critical approach" to their craft – not only studying phenomena from a spatial perspective, but reflecting on the dialectical relations between these phenomena and their spatial expressions (both material and discursive). As such it is not surprising that much contemporary geographical work on security follows the "critical turn" of security studies, whereby securitization itself becomes the object of analysis rather than a project to be supported. This fits within broader disciplinary concerns about denouncing unequal power relations and, in security-related geography more specifically, about seeking alternatives to oppressive and biased forms of security. The main questions thus relate to the spatial dimensions of securitization, while the main objective is to decipher better and denounce the "spatial logics" that support, justify, and legitimate the violence of particular security discourses and practices.

[8] See Alan Ingram, Geographies of Security, UCL Course Outline 2012: one of the few geography courses specifically devoted to a critical engagement with security and securitization.

To address these questions, and the referent objects studied, many geographers have turned to critical social theory. This is not to deny the importance of positivist work within the discipline (notably with respect to criminology, military-related geospatial analysis, and disaster or epidemiological studies); rather it is to point to the importance of critical engagements with security over the past two decades. Nor is this about denying the intrinsic value of security as a basic good, especially since many critiques of "security" explicitly denounce it for endangering the powerless. As such, critical perspectives need to avoid broadly condemning "security" and instead be more specific in the particular forms of security discourses and practices that they seek to denounce. Largely driven by feminism and poststructuralism, attention to security-related topics has mostly occurred within "critical geopolitics" and its many variants. Methodologies have mostly centered on textual analysis, especially official documents from the literature of security "think tanks"; however, there is now greater engagement with "the field" (either directly or through reporting and testimonies) as a result of the need for more embodied approaches and a search for (sub) altern perspectives.

Finally, geography's preoccupation with a progressive agenda as well as its combination of social theory and fieldwork observation grants the discipline the ability to deliver nuanced accounts with both conceptual and practical implications. Cross-fertilization with political science, sociology, and anthropology (and to a lesser extent with economics) is yielding fresh insights, methods, and data. This potential, however, has not been fully realized – in part because the discipline tends to follow individual research interests rather than to seek systematically to build a body of knowledge or pursue a policy agenda. The most innovative thinkers in geography also tend to remain within the realm of critique rather than provide and demonstrate the value of alternative conceptions of security. Thanks to debates within the discipline, this is changing, and there is greater interest in delivering concrete alternatives, notably in the areas of alternative forms of geopolitics and in quantitative studies of security. Often spearheaded by women in a discipline long dominated by men, this trend augurs well for geography's future contributions to security studies.

5 Sociology

Security and insecurities

LISA STAMPNITZKY AND GREGGOR MATTSON

In contrast to other disciplines, "security" has not traditionally been a central focus of sociological research.[1] This is not to say that sociologists have not studied problems, sites, interactions, and discourses that are relevant to what has elsewhere been classified as security.[2] But they have tended not to conceptualize their work as such.[3] Over the last fifteen years, however, this inattention to security has begun to shift, and sociologists have increasingly begun to frame their work around the concept. This has included those who study the terrains of security as it is understood in other disciplines – the realms of states, warfare, and political violence. But it has also included sociologists at the core of the discipline who research its traditional concerns of economic inequality, the family, and other social institutions.

---

[1] The situation in sociology resembles that of anthropology: "While other disciplines have dedicated journals, programs of study, and entire schools of thought to the security 'problem,' anthropology has largely refrained from joining the conversation, even as other global phenomena (e.g. human rights) have been prominent foci of anthropological scrutiny" (Goldstein 2010, 488).

[2] There are also works by nonsociologists that have been highly influenced by sociological approaches, for example, recent attempts to incorporate practice theory, and the theories of Pierre Bourdieu in particular, in international relations (e.g., Adler-Nissen 2012). And others have written on the "sociology" of international relations, scrutinizing the conditions of knowledge by which it was formed as something distinct from national interests (e.g., McSweeney 1999). Michael Skey asks what forms of belongingness nations provide in an insecure world, interrogating the microfoundations of the security that foreign policy is meant to provide, while Derek McGhee (2010) analyzes the degree to which concerns over security expose different conceptions of citizenship and human rights.

[3] There are rare exceptions, which date back decades. These include Altheide (1975), who discussed how security as gatekeeping restricting physical access to certain locations in the process results in the construction and reinforcement of racial and class boundaries, and Lowry (1972), who wrote on the interrelations of secrecy and security.

The study of security within sociology is thus bifurcated, with a small but robust tradition studying what we will call here *political* security in dialogue with other disciplines. Following Hobbes, scholars of political science and international relations focus on security as the key service provided by the state, most often referring to interstate war and subwar conflicts. Sociologists have engaged little with the concept of human security that emerged after the 1994 United Nations Human Development Report (e.g., Gasper 2005). Security-related research by sociologists has often focused on the production of expert knowledge and collective cultural interpretations of these problems, as well as about security and danger more generally, especially in regard to revolution, terrorism, state violence against domestic civilians, fear of crime, and disasters.

The disciplinary core of sociology, however, has more often focused on *in*securities of various sorts, particularly *social, economic,* or *interpersonal*. This division is a function of the historical division of the "objects of knowledge" among the social sciences by which professional incentives within disciplines are organized around particular objects and levels of analysis. Sociologists tend to study processes within particular societies, leaving the study of other countries to anthropology and transnational politics to political science. Furthermore, "security" is not a category in which sociology departments generally hire, although they do hire scholars who study crime, law, deviance, social control, and, more recently, global processes. This means that relatively few sociologists will focus their attention on what we are here calling "political security," at least until the interdisciplinary study of security makes claims upon the core of the discipline.

This chapter compares these two sociological conceptualizations of (in)security – political security versus social insecurities – including their main concepts, questions, and theories. We also highlight the research methods of exemplary studies, which like sociology itself span the range of quantitative and qualitative, case studies and comparative, social-psychological and historical, and various combinations of these. Within this methodological diversity of sociology we see no particular patterns regarding methods and findings, perhaps because of the infrequency with which sociologists study political security. We then evaluate these research traditions for their promise to provide insights for the interdisciplinary study of political security, identifying areas of potential cross-fertilization. We further suggest that scholars should distinguish between political security as an explicit object of discourse and practice and security as a broader category of cultural understandings of safety and disorder. We conclude that one of sociology's unique contributions are the tools to study the relationships among these different kinds of (in)security, connections that are lost when research focuses solely on external threats to the nation at the expense of internal, domestic processes.

Sociologies of (in)security

This section describes the recent engagements of sociologists with security and insecurity as subjective feelings and structural conditions at the level of the individual, the family, or the community.[4] These studies tend to reflect the fact that sociologists' commitments have long considered the role of gender, race, social class, sexuality, and other axes of difference in their effects on perceptions and implementations of security. At the most micro of levels, social psychologists and sociologists of emotion research security in terms of the attachments of children to their parents in the presence of family or economic stressors (see review by Thoits 1989). At the macrolevel, sociologists consider how citizen perceptions of security affect international policy, a topic to which we will return. For nonsociologists, we hope this review serves as a map of research traditions that have already grappled with some of the same epistemological and methodological issues that face contemporary security scholars. For sociologists, we hope it spurs more application of sociological insights to the problems of security.

Economic security is far and away the most robust engagement sociologists have with considerations of security and insecurity. Very few of these studies connect economic inequality to political security, however, representing a significant disconnection that future studies might address. The focus on the economy is particularly pronounced in English-language literature because the main defined-benefits program

---

[4] This review is based on a search for "security" in titles and abstracts of articles in 58 core sociology journals between 2000 and 2014. This netted 118 results, of which 63 were articles authored by sociologists. Of the 55 book reviews, several reviewed multiple books, and many books were reviewed in more than one journal. Not all books were authored by sociologists, but their review in core journals reflects their influence in their respective sociological subfields.

in the United States is called Social Security (key monographs include Amenta 2006; Béland 2005; Hardy and Hazelrigg 2010). However, the transnational project of the European Union has also provided a comparative focus to sociological analysis of economic stability politics (e.g., Hicks 2000; Muffels 2008).

Sociologists have long evaluated how government programs and changing work and retirement conditions affect measures of inequality and economic insecurity (e.g., Brady 2005). These include studying how low-income families respond to economic insecurity (e.g., Sherraden and McBride 2010). Domestic political opposition to entitlements programs has received sustained treatment as a cause and effect of income insecurity (Rogne *et al.* 2009), as has the global trend toward the privatization of government benefits (e.g., Quadagno 1998). Other trends that affect economic security include rates of immigration (Martin 2003) and the increase in casual labor at the expense of long-term work contracts (e.g., Bowles and MacPhail 2008). The relationships between these feelings of insecurity, general economic uncertainty, or rates of economic inequality and support for war or security policies are unexplored.

There is also a robust tradition of research on "food security," a concept sociologists study in three distinct ways: as it relates to community development, as a way of describing risks to industrial agricultural food systems, and as a means of describing hunger (see Mooney and Hunt 2009). Methodologically, these studies range across comparative statistical assessments of trajectories of country development (Scanlan 2003), interviews with farmers or patrons of farmers' markets, discourse analyses of scientific documents about organic food or foreign policy documents, and participant observations of community gardens or working family food preparation practices (e.g., Lawrence *et al.* 2013).

More recently, "precarity" has become the term of art to describe studies of economic insecurity: "the temporary nature of jobs, the dismantling of social assistance programs, and the deepening of social inequality" (Purser 2013, 74). This paradigm integrates research from the micro-, meso-, and macrolevels to view precarity as "a source of individual and social vulnerability and distress, affecting family, housing and communal security" (Wilson and Ebert 2013, 263). Especially prominent in studies of precarity are ethnographic engagements with part-time staffing agencies, documenting how this type of organization, which seems a valuable stopgap for the unemployed, actually "systematically exploits and reproduces structural vulnerability in the labor market" (Elcioglu 2010, 117). Sociologists also explore the impact of organizations on subjective perceptions of economic insecurity, ranging from unions (Martin 2003), employers (Appelbaum, *et al.* 2006), and the lobbying activities of special-interest groups (Lynch 2011), to the impact of globalization and supply-chain economics on employment conditions (e.g., Bender and Greenwald 2003).

Other researchers consider the implications of policies that also describe security as designated by US government programs. For example, the anthropologist Lorna Rhodes (2004) conducted an influential ethnography of inmate mental health in those US federal prisons designated as "maximum security" by studying control units, the "prisons within the prisons." She demonstrated forcefully how monsters and psychopaths are created in this process of harming some to create security for others: "Being in prison itself is bound to cause harm through either neglect or attention, the degeneration of inmates evoking a contrast with better days – national and institutional as well as personal" (Rhodes 2004, 119). The interconnections that ethnography permits across these levels – personal to national – are missing in other studies of security.

Similarly, schools have increasingly recategorized disciplinary problems as problems of security, rather than child behavior. Aaron Kupchik's four-school comparison combines ethnography with quantitative analysis to conclude that "much of the new homeroom security is a response to fear and general insecurities rather than careful, evidence-based deliberation" (2010, 9). He finds that such policies instead undermine the legitimacy of school discipline and reinforce inequalities between families who can influence administrators and those who cannot.

Amy Hillier's (2005) study examined how neighborhoods were assessed for investment risk in the 1930s. These "residential security maps," as they became known, were based on passersby assessment of housing stock, proximity to industry, heterogeneity by religion (especially the presence of Jews or Catholics), ethnicity (cooking smells, which could indicate investment insecurity), or the presence of African Americans. These maps became the basis of a host of public and private credit programs, entrenching inequality in the name of investor "security."

The media's role in personal perceptions of security and fear has long been a staple of sociological research (see Altheide 1975; Sacco 1995). More recently, sociologists have explored why citizens "are afraid of the wrong things," in Barry Glassner's (1999) influential formulation of how perceptions of risk far outstrip actual dangers. His dissection of media reports compares their coverage to the statistical prevalence of a wide range of topics ranging from pedophilia and political correctness controversies, to crack babies and crime. Glassner indicts media and politicians' accounts of dangers and bemoans the ability of experts and data to gain traction in public debates.

Sociologists working in this area also frequently focus on the social construction of knowledge *about* threats and dangers. For example, Lynn Eden (2004) analyzed how the effects of nuclear explosion were underestimated as a result of the organizational conditions under which this knowledge was produced. The social construction of dangers – the processes by which phenomena come to be seen as social problems – has multiple lineages within sociology, ranging from the emergence of drunk drivers as an object of fear and coercive social policy (see Gusfield 1996) to the chronic misplaced fears that American society is falling apart (Fischer and Mattson 2009). They also focus on misplaced fears over moral and sexual matters, often called "moral panics," which produce profound collective insecurity but also harmful policy responses that exacerbate inequalities (Altheide 2009; Hughes *et al.* 2011). At their most harmless, the responses do not address the underlying structural causes of the objects of concern. At worst, they punish the victims or vulnerable and misdirect public resources. "Sex panics," a subset of moral panics, feature responses against a sexual threat that target the already marginalized and do nothing to address the structural sources of danger nor actual perpetrators (e.g., Lancaster 2011).

Sociological contributions of security as policing and risk management occur largely within interdisciplinary fields of criminology and law and society. An influential model of security as existing along multiple nodes among which the state is only one was developed by the British criminologist Clifford Shearing (see Chapter 9). Criminologists in particular have a long tradition of robust empirical research documenting distinctions and interaction effects among objective crime rates, crime reportage, and subjective perceptions of crime and insecurity (e.g., Lane *et al.* 2014). Criminologists have also applied traditional sociological understandings of crime to terrorism. Gary Lafree and Laura Dugan (2004) answer the question "How Does Studying Terrorism Compare to Studying Crime?" arguing that "criminological theory, data collection, and methodological approaches are highly relevant to terrorism research and that applying criminological methods to the study of terrorism could rapidly increase our knowledge of terrorism and our understanding of its causes and consequences" (2004, 53).

Bernard Harcourt (2001) critiques the paradigm of "broken windows" policing, arguing that it is premised upon a (false) view of the world in which "these sharp categories – of law abiders and disorderly – divide the world into two distinct realms" (Harcourt 2001, 125). Since the "broken windows" approach both is premised on false assumptions, and, as Harcourt shows, is not actually effective in reducing violent crime, why has it been so popular? The practice of "broken windows policing" itself creates new categories of "orderly" and "disorderly" subjects, reframing the way in which we view certain actions (such as loitering) as harmful in and of themselves, which then acts to make "order-maintenance policing" seem necessary and right in response (2001, 165). Titles like "Rational Fear or Represented Malaise" (Elchardus *et al.* 2008) and "Theorizing Fear of Crime: Beyond the Rational/Irrational Opposition" (Lupton and Tulloch 1999) summarize the robust findings that social inequalities affect dramatic mismatches between actual rates of victimization and perceptions of threat. This line of research has particularly explored axes of inequality on this gap between perception and victimization, especially in differences by gender, age, race, and class.

At the intersection of criminology and urban sociology, fear and perceptions of security are embedded in physical places and how we talk about and remember them (see reviews by Leverntz 2012; Loader and Walker 2007; Taylor 1995). Researchers have long observed that neighborhood changes affect perceptions of crime even in the absence of actual changes in crime rates (e.g., Taylor 1995). In particular, increases in black and Latino residents spur increases in fear for community security (see Lane *et al.* 2014). Similarly, perceptions of social integration and closeness to neighbors affect both fear of crime and general feelings of happiness (Adams and Serpe 2000; Lotfi and Koohsari 2009).

Urban sociologists have also studied the effects of this fear on residents, ranging from the withdrawal of residents from the streets

(Miethe 1995) to the rise of gated communities and other privatized neighborhood security measures (Vesselinov 2008). This tradition also distinguishes among perceptions of fear, trust, and security (Walklate 1998), including the distinction between fears for the self and fear on behalf of others, so-called altruistic fear of crime on behalf of hypothetical children, for example.

Ethnographies of gated communities by anthropologists have been especially influential within sociology for conveying the complex motives residents have regarding physical insecurity. Setha Low (2004) performed a comparative ethnography of residents in Phoenix and Mexico City. She found that residents seek a dual sense of security of "protecting the individual from physical harm as well as providing the sense of psychological well-being," interpreting their desires as not necessarily for gates themselves; rather, "it is through the symbolism of gates and walls that the desire of gated community residents to re-create their childhood environments becomes intertwined with security" (2004, 90). Teresa Caldeira (2000) compared poor, middle-class, and wealthy residents of Sao Paolo, examining how all residents responded to fears of crime by closing themselves off in different ways, ranging from gated condominium communities to gated minds: "People feel restricted in their movements, afraid and controlled; they go out less at night, walk less on the street, and avoid the 'forbidden zones' that loom larger and larger in every resident's mental map of the city" (2000, 297). Demographic and fiscal analyses show the interrelationships of race, place, and perceptions of crime and security on rates of economic investment and gentrification (Hwang and Sampson 2014).

While others debate the degree to which a strong and competent security apparatus is necessary for democratic states, sociologists mainly study the decentralization of security *beyond* the state. These include the demands of private corporations, consumer demand for private security services, and organizations ranging from neighborhood associations to vigilante groups (see Wood and Dupont 2006). This shifting balance between private and public security forces has been the subject of considerable research (see Loader and Walker 2007; Sherman 1995). If state security forces are problematic, even more so are the unaccountable and unabashedly biased corporate ones. Another challenge to local, accountable policing forces is the spread of transnational policing agencies that relieve national agencies of blame for harsh practices against migrants, shifting responsibility to intergovernmental bodies such as EUROPOL that are detached from domestic politics and interests.

This "commodification of policing and security" has several origins, including the spread of consumer culture, the rise of a private security market, and the weakening sense of democratic citizenship (e.g., Loader and Walker 2007). One result is that consumers demand visible policing practices that make them feel safe rather than prevent or solve crimes, for example. The transnational character of corporations means that the implementation of corporate security has its own logics of implementing an internally consistent policy across multiple jurisdictions (see Walby and Lippert 2014). Dissatisfaction with state security can also lead to vigilante citizen security groups, such as the self-described Minutemen, who patrol the United States border with Mexico to deter immigration (Doty 2007).

This section has recounted sociological engagements with security on its traditional disciplinary terrain, what we have characterized as the *sociology of insecurity*. These range from research traditions with little intersection with political security, such as work on economic inequality, that present potent future research possibilities. Other areas, such as the work on fear of crime, offer significant possibilities for theoretical cross-fertilization with political security because of its relative maturity and robust empirical findings. This is not to say that sociologists have not engaged with "security" as such, a topic to which we now turn.

The sociology of political insecurity

Sociologists have long studied war, conflict, protest, and revolution: topics that could be situated within a framework of security (and often have been by scholars in other disciplines), yet sociologists have most often not framed their research into such topics as being primarily about "security." These include classics of political sociology about revolutions and the rise of states (see Walder 2009) and more recent works about the role of war in state formation (Tilly 1992; Wimmer 2012). Similarly, sociologists have studied war, insurgency, and soldiers, but largely in the subfield of military sociology (e.g., Kestnbaum 2009), with these studies of the military as an institution dating back to the "American soldier" studies that emerged out of World War II (Stouffer 1949).

More recently, there has been renewed interest among sociologists in studying empire, imperialism, and colonialism (e.g., Steinmetz 2013). Gurminder Bhambra (2007) criticized sociology's generalizations of modernity that ignored Europe's colonial needs for, among other things, security for trade. Julian Go (2012) provides a devastating empirical examination of the ways in which American imperialism is not unique but repeats the British Empire's economic and military patterns. Again, however, these topics have not been framed primarily as studies of political "security."

Finally, sociologists have also addressed violence as a general social phenomenon. Malesevic (2010) situates violence within classical and contemporary social theory, discusses the social role of war and violence in modernity and premodernity, and analyzes how war both draws upon and affects nationalism, social inequality, and gender divides. The social theorist Randall Collins produced a magisterial (2008) work on violence that, as the title suggests, was almost entirely focused on person-to-person violence. Collins suggests that when, and how, violence occurs can be understood through an analysis of the interactional relations among small groups at points of conflict. In contrast to Collins's microsociological approach, Michel Wieviorka's (2009) book is a sweeping account of how we should understand the role of violence in modern society and (re)establish it as central to social theorizing, addressing sources of political violence, the role of violence in the formation of states, the role of the media, interpretations of violence, and their interconnections.

More recently, however, sociologists have increasingly taken an interest in the more "political" or state-centered forms of security. These include studies of topics that tend to fall within the definition of security used by other disciplines, as protection from violence when the state is a key actor. In particular, sociologists have tackled the relationship between security and such topics such as terrorism, state violence, security expertise, disaster and catastrophe, and violence as a social phenomenon.

Since 2001, sociologists have taken a particular interest in "terrorism" (an early review of this literature is that by Turk 2004). Whereas much of the extant literature on terrorism by nonsociologists has treated it as a problem sui generis, sociologists have drawn insights from the discipline's tradition of studying social movements and social protest, introducing new theoretical and analytical approaches, and providing useful correctives to the "problem of definition," which has tended to stymie the field (e.g., Beck 2008; Bergesen and Han 2006; Kurzman 2011; Tilly 2006). Other sociologists have emphasized the production of discourse about "terrorism," focusing on the processes of knowledge and culture by which threats of terrorism are classified and produced (e.g., Altheide 2004; Bail 2012; Miller and Mills 2009; Stampnitzky 2013a). For example, Colin Beck and Emily Miner analyze how governments formally designate some groups and not others as "terrorists," finding that groups that engage in violence against civilians are more likely to be formally designated as terrorists by states if they "target aviation" or if they have an "Islamic ideological basis" (2013, 837).

Robin Wagner-Pacifici's *Discourse and Destruction: The City of Philadelphia versus MOVE* (1995) analyzes the events that led up to the violent confrontation between an urban police force and a radical black separatist group that ended with eleven members of MOVE dead and the destruction of an entire city block. Through interviews, hearing testimony, and an analysis of government documents she makes sense of the rival ways that city officials classified MOVE, how the classification of terrorist won, and how escalations in narrative served interests on both sides, leading to conflict. Wagner-Pacifici's account warrants particular attention for the ways in which the melodramatic language of war was deployed at the municipal level, labeling MOVE children as feral or young terrorists. These narratives, playing out in the otherwise dispassionate context of bureaucratic memos and lawyer-speak, justified an intervention that remains controversial to this day.

By treating terrorism as a variation of social protest and conflict, sociologists have made contributions such as theorizing under what circumstances groups will engage in or refrain from using terrorist tactics. Jeff Goodwin (2006a) draws on sociological theories of rebellion and revolution to argue that terrorism is most likely to occur when (potential) proponents of such acts see civilians (potentially to be targeted) as categorically different from them, and as complicitous with the state that is their target, and, conversely, so long as insurgents see civilians as potential supporters, they will not be attacked. Further, he suggests that when states blur boundaries between government actors and citizens, or between military and civilians, it becomes more likely that potential terrorists will do the same, that the presence of affective ties between insurgents and privileged groups will tend to work against the likelihood of categorical terrorism (Goodwin 2006b).

Charles Kurzman (2011) takes a counterintuitive tack in *The Missing Martyrs: Why There Are So Few Muslim Terrorists*. The question he poses is this: "If there are more than a billion Muslims in the world, many of whom supposedly hate the West and desire martyrdom, why don't we see terrorist attacks everywhere, every day?" (2011). An expert on social movement theory and the Iranian Revolution, Kurzman answers his question using interviews, surveys of public opinion, political documents, and casualty statistics. He finds that the major deterrents against terrorism are Muslims themselves, among whom terrorist movements are thoroughly marginal. Despite widespread anger against Western government interference, terrorist attacks overwhelmingly turn Muslims against radical Islamists. Kurzman argues that the best way to win hearts and minds is to listen to liberal Muslims, even when their advice is to not embrace them too closely: "If anybody is going to be discredited by association with American hegemony, Muslim liberals may prefer it to be their rivals" (2011, 161).

Sociologists have also studied state violence, including torture and other human rights violations often perpetrated in the name of "security." These have included comparisons of state violence in Serbia and Israel (Lazreg 2008) or Lisa Hajjar's (2013) recent overview of torture, which compares its use in ancient, colonial, and neocolonial contexts. She summarizes the sociological answers to such questions as torture's prevalence, why organizations torture, whether torture works, why accountability is so difficult to enact, and the uses of human rights to prevent it. James Ron (2003) uses interviews, fieldwork, and documents to conduct a comparative analysis of state violence in Serbia and Israel, to develop a theory of why states will engage in more or less brutal forms of repression: why states will sometimes engage in ethnic cleansing, and at others in what he labels "ethnic policing," showing that it is important to study not just when or whether states will engage in violence, but how and why.

Studies of disaster and catastrophe represent another frequent topic of study for sociologists (see Freudenburg *et al.* 2012), a research tradition summarized succinctly by the title of a volume about Hurricane Katrina: *There Is No Such Thing as a Natural Disaster*

(Squires and Hartman 2006). This subfield has a long and distinguished history within sociology, starting with Kai Erickson's (1976) study *Everything in Its Path*, an analysis of the Buffalo Creek flood in West Virginia that killed 125 and displaced more than 4,000. Through his own interviews and by analyzing tens of thousands of pages of transcripts collected by the survivors' legal team, Erickson described the factors that influenced the trauma of survivors, claiming that what psychiatrists were diagnosing only measured individual trauma, when survivors were actually mourning a lost communality and the everyday ties disrupted by their haphazard relocation to trailer camps. Erickson introduced the influential distinction between disasters not only as acute events, but also as chronic conditions, such as poverty, individual isolation, or racism.

Eric Klinenberg's (2002) *Heat Wave* was an influential work in this tradition that studied how social inequalities structured the mortality rates and reportage of the 1995 Chicago heat wave that killed more than seven hundred people. Through interviews, an ethnography of a major newspaper newsroom, and detailed analyses of epidemiological reports, he showed that the thirtyfold difference in death rates between African American and Latino men was largely the product of living alone, an uncommon situation among the latter.

These classics underpinned an explosion of such studies on the aftermath of Hurricane Katrina that analyzed the failures of the US government. Two especially influential edited volumes contained mixed-method studies of the way stratification and inequality affected the decisions that caused and exacerbated the hurricane's destructiveness, inequalities that were subsequently magnified by the unequal responses by government and nonprofit agencies (e.g., Bankston *et al.* 2010; Squires and Hartman 2006).

Sociologists have often studied disaster as an organizational problem. Vaughn (1997) analyzes the 1986 *Challenger* shuttle explosion as not merely a technical failure, but the result of an organizational structure that made it difficult for certain types of information about risk to be communicated effectively. Perrow (1984)'s *Normal Accidents* posits that certain types of failures are unpreventable in complex systems such as nuclear reactors, and that expectations that accidents will not occur are unrealistic. He documents how redesigns that implement redundancies into the system might appear to solve such problems, but such reworkings will themselves introduce new potential points of failure. Lee Clarke's (1999) *Mission Improbable* considers the similarities among terrorism, nuclear accidents, and assassinations, arguing that organizations construct "fantasy documents" that make us feel that there are emergency plans but can ultimately make us less safe by pretending that the unknown is known.

Further areas studied by sociologists that could fall within the domain of "security" studies include the intersections of science, technology, and safety. For example, Jeanne Guillemin (2005) has studied the ways in which expert knowledge about biological agents transformed them into potential weapons, information that both created security threats and had to be protected as a threat to security itself. David Lyon and David Wood (2012) assess the mixed empirical results of surveillance tactics to provide security, ranging from closed-circuit television and computer privacy safeguards to biometrics and credit card tracking, topics taken up in Torin Monahan's (2006) edited volume as well. The ways in which safety and security are themselves embedded within commonsense cultural understandings are reviewed by Susan Silbey (2009), who argues that claims that a "safety culture" can be created are belied by sociological understandings of culture as emergent and indeterminant.

Sociologists, following Ulrich Beck's (1992) influential theorization of modernity as the assessment and anticipation of risk, have also theorized security in these terms (see review by Elliott 2002). Studies in this "risk society" tradition analyze how the disruptions caused by globalization are "prejudged" by governmental and corporate actors, meaning that understandings of risk have their own effects beyond the underlying processes of globalization. Some suggest that all sites of social uncertainty and risk can be incorporated under the umbrella of security studies. Bajc (2013) anticipates a time when the voluminous data collected by government agencies will be turned over to researchers, allowing "the creators to divide the world into taxonomies in such a way that each person can be unambiguously positioned into a single category, information related to such category accumulated methodically, and specifications devised on how to act on this information" (Bajc 2013, 619). But others have countered that states have commonly failed at such attempts at rationalization, because problems of security tend to overflow customary categories and logics as a result of the ease with which nonexperts can make claims about it (de Goede 2008; Stampnitzky 2013b).

For a sociology of (political) security

Why should sociologists study security? What are sociology's unique contributions to its study? And in what ways might sociologists connect the insights at the core of their discipline to the interdisciplinary debate? For sociologists to contribute, their research needs to move from a sociology of insecurity to a sociology of security. To state it another way, sociologists need to leverage their understandings of insecurity as a subjective perception to study how it is made real by institutions and practices. Key areas in which this work might be carried out are in the questions of what is done in the name of security, how certain phenomena but not others are classified as security problems, and the processes by which practices of "security" travel from one social field to others.

Among the key contributions of sociological approaches to political security are answers to the question, Why is studying security so difficult? The problem stems in part from the concept's polysemy (Ranasinghe 2013; Stampnitzky 2013b; Valverde 2011; Zedner 2003). Yet, as Joseph Masco notes, the term "is almost never defined by those in the political arena who rely almost entirely on it. It is rather more commonly evoked as a self evident good, a rationale for wide-ranging and (particularly in the United States) often quite extreme political visions" (Masco 2010, 509). This bifurcation thus suggests that there are two epistemologies of security in contemporary scholarship that structure the way it is studied. One is to study security as an objective, real state of affairs; a course that requires accepting or refuting the political definitions on their own terms. The alternative is to study security as a terrain of discourses and practices that are applied by powerful actors to different sites at different points in time, looking for places where security could have been invoked but was not, the irregular application of security practices, or the way actors or institutions resist some definitions of security over others.

In the objective tradition of security as realpolitik, sociologists have used their traditional disciplinary tools to measure the realities of security, although they have not conceived it in the terms of the interdisciplinary study of political security. For example, sociological studies of "family security" use the word as a synonym for stability. This suggests fruitful opportunities for connecting the microworld of family economic insecurity to broader questions of political insecurity.

We know less about how perceptions of security threats vary among people of different social classes, or whether rates of economic inequality affect population-level perceptions of political security, or how changes in "family security" affect public opinion in favor of war, the curtailment of civil liberties, or other political interventions.

In the subjective, social constructionist tradition, security has been studied as a terrain of discourses and practices that can only be understood in particular contexts at limited historical moments. Some of the strongest, and most distinctive, contributions of sociologists to the study of security stem from such analyses of the production of knowledge and cultural interpretations about security. These range from studies of how individuals understand security threats, to studies of societal commemorations, to analyses of the production of official discourses about "security."

Tamar Liebes (1992) provided an influential analysis of how Israelis developed political worldviews about security in response to media consumption. Through interviews, she found that viewers of television news tended to develop more "hawkish" security views. This was not necessarily because news shows were deliberately biased, but because "dovish" positions depended on communicating ambiguities that were less powerfully communicated through television than the seemingly more straightforward "hawkish" positions.

Later, Andrew Perrin (2005) analyzed a stratified random sample of more than one thousand letters to the editor published in major newspapers before and after the September 11, 2001, attacks. He coded the letters for statements regarding authoritarianism and anti-authoritarianism to understand how the threat posed by terrorist attacks affected the political attitudes of ordinary people. Rather than a simple rise in authoritarianism in response to the attacks, he found an increase in both discourses, arguing that they "are paired elements of political culture that are invoked together in the face of a national threat" (2005, 167).

Mohr and his collaborators (2013), on the other hand, analyzed the framing of security threats at the national political level by studying the texts of US National Security Strategies. They did this by analyzing the texts via computer-automated textual coding, applying Kenneth Burke's concept of a "grammar of motives" to the documents. Christina Simko (2012) analyzed the production of collective meanings about security threats in social commemorations, analyzing all presidential speeches about 9/11 and the speeches given at annual memorial services at the Pentagon, in Manhattan, and in Shanksville, Pennsylvania. She found that site-specific meanings were durable, affecting subsequent performances even by political rivals: Presidents George W. Bush and Barack Obama, though from different parties and political leanings, used the same tropes at different sites, indicating that the meanings of the attacks remained "tragedy" in Manhattan but "sacrifice" at the other two sites. Her research suggests the power of initial interpretations of disasters to shape future responses.

Much of the work in this area focuses on the production of public knowledge about – or denial of – security, insecurity, danger, or other threats. Stanley Cohen's (2001) *States of Denial* connected individual states of denial, such as denial of alcoholism, to societal-level denial of political atrocities. From case studies ranging from "passive bystanders" and "compassion fatigue" to genocides and truth commissions, he derives the lesson that the value of "inclusivity" must be promoted and "passivity" shamed if information about horrors might lead to political interventions. Sutton and Norgaard investigated denial at the individual and social levels through in-depth interviews to answer the question "Why and how do individuals distances themselves from information about their government's participation in torture and other human rights violations?" (Sutton and Norgaard 2013, 495). They found that varieties of denial are shaped by social and political contexts.

Similarly, Jared Del Rosso (2011, 2014) examined the social "denial" of torture in texts produced by the war on terror, advancing work done earlier by Gregory Hooks and Clayton Mosher's (2005) analysis of official justifications given for torture at Abu Ghraib.

Rachel Wahl, in contrast, conducted interviews and fieldwork with law enforcement officers to elicit their explanations for "why they torture." She found that police "torture more widely than their own conceptions of justice allow, but see this as an imperfect implementation of their principles rather than a violation of them," a finding that contrasts with understandings that human rights ideas are merely imperfectly understood in local contexts (2014, 807). Torture is thus not necessarily a failure of human rights, but may be used in service of them.

A related area where sociologists have also made significant contributions is the production of security knowledge and expertise, a field that draws upon sociology's traditional focus on occupational legitimacy and professionalization (e.g., Eyal and Pok 2011). Gil Eyal (2006) analyzed the interconnections of academia and the military in Israel, asking why academic scholars of the Middle East would become involved in military intelligence work. He traced how the social structure of the expert field led certain types of experts to influence policy and public discourse more than others, and finding that, as one group of experts, the "Arabists," were usurped, this led to changes in both how Israeli national identity was constructed, and how Israel constructed security policies against the Palestinians.

Lisa Stampnitzky (2013a) analyzed the changing production of expert knowledge about political violence arguing that the category of "terrorism" and the role of the "terrorism expert" have been coproduced. On the basis of interviews with contemporary security experts, archival research on the history of knowledge production about terrorism from the 1960s until the 2000s, and a network analysis of the participants in terrorism conferences, Stampnitzky traced the shifting definitions of what constituted terrorism in relation to the institutional origins of the claimants. She found that experts were unable to define terrorism with any degree of specificity, leaving them unable to prevent political or media figures from anointing acts as terrorism that did not meet any consistent criteria. Stampnitzky argues that this reveals that terrorism, as a social problem, is inseparable from the experts who arose to talk about it, meaning we must attend closely to the ways in which problems and experts are intertwined.

In addition to the study of expertise itself, sociologists have studied how policy makers construct meanings of danger and threats, and the technologies through which they do this, as in Gregoire Mallard and Andrew Lakoff's (2011) study how "techniques of prospection" are used by leaders to imagine future threats. Similarly, Melinda Cooper (2010) has studied how the forecasting technique of "scenario planning" has traveled from the world of security and disaster planning to other realms, such as finance.

Perhaps the most unique contribution of sociologists lies in those innovative studies that connect perceptions of security to international relations. For example, Joane Nagel (2011) provides an optimistic account of climate change policy despite widespread skepticism in the US population that climate change exists, is caused by humans, or requires policy response. By her account, the adoption of climate change policies among two of the most conservative elite communities – the military and international corporations – means that American policy will address climate change despite popular skepticism. Her assessment was later confirmed by media reports, highlighting the advantages of applying the sociology of risk perception to traditional considerations of political security.

These studies of collective understandings of security are akin to, but not exactly the same as, "securitization theory" as studied by political scientists (see Bourbeau 2014; Buzan *et al.* 1998). In this case, sociologists might study how "securing the family" became a concern in the early twenty-first century among religious conservatives in American suburbs. Similarly, sociologists might study why the military has been the primary site of American concerns about security and *not* the family, and how this application of security to some domains over others is produced, and by whom. Sociologists have indeed studied why some sites rather than others have become "securitized." For example, climate change has recently been defined as a threat to national security by the US Department of Defense, complicating its relation to its traditional supporters on the conservative Right. While the objective tradition would accept this classification and use sociological tools to measure the ways in which climate change is a security threat, the subjective tradition (e.g., Nagel 2011) would problematize how the domains of environmental and military expertise became connected at a particular moment.

We argue that the sociological approach gives particular value to the latter. This is both because the former tradition is well represented by other disciplines both theoretically and empirically, and because sociologists are already working in ways that challenge the first approach. The fact that sociologists are already studying so many disparate objects, sites, and institutions in the name of "security" already suggests that it is an inherently unstable object. A coherent way to move forward from this bifurcation would be to foreground the traditional sociological contributions to the construction of social problems to study the problematization of security itself.

To study what is done in the name of security, sociologists should study the discourses, practices, institutions, and policies that determine the content of security in particular contexts. Key questions that orient this line of future research are the following: What is the object of security, how is it produced, what does it govern, and what are the effects? The contemporary classics that should provide foundations include the work of Stephen Collier and Andrew Lakoff (2008) on how "critical infrastructure" became a concept that governments and corporations must assess in terms of security.

Similarly, Melinda Cooper and Jeremy Walker (2011) contend that the concept of "resilience," first a governmental antidote to security, smuggled those concerns into mainstream social scientific research. As they summarize: "We trace the genealogy of 'resilience' from its first formulation in ecosystems theory to its recent proliferation across disciplines and policy arenas loosely concerned with the logistics of crisis management." We concur that these processes by which practices of "security" travel from one field to another (as also deftly illustrated by Jennifer Light's (2003) research on how technologies of warfare and urban combat became incorporated in mainstream urban planning) should be another key domain for sociological investigation.

Another model is Harvey Molotch's (2012) *Against Security*, which deftly traces how "security" is produced through social and environmental practices – sometimes resulting in less, rather than more, safety. His wide-ranging book incorporates interviews, ethnography, and analysis of government documents that cover a host of sites that scholars of political security would recognize – subways, airports, and the Ground Zero site in Lower Manhattan. But he begins his discussion with public restrooms, using them to exemplify how they are sites of "ambiguous dangers," especially for women, that have attracted lots of possible solutions except the one that might actually make women safer: gender-neutral bathrooms. This illustration grounds Molotch's discussions of practical physical changes (wider stairwells) and policies that empower individuals with the flexibility to respond to novel circumstances.

In conclusion, sociologists have particular contributions to make to the interdisciplinary study of security by (1) connecting their core disciplinary concerns with domestic insecurity to broader political insecurity and (2) by problematizing the interdisciplinary engagement with security as an objective phenomenon. The former synthesis is open ground waiting to be explored. The latter overlaps with other disciplinary contributions to security studies. Fruitful understandings of security are unlikely to result from either objective studies that pretend there is no ambiguity about security, nor subjective studies that destabilize security so fully that they ignore the very real feelings, behaviors, and institutional responses that are organized around it. To understand how security is or is not the pursuit of war by other means, a rational response to ambiguous or distant threats, or some combination of the two, we need context-bound, empirical accounts of how security operates in specific institutional frameworks. Only through such research can the contradictions, discontinuities, and organizational logics that "security" enables be uncovered.

6 | *International relations*
Celebrating eclectic dynamism in security studies

PHILIPPE BOURBEAU, THIERRY BALZACQ, AND MYRIAM DUNN CAVELTY[*]

While security is hardly discussed in philosophy (as Jonathan Herington, this volume, points out) and while theories of security are politely neglected in law (as Wouter Werner, this volume, shows), it is the preeminent concept in international relations. Courses on security studies are taught in almost all undergraduate/graduate programs in international relations around the globe. There is at least one security specialist (and often, many more) in almost all departments of political science and international studies in North America, Europe, and Asia. Security is the primary focus of no fewer than four major journals in the field – *International Security*, *Security Dialogue*, *Journal of Conflict Resolution*, and *Security Studies* – and this list is expanding, with the newly created *Critical Studies on Security* (2013), the *European Journal of International Security* (2016), and the *Journal of Global Security* (2016). In the top twelve journals in international relations according to the 2012 *Thompson Reuters Citation Journal Report*, four are security-related journals. In short, security studies is a massive field of research in international relations.

In the past decades, debates surrounding security studies have evolved through several interrelated turns. Security has been structured, systemized, broadened, deepened, gendered, humanized, constructed, and privatized. Theoretical and empirical studies detailing the contours and the importance of each of these approaches to security abound in specialized journals. In this chapter, we want to celebrate this eclectic dynamism. Through our discussion, we will show that the diversification of referent objects, approaches, and research methods is a crucial vector in the development and relevance of security studies.

---

[*] For their comments and suggestions, we thank Keith Krause, Richard Price, Vincent Pouliot, and Juha Vuori.

Scholars have organized and reviewed this immense field of study in several ways. Some of the most influential reviews address how the various international relations approaches *understand* security (Williams 2013), how they distinguish between *types* of security (Collins 2013), and what are the security *problematics* (Baldwin 1997). Still others tackle the *evolution* of international security studies as a field of research (Buzan and Hansen 2009). Although the discussion we offer in this chapter will necessarily be influenced by these important contributions, we have a different set of objectives here.

We seek to offer an analytical review of the main research questions, theories, and methods driving security studies by analyzing three mistaken beliefs that persist in international relations scholarship: first, that security's typical referent object has always been and will always remain national security (or the security of the state); second, that scholars based in North America (and particularly in the United States) produce traditional/orthodox security studies, while those working in Europe are the architects and the gatekeepers of critical security studies; third, that critical approaches to security are incompatible with methods generally associated with positivist epistemology, whereas orthodox or traditional approaches to security cannot work with anything other than a positivist epistemology.

To be sure, a one-chapter survey of this enormous field of inquiry cannot hope to be comprehensive. There will certainly be those who criticize this overview for eschewing a particular strand of literature or for failing to provide sufficient bibliographical references for a particular approach.[1] It is important to keep in mind, however, that our intended audience is not necessarily international relations folks. Rather, the goal is to initiate an interdisciplinary dialogue on security; we hope that the discussion contained herein will provide newcomers to the field with a reasonable sense of the prominent schools of thought, authors, debates, concepts, questions, and answers that form the necessary basis for such an interdisciplinary dialogue to commence.

---

[1] In our effort to offer a synthetized overview of the field, several concepts or issues have been excluded or not significantly discussed, such as arms controls, nuclear weapons proliferation, terrorism, military doctrine, strategic studies, and ethnic conflicts. Readers should not see this as a theoretical statement on what constitutes a security issue.

Referent objects of security

One way to systematize security research in international relations is through the type of referent object that security researchers choose to focus on. In the post-Westphalian era and definitely since the birth of international relations as a discipline (Schmidt 1998), security actions have been and still are closely associated with the needs and security instruments of "the state," a political entity defined by a permanent population, a territory, a government, and the capacity to enter into relations with other sovereign states (see Montevideo Convention on the Rights and Duties of States, article 1) (States 1933). Security for that referent object is traditionally pursued by classical instruments of the state, most often the national army or other tools of statecraft such as diplomacy (Walt 1991).

This particular concept of national security (which connotes a fusion of the state with the nation) took form after the Second World War (with earlier roots; Baldwin 1995). It is built on a notion of the modern state that combines the importance of territorial sovereignty, a secular political identity (Walker 1990), the emergence of private property (Ruggie 1983), as well as modern nationalism (Anderson 1983; Mayall 1990). Within this construct, individuals grant the state the right to protect them, in the process giving away part of their individual rights in the service of collective security (Walker 1997). Therefore, security emerges as "a condition both of individuals and of states," with an inseparable relationship between the two (Rothschild 1995, 61). The combination of the norms of sovereignty with nationalism (linked to the conception of the nation as "imagined community"; Anderson 1983, 7) allowed for a notion of security that regarded the "inside" as different from the "outside" (Walker 1993). The inside is a realm of similarity, progress, and peaceful coexistence, whereas the outside is defined by difference, anarchy, and the constant danger of conflict (Waltz 1959).

For many scholars, security of the nation state is the analytical and normative focus, for at least two reasons: First, because of that inseparable relationship, securing the state means ensuring the security of the entities within that state, that is, its society, its values, and its interests (Buzan and Hansen 2009, 11). Second, because national security is linked to the survival of the referent object that is constantly threatened by the anarchic outside, national security is considered "high politics" – a politics above others (Keohane and Nye 1977).

Against this backdrop, security studies have prominently been defined as "the study of the threat, use and control of military force" (Walt 1991, 22). Often, this conception of security is attributed to the neorealist paradigm, which claims a strong position in security studies (cf. Legro and Moravcsik 1999). However, there is more diversity than that. First, the other "big school" in international relations, neoliberalism, has also produced much security-relevant literature that takes the state/nation as the main referent object and explains issues of cooperation rather than war (cf. Bennett and Stam 2004; Bueno de Mesquita *et al.* 2003; Doyle 1986; Gartzke 2007). Second, neorealism is highly diverse itself (cf. Wohlforth 2009b), with scholarship incorporating a wide range of issues and factors, effectively leading to a differentiation between offensive realism (e.g., Mearsheimer 2001), defensive realism (Taliaferro 2000–2001), and lately neoclassical realism (Rose 1998).

Importantly, however, and even with researchers looking inside states for the domestic and ideational causes of war and peace especially after the end of the cold war (Glaser 1994–1995; Posen 1993; Van Evera 1999), both big schools of international relations, despite their diversity, have something in common: They assume a notion of the state that universally applies throughout the international system. Crucially, they take for granted that the external realm of politics is different from the internal; that state interest and the interests of their societies align; that states are (more or less) rational actors, whose actions can be understood through scientific means (Deudney 2007; also Buzan and Hansen 2009, 30–32). In other words, the central importance of "the nation state" as referent object was never questioned.

In the last three to four decades, some security studies scholars have started to engage critically with this dominant conception of national security (and the referent object of "the nation state") and diversify it in at least three ways: The first move is called "widening" and entails a move away from security as the study of the threat, use, and control of military force. The second is called "deepening" and looks more closely at the relationship between the state and its citizens. The third breaks with the tradition of seeing security mainly as outward oriented and looks more closely at how security also works on the inside and how these distinctions between the inside and outside became porous.

First, researchers suggested that security was also of relevance in other issue areas (or "sectors") besides the military such as the environment, the economy, or society (cf. Buzan 1983; Matthews 1989; Ullman 1983).

The reason behind this move was their belief that security was (and should be) much more than just military security. In part, this move was paralleled (and influenced) by changes in practices to adopt doctrines of comprehensive security on the level of governments and international organizations as well as influenced by important events such as the oil crisis of the 1970s or environmental degradation in the 1980s. The second move by the "deepeners" served to add more units of analysis to the traditional state-centric view; most explicitly, they have introduced the idea that there are five levels of depth to security: international systems, international subsystems, units, subunits, and individuals (Buzan *et al.* 1998, 5f)

Foremost, wideners and deepeners focused on the what and the who of security: That is, they discussed the legitimacy and practicability of different security issues/referent objects. Second, scholars also inquired into the metapolitical implications of this widening of security politics. Some scholars argued that the extension of security politics to new domains was colonizing the public space with unwanted logics of zero-sum thinking (Deudney 1990), inclusion and exclusion (Booth 1991b), or exceptional politics (Waever 1995). Prominently, some deepeners have advanced the notion of *human security*, which has been defined narrowly as freedom from fear (cf. Mack 2004) or broadly as freedom from want (cf. United Nations 1994) and is essentially a type of security that is desirable because it "distances itself from the exclusive grip of a state-determined concept and becomes security relevant to people" (Hoogensen and Stuvoy 2006, 219). Again other scholars have focused on particularly vulnerable subjects such as children (Rosen 2005) or have introduced a specific focus on women (and later gender) into the study of international relations (i.e., Enloe 1989; Steans 1998). Similarly, other scholars have focused on challenging the unproblematized link between the state and security from the perspective of non-Western settings (Ayood 1995). The assumption that state-provided "national" security is something desirable only counts if the notion of state is based on a working social contract, which is not a given in many areas of the world.

Of course, these contributions to security studies are highly diverse in their metatheoretical leaning and in the methods they use. What they have in common, though, is that they took an explicit position against the traditional and dominant concept of (national) security as described earlier, especially in the 1980s and 1990s. Such positioning was indeed necessary just because the other notion of national security with its referent object was so dominant. The result of this differentiation was a conflict of the traditionalists versus the wideners-deepeners (Krause 1998; Mearsheimer 1994–1995). From that conflict emerged another differentiation: a group of scholarship labeled "critical" (often by its proponents) (Krause and Williams 1997). While the label "critical" means different things to different scholars (cf. Mutimer *et al.* 2013), most of them share an interest in taking up various unquestioned and taken-for-granted aspects of security. By opening them up to analytical and normative inquiry, they initiated important conceptual debates on the deeper politics of security. This is discussed here as the third move.

Though critical scholarship is very diverse, many scholars within that research tradition would probably agree that the definition of referent objects is an unavoidable political act. It is unavoidable since any threat/danger discourse must eventually be tied to some kind of endangered entity in the political process to become meaningful and/or actionable (Buzan *et al.* 1998). At the same time, this necessary selection of referent objects is always political, since it entails a larger argument about legitimate claims to protection (Buzan 1991, 13). Fundamentally, the definition of who or what exactly is threatened promotes or relegates political subjects to different privileged or silent positions, assigning legitimate claims to protection to some, but not to others. Importantly, however, there are quite a few critical scholars who would agree that (international or national) security is related to the highest possible political and social stakes; in other words, it is about existential issues such as survival, so that the protection of securitized referent objects legitimizes extraordinary emergency responses (Buzan *et al.* 1998; Waever 1995). That is why turning issues into security issues always entails a danger of undemocratic procedures, and processes of securitization need to be scrutinized carefully.

However, there are other security scholars who focus on security that is no longer primarily about threats and battles against an enemy, but are characterized by an inward-looking narrative about vulnerabilities. They question the perception of security as "exceptional" and linked to "extraordinary" means and suggest that security is also about routine processes in bureaucracies by means of which it is sought and produced (c.a.s.e. collective 2006, 469). In line with this, scholars inspired by Continental philosophy have advanced different notions of security, often lying outside the "state/legitimate-violence complex" (Lobo-Guerrero 2008). This type of security studies is often influenced by the concept of risk (Williams 2008), which has moved into the field of security via other disciplinary approaches that have focused on risk for decades (Petersen 2012). Particular to risk narratives is the understanding that national security is not (or no longer) defined by known and current threats, but rather by potentials of unforeseeable (potentially catastrophic) harm. This is still security, but a security of a different kind, which is empowering a range of specific government rationalities, be it the permanent surveillance of populations, precautionary arrests of suspects, or preemptive invasions of foreign countries (Aradau and van Munster 2007).

In this world of nonexceptionality, there is no single essence of security that researchers adhere to – in contrast to the traditionalists. Also, security is not mainly the domain of security elites and politicians. Instead, the research focus shifts to everyday security practices, to less traditional security actors such as civil protection agencies, and to actors outside government that have a central role in the creation of danger knowledge and everyday security (cf. Hagmann and Dunn Cavelty 2012; Huysmans 2006). Security is not understood as a condition that is binary – meaning that one is either secure or not – but as a future state of being that is continually approached through risk management or other routine practices such as surveillance, which solidifies security's ubiquity in the everyday (Bourbeau 2014; Huysmans 2014). In terms of referent objects, moving away from one essence of security and focusing more on routine practices than on exceptionality open up the field of security studies to many different issues, including the financial system (Kessler 2011), drugs (Andreas 2008), the environment (Floyd 2010), migration (Bourbeau 2011), urban spaces (Graham 2011), or cyberspace (Dunn Cavelty 2013).

Importantly, the state is still there – but it is by far not the only or the most important referent object within these diverse issue areas. Scholarship within the tradition of the "third move" accepts more amorphous and ambiguous characteristics of national security, composed of a mixture of security problems – international, local, regional, domestic, and global security issues are intertwined, put on par, and sometimes not even differentiated conceptually. Its referent objects populate a national security spectrum that connects global threats right down to personal safety. Its referent object is often not the population or life more broadly but technical and social systems that are designated vital to collective life. The sources of insecurity (classically, the "enemy") are moved to the background, as the stability of technical and societal systems becomes a main aim of security interventions. Many different actors, state and nonstate, are responsible for this type of security. Clearly, however, the second, amorphous and ambiguous type of security is not "the" new paradigm. Security practices neither shift from one ideal type to another nor are universal or without alternatives. Traditional national security – state, government, and elite-centered – still prevails as a dominant tradition in many universities around the world. Yet, this other type of security has been gaining traction recently and stands in at times competing and at times convergent relationship with other types of security.

Theories, geographies, and practices

While international relations' literature has seen an explosion of referent objects of security in the past three decades, as the previous section describes, the second preconceived idea that we want to tackle and debunk is the often-heard claim that a geographical division exists within security studies: Scholars based in North America (and particularly in the United States) produce mainstream/traditional security studies, while scholars working in Europe are the originators and defenders of critical security studies. Countless times while presenting at conferences we have heard US-based scholars dismissively label European security researchers as "critical" and "nonscientific" scholars. Similarly, you only need to sit in a panel or two at the British International Studies Association annual conference to hear colleagues discuss the "ludicrous" scientific efforts of US-based scholars, who are "trapped in the folly" of a mainstream, rational-choice imperialist approach to security.

If we look at major journals in the field, we can certainly observe trends that seem to corroborate these anecdotal findings. One of the top journals in the field, *International Security*, published by the Harvard Kennedy School of Government, is resolutely traditional and only rarely (if ever) publishes articles that explicitly adopt a critical approach. Equally, you would be hard-pressed to find many articles opting for an "offensive" realist perspective in the most well-regarded critical security studies journal, *Security Dialogue*, published by the

Peace Research Institute of Oslo. In short, the field of security studies is often portrayed as a 2 × 2 field: North America/orthodox versus Europe/critical.

We argue against the usefulness of this geographical demarcation as a tool with which to analyze the past, present, and future of security studies. In providing an overview of the influential theories of security, we hope to show that the diversity of approaches across geographical locations is so well established that it is hard to sustain a simplistic distinction based on theoretical orientation and location. To be sure, we are not arguing that there are no traces of geographical divisions remaining in the field. Undoubtedly, geographical divides are still present in general and for certain subfields of security studies. Yet, we argue that the chasm has shrunk to a point where one can seriously question the usefulness of a geographical representation of the field as a whole.

The dominant theory in security studies has been for a very long time the realist one. Of all the variants of realism, structural realism (or neorealism) has been the most influential. It is widely accepted that structural realism emphasizes four core elements: States are seen as rational actors and by far the most important actors in the international system; there is not an international authority that can prevent the use of force between states (the system is then said to be anarchic); each state cannot take for granted its security and thus, is responsible for ensuring its own survival, most notably through the nurturing of material capabilities; the balance of power (the formation of alliances with certain states to counter the threat of other states) is the defining mechanism that regulates the international system and explains war and peace. The books *Man, the State, and War* (1959) and *Theory of International Politics* (1979) by Kenneth Waltz are largely considered to be the best representatives of this school of thought.

Disagreements exist within the realist tradition as to whether states, in their quest for survival, seek only a certain (minimally necessary) amount of military power – a position known as "defensive realism" – or whether they seek to maximize infinitely their power – a stance labeled "offensive realism." Defensive realism holds that the international system provides incentives for competitive behavior only under certain conditions. The security dilemma (the idea that the actions chosen by a state to increase its security in fact decrease the security of others, thereby provoking a spiral model in which interactions between states fuel competition and insecurity) is central here. Under anarchy, states may pursue an expansionist policy because their leaders perceive that it is the only viable and effective course of action to guarantee national security. One of the major challenges in world politics then becomes communication; according to defensive realists, how leaders signal their intentions to other leaders and how these intentions are perceived on the international stage can go a long way toward explaining security policies and war. To support this argument, several scholars have sought within states for domestic causes of war/peace and have imported to the conversation insights and concepts traditionally associated with psychology, such as perception, revenge, reputation, and in- and out-group relations (Jervis 1976; Löwenheim and Heimann 2008; Mercer 1995; Taliaferro 2004; Wohlforth 1993). Defensive realists strongly believe that, under most circumstances, the best strategy available to leaders is restraint (Glaser 1997; Taliaferro 2000–2001). Scholars indeed argue that states understand, through a rational cost/benefit choice, that excessive power is counterproductive because it gives rise to hostile alliances. A state should therefore seek to possess enough (military) power to ensure its survival, but not more (Glaser 2010; Waltz 1979).

Offensive realism shares with defensive realism the idea that states face uncertainty about other states' intentions, but contends that in facing this uncertainty, states should assume the worse. Offensive realists argue that since no international authority exists, a state can never be sure that a peaceful moment in world history (the end of the cold war, for example) will remain peaceful in the future (Mearsheimer 1990). As a result, the international system compels states to maximize their relative power position; all states are continuously striving to gain more power at the expense of other states. Hence, according to the tenets of offensive realism, states' relative capabilities are of overriding importance and the best strategy to ensure national security is to be the dominant/hegemonic power (Mearsheimer 2001).

Many of the concepts and research questions that first emerged within the realist perspective are still at the heart of the discipline today. Indeed, the causes and consequences of the security dilemma are actively debated in the field (Booth and Wheeler 2008; Jervis 1978; Posen 1993; Tang 2009). Debates about the utility and the veracity of deterrence (which, to simplify, refers to threats of military retaliation by leaders of a state to convince leaders of another state not to resort to the use of military force in their pursuit of foreign/security policy) abound in specialized journals/press (Achen and Snidal 1989; Morgan 2003; Quackenbush 2006; Sartori 2005; Zagare and Kilgour 2000). Likewise, the questions of (a) whether states balance against each other or bandwagon (i.e., align with a threatening state to avoid prevent attacked by it) and (b) whether balance of power is indeed the central mechanism regulating the international system still capture a great deal of academic attention (Brooks and Wohlforth 2008; Eilstrup-Sangiovanni 2009; Levy and Thompson 2010; Pape 2005; Paul 2005; Schweller 2006; Walt 2009; Wohlforth et al. 2007).

To be sure, a considerable number of influential realist scholars are based in the United States, yet there is no shortage of such scholars in Europe either. European countries house many prominent researchers in the field of strategic studies, which has deep links with neorealism. One such scholar, Lawrence Freedman (2012), recently argued that the realist tradition might constitute the best starting point for a revival of strategic studies. Along the same lines, Hew Strachan of the University of Oxford published a passionate defense of strategic studies in which he decries that strategic studies has been replaced by security studies and that war has been "wrenched from its political contexts" (Strachan 2013, 42). Moreover, as Andrew Linklater and Hidemi Suganami (2006) argue, a book by two of the most well-known UK-based international relations scholars – Barry Buzan and Richard Little (2000) – can be seen as a corrective to Waltz's structural realist theory.

The realist theory was seriously challenged in the mid-1980s with the publication of two groundbreaking books and one seminal article: Barry Buzan's *People, States and Fear* (1983), Stephen Walt's *The Origins of Alliances* (1987), and Alexander Wendt's (1987) article "The Agent-Structure Problem in International Relations Theory." While Buzan and Walt agreed with the basic neorealist contention that anarchy is the defining feature of the international system, they both depart from it in substantial ways. On the one hand, Buzan argued that military security is merely one aspect of security and that a comprehensive understanding of this topic needs to take into account other sectors, such as political security, economic security, environmental security, and societal security. Walt, on the other hand, contends that states do not balance each other on the basis of systemic power distribution, but rather on the basis of threat; this perspective introduces a subjective dimension into the realist scholarship. Looking back on this period, many security scholars have suggested that the solidity (some would say the rigidity) of realism's premises began to crack from this point.

Wendt's article imports the agent-structure debate from sociology into security studies. In this article, he convincingly argues that much of international relations literature (and especially Waltz's theory) wrongly postulates that the international structure can only constrain states, and thus generates interstate regulation based on the distribution of military power. Employing Anthony Giddens's concept of structuration, Wendt contends that structure also constructs state identities and interests. In a subsequent article, Wendt criticizes the mainstream theories of the time for postulating that the anarchic international structure causes states to adopt self-help mechanisms to ensure their own security. Self-help and power politics, argues Wendt, are processual, not essential, products of international anarchy; hence "anarchy is what states make of it" (Wendt 1992, 395).

The diversification of security studies shifted into high gear in the 1990s. The publication of landmark studies such as Ken Booth's (1991) article on security and emancipation, J. Ann Tickner's (1992) article on feminism and security, David Campbell's (1992) book on the role of identity in security policy, and R. B. J. Walker's (1993) book on sovereignty set the stage for the publication of three books that have significantly contributed to the development of alternative approaches to the realist standpoint on security.

A first "game changer" was Peter Katzenstein's (1996) edited volume *The Culture of National Security: Norms and Identity in World Politics*, whichk sought to challenge the material-based neorealist explanation of national security and to present an alternative approach based on ideational factors. The book aimed to deal a major, potentially fatal, blow to neorealism by demonstrating, in the context of the hard case of national security, that an ideational explanation trumps a material one. In setting up its battle with neorealism Katzenstein's book even gave the method home advantage to its theoretical opponent by adopting a largely positivist epistemology.

The Culture of National Security is one of the first books to have adopted a constructivist approach to security. In broad terms, constructivists posit that both knowledge and social reality – including the reality of security – are social constructions. Constructivism understands security as a project under construction, as becoming rather than being. Culture, identity, and norms are at the center of the constructivist "tool kit" for understanding and explaining contemporary security policies (Hurd 2007; Price 1997; Reus-Smit 2004).

Katzenstein's book was a seminal yet polarizing volume.[2] Some scholars felt that the book considerably shook the then-dominant approach and established constructivism's usefulness and legitimacy in security studies. By framing the development of constructivism through a dialogue with the dominant approach, the book has been highly influential in promoting constructivism as an important approach in security studies (Adler 2012; Barnett and Duvall 2005; Finnemore 2003; Tannenwald 2007). Advocates of this approach would later be labeled "conventional constructivists" – although it remains unclear to what extent they would themselves agree with that categorization. For others, Katzenstein *et al.*'s decision to open the possibility of working within the epistemological framework of the mainstream approach was a regrettable move that positioned "conventional constructivism" as a supplement to neorealism. This strand of scholarship is sometimes referred to as "critical constructivism" (Fierke 2007).

The distinction between conventional and critical constructivism is sometimes made in conjunction with a geographical divide between North America and Europe, respectively. Yet, here again, we question the usefulness and to some extent the accuracy of this dichotomy. In the first place, the fact that several critical constructivists are based in North America and that many conventional constructivists are affiliated with European universities renders this geographical division debatable. In the second place, it remains unclear what is gained by advocating such a locational division, which runs the risk of further entrenching disciplinary tendencies in isolation and compartmentalization.

A second groundbreaking international relations work published in the 1990s is Keith Krause and Michael C. Williams's edited (1997) volume *Critical Security Studies: Concepts and Cases*. Careful not to

---

[2] For example, a team of scholars published a book a short time later entitled *Culture of Insecurities: States, Communities and the Production of Danger* (Weldes *et al.* 1999). Many saw the book as a direct response (and rebuttal) to *The Culture of National Security*.

produce an orthodox or rigid view of critical security studies, they offer a broad definition of *critical* security studies(1997, x–xi) that is "meant to imply more an orientation toward the discipline than a precise theoretical label"; this definition encompasses the work of a wide range of scholars working in such approaches as poststructuralism, feminism, neo-Gramscian, and Foucaultian. Krause and Williams start from the standpoint of Robert Cox's (1986) distinction between problem-solving theories and critical theories: The former do not question the prevailing social and power relationships when conducting research, while the latter problematize these same relationships by analyzing their origins and their evolution. Krause and Williams's book seeks to employ this distinction to address *what* is studied when scholars study security, and *how* security is studied. This book has been influential in developing an alternative approach to the traditional/orthodox one and in stimulating the incorporation of nonmilitary issues in the realm of security studies.

Critical approaches to security have indeed burgeoned in the past two decades. A particular focus of interest has been the analysis of the (social) power relations that underpin security policies, especially in liberal states: Various scholars have contended that security should be understood as (i) a collection of discourses that serve to empower and reproduce gender-biased hierarchies (Shepherd 2008; Sjoberg 2013; Sylvester 2007a); (ii) a powerful political technology for social (and political) control (Burke 2007; Dillon and Reid 2009); or (iii) a series of routinized practices carried out by security professionals to create a governmentality of unease (Bigo 2002).

From the beginning, critical security studies has never been an exclusively European field of research. In fact, several of the pioneers of the critical security perspective are Canadian. The newly created journal *Critical Studies on Security* is based at York University in Toronto, Canada. In addition, several central figures of critical security studies are – or have been for a long time – based in the United States (Ashley and Walker 1990b; Debrix and Barder 2011; Der Derian 1995; Doty 2007; Sjoberg 2013; Steele 2008).

A third book that has had tremendous impact on the development of security studies imported speech-act theory into the field of security studies. In *Security: A New Framework for Analysis*, Barry Buzan, Ole Waever, and Jaap de Wilde (1998) introduced a new approach that became known as the "Copenhagen school." The authors contend that to label something as a security issue imbues that issue with a sense of significance that legitimizes the use of emergency measures extending beyond the usual political processes. A security speech act not only describes a state of affairs but also determines appropriate ways of acting and participating in relation to that state of affairs. The process of securitization then becomes what in "language theory is called a speech act. It is not interesting as a sign referring to something more real; it is the utterance itself that is the act. By saying the words, something is done (like betting, giving a promise, naming a ship)" (Buzan et al. 1998, 26). In a powerful rebuttal to the realist tendency to understand security as objectively given, the authors presented a cogent framework for investigating who securitizes, on what issues, and for whom. In contrast with many critical security scholars of the time, who did not feel the need to establish a demarcation between practices that relate to security and those that do not, Buzan et al. argued that security is related to existential threat and survival.

Securitization has been one of the most active fields of research in security studies in the past few decades. Although European security scholars were the quickest to contend with the Copenhagen school (Balzacq 2005; McDonald 2008; Stritzel 2007; Vuori 2008; Williams 2003), it was not long before Canada-based, United States–based, and Australia-based scholars joined the debate (Alker 2006; Bourbeau 2011; Curley and Wong 2008; Hayes 2009; Nyers 2009; Salter 2008). If initially much of the discussion centered on speech-act theory itself, as well as the political roots and philosophical underpinnings of the framework, much of the recent debate has focused on the notion of security performativity and the ethics of desecuritization (Bourbeau 2014; Browning and McDonald 2013; Floyd 2014; Hansen 2012; MacKenzie 2009).

After several decades of debate, international relations' take on security is now an eclectic mix of theories and approaches. If, in the 1990s, several observers were openly asking whether realism had a future and whether "anybody was still a realist" (Legro and Moravcsik 1999), the 2000s saw formidable rebuttals of that line of questioning from multiple realists (Feaver et al. 2000; Glaser 2003; Schweller and Wohlforth 2000; Walt 2002). For example, Mearsheimer's *The Tragedy of Great Power Politics*, published in 2001, mounts a powerful defense of the realist approach to security studies. Working with the assumption that great powers "are always searching for opportunities to gain power over their rivals, with hegemony as their final goal" (2001, 29), the book has undisputedly been influential in further developing the realist approach to security – compelling realism-attuned scholars to distinguish, as we have seen, between defensive and offensive realism. Others have abandoned structural realism's assumption that states are unitary actors and have put forward a renewed, neoclassical approach, which postulates that domestic politics and internal characteristics of states are a fundamental vector explaining how states respond, overrespond, and underrespond to security threats (Lobell *et al.* 2009; Schweller 2006).

While realism is certainly far from being dead, it has nonetheless lost its former unquestionably dominant position in the field. Indeed, studying security from an international relations perspective is particularly exciting these days, because we are potentially witnessing an important shift: Constructivism (broadly defined) is replacing realism as the dominant approach.[3] According to the latest TRIP survey of international relationships scholars (2012) the most frequent response to the question "Which paradigm best describes [your] approach to the study of international relations?" was "constructivism." This is true both in the United States and in Europe. To be sure, this is only a single snapshot of a complex reality; many other proxies should be analyzed before making a definitive statement. Nonetheless, the TRIP data are indicative of a trend toward general acceptance that the world we are living in – and in the context of which we understand security – is socially constructed.

Studying security nowadays is also exciting for another reason – and it is perhaps this reason that best illustrates the fact that a clear-cut distinction between North America/orthodox and Europe/critical scholars is becoming a thing of the past. We are potentially witnessing the emergence of another "game changer" perspective in security studies: The practice turn has come to security studies shores. Of course, a focus on practices is not entirely new. A practice approach has indeed been employed for decades by scholars to highlight the role of practices in creating the structure of the logic of anarchy (Wendt 1987), the textual interplay behind world politics (Der Derian and

---

[3] It is exciting not, primarily, because of the outcome (whether constructivism will indeed become the "new" dominant approach), but rather because the tectonic-theoretical plates are moving, a phenomenon that always makes for stimulating debates in any field of research.

Shapiro 1989), the importance of practices in constituting international norms (Price and Tannenwald 1996), the idea of a multibased diplomacy (Neumann 2002), and the cultural and symbolic form of power in security policies (Gheciu 2005; Williams 2007).

Yet, few would disagree that the practice approach truly came into its own in the late 2000s with the publication of Vincent Pouliot's seminal (2008) article "The Logic of Practicality." Pouliot, a constructivist trained and currently working in Canada, argues that most of what people do in world politics is not the result of rational decisions (as realism claims), nor of norm following or Habermasian communicative action (as strands of constructivism contend), but of routinized and inarticulate know-how that makes what is to be done appear commonsensical. Pouliot's article was followed by a coedited book with his former supervisor that drew together scholars (based in the United States, Canada, Denmark, United Kingdom, and Australia) employing a practice approach to issues ranging from deterrence, balance of power, emotions, and media performativity, to the privatization of global security (Adler and Pouliot 2011).

The jury is still out as to whether these contributions, which seek to establish a practice approach in international relations/security studies, will be capable of steering the field toward a more pragmatic international relations scholarship. Yet there is little doubt that questions of how, when, under what conditions, and why practices permeate security policies will attract a great deal of scholarly attention in the near-future.

Epistemology and methods

We have argued that, since the end of the cold war, the field of security studies has been shaped and guided by the relation among conventional (classical or traditional or orthodox), constructivist, and critical approaches to security. Thus, in the previous sections, we insisted upon the transformations in our understanding of referent objects of security and of our theoretical lenses to study security. To a certain extent, the discussion in the first section was primarily about ontology, in the sense that we emphasized what security problems were and how decisions about their "reality" came about. But, as often, ontology related questions are loaded with epistemological concerns, which in turn affect methodological choices. In *The Conduct of Enquiry in International Relations* (2011), Patrick T. Jackson has been instrumental in demonstrating that, despite divergences about what they mean by it, debates around epistemology often mirror broader discussions on the scientific character of a given scholarly endeavor. The problem is that these quarrels usually lead to dead ends, as epistemological questions are turned into "commitments." In turn, these commitments are translated into methodological terms, which unfortunately limit the room for dialogue between theories that claim to belong to separate epistemological families and live by different methods.

In this section, the myth (or caricature) that we want to challenge is the following: Critical approaches to security are incompatible with methods generally associated with positivist epistemology, whereas orthodox or traditional approaches to security cannot work with anything other than a positivist epistemology.

If ontology deals with the emergence, evolution, and transformation of entities – observable or not – that populate global politics, epistemology asks what kind of knowledge claims can be made about these entities and the consequences, if any, they have for practice (Chernoff 2007; Wight 2006). In brief, the discussion pitches positivists against postpositivists.

Neo-utilitarian theories (i.e., realism, liberalism, and their "neo" variants) are commonly defined as positivist approaches, just as critical theory and postmodernism are regarded, respectively, as postpositivist and antipositivist. But constructivism defies easy classification. Though constructivists work with largely similar basic ontological assumptions, they have quite different opinions as regard epistemology; different strands emphasize alternative stances and inevitably discount others. Fundamentally, constructivists are united in an opposition to empiricism – meaning that experience is the final test for our knowledge claims – and behaviorism – meaning that the rationale that undergirds actors' explanation of their behavior is of no relevance (Smith 1996, 35ff.). The vast majority of constructivists argue that "theory does not take place after the fact. Theories, instead, play a large part in constructing and defining what the facts are" (Zalewski and Enloe, 1995: 299; see also Guzzini 2000, and Price and Reus-Smit 1998).

However, these commitments cannot bridge the gaps between modern and postmodern constructivism, as each invokes a specific epistemological argument. The postmodernist or critical variant is decidedly interpretivist, while the modernist encourages both realist and positivist epistemologies (on this distinction, see Bevir and Rhodes 2002).

Postmodernist constructivists develop a skeptical take on core notions of positivism such as truth, objectivity, and reason. Following this approach, to study world politics requires students to sort out the social discourse within which actions are designed and acquire meaning. The epistemological implication is that understanding, not explaining, constitutes the primary activity of social science (Hollis and Smith 1990).

Modernist constructivism, on the other hand, is compatible, though not coterminous, with interpretivism. For instance, Kratochwil (1989) and Onuf (1989) hardly adhere to the language of causality, falsity, or truth usually associated with conventional constructivism. They argue, instead, that explanation could be expressed in terms of reasons, not causes, that is, in terms of "how possible" claims (Fierke 2007). Within modernist constructivism, scientific realist and positivist strains occupy a distinctive epistemological space. On the one hand, those who adopt scientific realism (e.g., Wight 2006) attempt to explain both the causal and the constitutive effects of unobservables in world politics (e.g., structures or processes). In this regard, ontology predates epistemology. On the other hand, those who defend a positivist posture encourage the use of the traditional language of causality and covering-law techniques (Wendt 1999). What distinguishes a realist from a positivist approach to epistemology is thus essentially the fact that the former acknowledges the existence of unobservable entities, while the latter does not (compare Carlsnaes 1992; Ruggie 1998). However, the boundaries between scientific realist and positivist strands are permeable. In fact, many constructivists use scientific realism and positivism, sometimes interchangeably. Wendt (1995, 75), for instance, asserts that "constructivists are modernists who fully endorse the scientific project of falsifying theories against evidence."

Method

One of the consequences of these epistemological disagreements is that critical studies on security tend to overlook methods that are usually associated with positivist epistemologies. For instance, in their otherwise excellent volume, Mark B. Salter and Can Mutlu (2013) disregard any method that is usually associated with a positivist epistemology (e.g., content analysis, process tracing). In the realm of critical approaches to security, then, the two dominant methods used are discourse analysis, which has different shades (Hansen 2006), and ethnographic research, which is practiced, for instance, by students who work on border security (Andreas 2009; Bigo 1996; Léonard 2010). That said, both critical scholars and neo-utilitarians, often rely on case study and when they do resort to comparative analysis, they favor small-n studies. Yet, neoutilitarian scholars usually stick to their covering-law technique (Mearsheimer 2001; Waltz 1979). For instance, Glaser's (2010) work on competition and cooperation in world politics attempts to develop a deductive approach to states' security policies and derives from it a set of assumptions that are supposed to characterize states' behavior. Put differently, there seems to be a tacit consensus that critical studies are not amenable to approaches that lend credibility to traditional views of security. As such, the "epistemological chasm" is translated into a methodological divide (Silverman 1997, 94). In particular, critical security studies treated issues pertaining to methods in two main ways. First, some scholars held that the construction of methodological standards was dangerous because those standards prevent alternative experiences from being taken into account in the research process (Ashley and Walker 1990a; Campbell 1998). Because this approach has proven unproductive, a second position has been developed, which argues that security studies is best understood through the lens of qualitative methods (cf. Salter and Mutlu 2013; Shepherd 2013). In this context, for a long time, critical studies on security, in general, and securitization studies, in particular, were usually associated with methods that fall within the conspectus of interpretive epistemologies, which often relied upon an inductive approach to scientific inquiry (Vuori 2014).

To understand the divide between different methods that is said to embody the barrier between critical and traditional views of security, it might be useful to refer to the guiding principles that underpin them. Typically, traditional approaches relied on quantitative research, whereas critical approaches to security offered more, if not exclusive space to qualitative views. Thus, on each side of the divide, one type of research seems to dominate and tends to overstate its own value, with detrimental effects on the dialogue between corresponding methods. However, this debate should not be regarded as restricted to security studies; anyone who enters the field will discover that it is actually a discussion that traverses and structures social sciences, including political science and international relations (King, Keohane, and Verba 1994).

International relations: Celebrating eclectic dynamism   131

Moreover, critical scholars often treat quantitative research as quintessentially the study of data set observations while they regard qualitative approaches as concerned with understanding "how" phenomena take a particular shape, and the meaning actors attribute them. The study of data set observations is concerned with observation in the sheer statistical sense and aims to develop correlations of data across cases. This approach has been very influential in the literature on deterrence, war, and the balance of power (e.g., Niou, Ordeshook, and Rose 1989; cf. also "the correlates of war project," Singer and Small 1972). In a recent study, Vipin Narang (2014), for instance, attempts to code the sources of nuclear postures in the modern era. Such a technique allows him to design hypotheses that are then tested across a wide range of cases (China, France, India, Israel, Pakistan, and South Africa). In this respect, data set observations are meant to "increase the number of observable implications of a theory" (George and Bennett, 2005, 13). For quantitative approaches to security, therefore, the challenge is to widen the scope of their N, so that data collected enable researchers systematically to probe causal inferences (i.e., the value of one variable impacts on the other). The most common approach to a quantitative view of security remains that which follows in the footsteps of Thomas Schelling (1960). For example, in a nice analysis of trust and mistrust in the cold war, Andrew Kydd (2005) uses game theory in order to explain why trust obtains in certain security situations, and not others. In many ways, the emphasis on game theory is one of the key characteristics of orthodox or traditional security studies, as evidenced by the work published by the *Journal of Conflict Resolution* since its creation in 1957.

Not all positivist scholars, however, clothe their subject within a quantitative frame. Indeed, some orthodox scholars adopt a positivist perspective but not the data set observation of quantitative approaches, placing them a little closer to, though without aligning them with some qualitative approaches to social phenomena. On this view, most articles published in *International Security*, while adopting the vocabulary of positivism, do not delve into quantitative technicalities. Those articles' strength does not necessarily depend on correlation based inferences, but primarily on a causal process observation, that is "an insight or piece of data that provides information about context, process, or mechanism, and that contributes distinctive leverage in causal inference" (Collier, Brady, and Seawright 2007 277; Fazal 2014).

Often, indeed, they concentrate on "sequential processes within a particular historical case" (George and Bennett 2005, 13). Many conventional constructivists map their work on this approach. Hence, they confront the same problem, that is, the existence of the cause that they claim affects an outcome. For instance, when Nina Tannenwald (1999) brings the nonuse of nuclear weapons to rest on the existence of a nuclear taboo, which is a cause for nuclear restraints, she collects data that seem to concur with her initial intuition. However, this does not "test" the presence of a nuclear taboo; rather, it supports its presence.

A new strand of security studies examines how qualitative and quantitative approaches can be combined, while respecting the specificities of each technique, but with an eye toward developing a richer perspective on the issue at hand. Unfortunately, it is not common to encounter works that go beyond appeals to integrating these approaches. We therefore provide an illustration of a recent attempt to cross-fertilize the distinctive research methods. Bourbeau (2011) demonstrates the usefulness and added value of thinking about research methods for the study of the securitization process along these lines in his comparative analysis of the securitization of migration in Canada and France. In the same lineage, Balzacq (2011) argues that there is nothing so specific about securitization that it makes it incompatible with quantitative approaches. The upshot of these sets of arguments is that security problems can be captured using a variety of methods, quantitative and qualitative. The fact that an approach uses qualitative methods does not align it immediately with a critical view of security. In this light, Balzacq (2014) suggests that students of security should resort to triangulation of methods. In the case of securitization, for instance, relying upon one single method has provoked two pathologies in securitization studies. First, it led to confirmation bias. Second, perhaps as a consequence, it delayed the advancement of the theory.

Some methods, we know, are better equipped to deal with some types of research puzzles than others. In Figure 6.1 (adapted from Gorard and Taylor 2007, 7), it appears that each method provides distinctive evidence about the phenomenon examined (A, B). Less acknowledged yet is the fact that combined, methods generate an original perspective, C, that is different from A and B. In other words, by ignoring possibilities offered by triangulation, securitization has missed other perspectives (A and C). In terms of theory development,

International relations: Celebrating eclectic dynamism 133

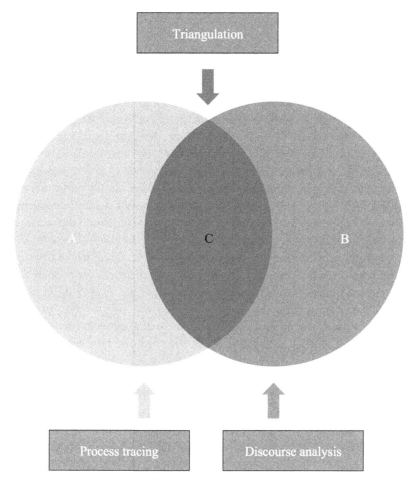

Figure 6.1 A visual model of triangulation by method.

the consequences are numerous, but it is urgent to raise one here. By leaving out "A" and "C," researchers are less lucid on how and when to rule out rival accounts, and the extent to which those sharpen the scope of their theories.

In the field of securitization, there have been sustained calls for triangulation, as a way of strengthening the results generated by this field (Bourbeau 2011). In order to show how this might help a theory's development and dialogue with others, Balzacq (2014) has proposed an example of triangulation by methods, articulating two types of methods that are usually associated with different epistemological stripes, namely, discourse analysis and process tracing. In fact, discourse analysis and process tracing capture different aspects of the object of study. In particular, the core of process tracing is to examine social mechanisms that brought a social phenomenon into being. According to Hedstrom and Swedberg (1998, 25), social mechanisms are "a set of hypotheses that could be the explanation for some social phenomenon, the explanation being in terms of interactions between individuals and other individuals and some social aggregate." In short, process tracing deals with issues of interactions, causal chains linking the independent variable(s) to the outcome of the dependent variable, and the conditions under which such causal paths obtain (Checkel 2008). In this sense, process tracing can be a cure to confirmation bias. In fact, the explanation of process tracing lies in the strategy of condition seeking, which asks, "Under what conditions does securitization occur?" Process tracing fares better than discourse analysis in that regard, as the latter often concentrates on whether securitization has happened or not, and how it has taken shape; less frequently, if ever, does discourse analysis ask why. This is where, we surmise, process tracing is probably at its best. The point is that the concern with the question of whether securitization has occurred and how has led some scholars to assume (among other things) that accumulating facts in order to confirm the desired outcome (i.e., successful) was the summum bonum of securitization studies. In brief, discourse analysis is strong in understanding how securitization operates, but weak in uncovering why certain securitizing moves succeed and when. By contrast, two techniques capture the significance and specificity of process tracing: condition seeking and design strategy. First, condition seeking aims to sort out "limiting conditions for a known finding." The aim of design strategy is, on the other hand, to discover "conditions that ... produce a previously unobtainable result" (Greenwald *et al.* 1986, 211). This means, for example, that within the conspectus of process tracing, failed securitizing moves are outcomes worthy of investigation, in part because they enable us to explain why other moves were successful and, in part, as a consequence, because the knowledge culled from failed securitizing moves can "enrich the general theory" of securitization (George and Bennett 2005, 215). In this light, process tracing is decisive both in constructing and in testing theories.

However, the nature and particular blend of triangulation one articulates depend on the purpose of the study. Yet, it is generally argued that triangulation by method remains the most common form of triangulation to which social scientists resort. Kopinak (1999, 171) defines multimethod triangulation as the procedure of "gathering information pertaining to the same phenomenon through more than one method, primarily in order to determine if there is a convergence and hence, increased validity in research findings." In our view, the basic idea here is that when a phenomenon is approached from more than one perspective, something new results. In other words, triangulation is not, at least not essentially, about using other methods to "inspect" or "test" the result obtained through a different method. The most productive character of methodological triangulation emerges when and if researchers acquire a new vision of the phenomenon examined or aspects of it, at variance with the one enabled by another method. That is, triangulation works best when methods are treated less as substitutable than as complementary techniques.

Conclusion

If, as is often stated, culture, space, and liberty are the signature concepts of anthropology, geography, and philosophy, respectively, security is usually regarded as one of the defining concepts of international relations. Unsurprisingly, then, security is a topic that is much debated in international relations literature. Debates breed diversity and, for our part, we think that this eclectic diversity is one of the chief strengths of international relations.

As we have highlighted in the previous sections, all the current approaches to international relations engage with the topic of security. The vast majority of textbooks on security include chapters on realism, liberalism, constructivism, critical theory, gender, and poststructuralism. We believe that this situation should be celebrated not only because it legitimizes, solidifies, and stimulates debates and dialogues across particular standpoints on security, but also because it testifies to the health of international relations' take on security. While we have organized our discussion of the literature on security through an analysis of three myths, we have tried to underscore some of the strengths that international relations offers to a multidisciplinary approach to security.

Another strength of the current scholarship is that scholars are now focusing on what unifies them instead of what separates them.

For instance, whereas much of the discussion in the early 2000s centered on disagreement concerning the boundaries of critical security studies and the meaning of the label "critical" (Booth 2005), recently, there has been a return to the broader and more encompassing definition of critical security studies espoused by Krause and Williams (1997). As Browning and McDonald (2013) argue, talking about critical security studies means analyzing the social construction of security through, notably, problematizing the role of knowledge, politics, and representations in contemporary security policies. Similarly, some scholars have argued that "moving forward together" – that is, searching for similarities rather than differences between approaches – consolidates the scholarship and permits a better connection between theoretical models and contemporary security politics (Bourbeau 2014; Sylvester 2007b). Others, including James Fearon and Alexander Wendt (2002) and Jeffrey Checkel (2012), have argued that a "pluralist" or "bridge-building" approach provides scholars with a better understanding of world politics. In sum, an increasing number of scholars are recognizing the need to cut across traditional divides and to shift the discussion toward the factors that unite security scholars rather than those that divide them.

Another significant strength of current international relations scholarship on security is the growing acceptance that "more is better" – to paraphrase a central debate in the field (Sagan and Waltz 2012) – when it comes to the choice of methods one uses to conduct a study. Clearly, the embracing of a plurality of methodologies nourishes a constant renewal in debates within the field; certain approaches are more strongly associated with certain methods, and thus scholars feel compelled to discuss work employing "their" method from a different theoretical standpoint. The encouragement of multiple methodologies also facilitates and induces interdisciplinary dialogue, as scholars who share the same methodology feel encouraged to enter into a cross-disciplinary discussion on their particular security issues.

In sum, the subfield of security studies has started to renew itself on multiple fronts and appears to be in a superb position to embrace, tackle, and push a multidisciplinary approach to security. This is certainly no small achievement given the history of the field, and we believe it is a development that holds great promise for the future of the scholarship.

7 Psychology
The phenomenology of human security

THOMAS C. O'BRIEN AND LINDA R. TROPP

Psychological perspectives are critical for understanding the concept of security because they explain and predict processes that may promote violent conflict or peaceful relations between nations and other groups (Bar-Tal 2007; Carroll, Wichman, and Arkin 2006; Huddy, Feldman, and Weber 2007; Leidner, Tropp, and Lickel, 2013). Psychological approaches examine these processes on multiple levels, such as relations between ethnic or religious groups within a nation as well as relations between nations.

The factors that motivate people's behavior and decision making, whether in relations with other groups or in support of national policies, are far more complex than a rational calculation of costs and benefits. Psychology has specified a range of biases that influence human behavior and decision making, in particular with regard to the groups with which people identify and in which they categorize others (Tajfel *et al.* 1971; Tajfel and Turner 1986; Turner *et al.* 1987).

Psychological contributions to the study of security focus on structural and subjective factors that predict people's perceptions and feelings of insecurity, the consequences those feelings of insecurity have on their attitudes and behavior (Bar-Tal and Jacobson 1998; Huddy *et al.* 2007), as well as the factors that may be necessary to enhance their sense of security. An underlying premise is that insecurity – whether actual or perceived – is an undesirable psychological state. Correspondingly, the need for security motivates people to diminish this state, prompting attitudes, emotions, and behaviors that can promote or hinder positive relations between groups (Huddy *et al.* 2007;

Acknowledgements: This material is based upon work supported by the National Science Foundation Graduate Research Fellowship Program awarded to the first author under Grant No. 1451512. Any opinions, findings, and conclusions or recommendations expressed in this material are those of the author(s) and do not necessarily reflect the views of the National Science Foundation.

Skitka *et al.* 2006). For the purposes of this chapter, we use the term "groups" to refer to large collections of individuals who categorize themselves, or whom others categorize, on the basis of ethnicity, race, nationality, political orientation, religion, or other categories that society recognizes as constituting meaningful groups (see Roccas and Elster 2012). The psychological need for security may lead people to identify more strongly with certain groups (e.g., Hogg 2010) or to antagonize or avoid members of other groups, as contrasted to building positive relationships across group boundaries (e.g., Leidner *et al.* 2013; Pettigrew 1998).

The current chapter focuses on theory and research from social and political psychology, and in particular the processes that pertain to relations between groups. We organize our review of theory and research around three central questions relevant to the psychological study of security:

- What are security and insecurity from a psychological perspective?
- What psychological factors predict feelings of security and insecurity between groups?
- What strategies could enhance feelings of security and promote positive relations between groups?

In this chapter, we discuss more in depth the methods that social and political psychologists use to address these issues empirically. Next, we discuss each of the questions outlined previously. At the end of our chapter, we describe strengths and limitations in how psychologists study security concerns, as well as the potential for integration of psychology with other disciplines to enhance the study of security.

Research methods in social and political psychology

Social and political psychologists address research questions using multiple methods. The vast majority of social psychological studies are quantitative and use cross-sectional, experimental, or longitudinal research designs (Maruyama and Ryan 2014). Psychologists can use these methods in field or laboratory settings, and each approach has a unique set of benefits and drawbacks. Researchers often combine methods to enhance the validity and generalizability of findings about relationships between variables (e.g., correlation) or evidence demonstrating that one variable causes change in another variable (e.g., causation).

Social and political psychologists use quantitative methods to predict and explain psychological processes so they can generalize to other contexts. They can also use qualitative research to enrich understanding of individuals' experience. In pursuit of a rich understanding of the experience of security and insecurity for particular individuals, contexts, and communities, qualitative methods used widely in fields such as anthropology and sociology may be more appropriate (see Goldstein, this volume; Ragin, Nagel, and White 2004).

The use of laboratory experiments in social psychology is popular because they have strong internal validity – that is, they have the potential to demonstrate causal relationships between variables while controlling for possible confounds that other variables pose (Wilson, Aronson, and Carlsmith 2010). For example, psychologists can use experimental methods to test whether, at its most basic level, group membership would cause bias even if it were seemingly arbitrary, and divorced from long-standing ties with fellow group members or conflicts with other groups. To answer the question, Tajfel and his colleagues (Tajfel *et al.* 1971; see also Pinter and Greenwald 2011) devised the minimal group paradigm. In this paradigm, experimenters randomly assign participants to laboratory-generated groups, so that their group memberships are free of any preexisting individual or context variables. In one version of the minimal group paradigm, researchers instructed participants to estimate the numbers of dots on a screen. Regardless of participants' actual responses, half of the participants were told that they were overestimators, and the other half that they were underestimators. Researchers then assessed outcomes such as attitudes toward each group or allocations of resources to members of their own group and the other group. Numerous studies conducted in many countries show that participants tend to report more positive attitudes toward – and give greater resources to – members of their own group than the other (Brewer 1999).

Although laboratory experiments have strong internal validity, one could easily argue that research findings from such studies have weak external validity; they may not generalize to other kinds of groups and settings (Campbell 1957; Paluck and Cialdini 2014; Wilson *et al.* 2010). Thus, social psychologists balance using controlled research designs with strong internal validity for theory building with studies that have greater external validity. Social psychologists can thus generalize findings more effectively to real world settings. They can accomplish this by using a combination of studies that test effects among both minimal, randomly assigned groups and members of real ethnic, religious, and national groups (e.g., Saguy *et al.* 2009).

Experimental studies in field settings can be more readily interpreted in and applied to the contexts and populations of interest (see Paluck and Cialdini 2014). Like laboratory experiments, field experiments can test casual relationships on psychological processes relevant to the study of security. Field experiments may have less internal validity than laboratory experiments because researchers can control fewer aspects of participants' experience, but this aspect of field experiments may strengthen their external validity (Campbell 1957; Wilson *et al.* 2010). For instance, Paluck (2009) used random assignment to test whether exposure to a media program promoting reconciliation could change Rwandan participants' attitudes, perceived norms about intergroup relations, and cooperative behaviors. The researchers assigned participants in matched regions of Rwanda to listen to one of two radio soap operas, one promoting positive health behaviors (control condition) and one promoting positive intergroup relations through stories about reconciliation (experimental condition). After a year of listening to episodes of the respective program each month, the researchers assessed dependent variables using surveys, focus groups, and behavioral observations. Results suggested that Rwandan participants who listened to the reconciliation program were less likely to oppose intermarriage between their and other religious, regional, and/or ethnic groups; were more likely to express empathy for victims of the Rwandan genocide; and demonstrated more cooperative behavior (Paluck 2009).

Cross-sectional studies are useful when it is impractical or unethical to study the phenomena of interest through experimental means, although the evidence for causation is less strong. For example, with a massive sample of US participants, Huddy and her colleagues showed that feeling insecure about terrorist attacks interacted with the threat participants perceived to predict their support for various domestic and foreign policies. Among those who reported feeling less secure and confident when thinking about terrorist attacks, the threat they perceived from outgroups was particularly predictive of their support for requiring US citizens to hold national I.D. cards, for the US government's conducting special surveillance of Arabs and Muslims, and for US foreign policies in reaction to 9/11 (Huddy *et al.* 2007).

Are psychologists in consensus on methodology?

Psychologists studying issues relevant to security take different methodological approaches, as we have described. A general principle is that the method selected depends upon the nature of the research question, as well as the researcher's interest (Reis and Gosling 2010). Thus, a researcher's inclination to use laboratory methods versus field methods, or experimental versus survey methods, likely reflects differences in interests and in how the researcher frames the research question.

An important methodological critique in behavioral science research concerns the disproportionate focus on "western, educated, industrialized, rich, democratic" populations (Henrich, Heine, and Norenzayan 2010). Psychologists differ in their attitudes regarding the importance of studying psychological processes outside the laboratory and with diverse populations (see commentaries to Henrich *et al.*'s 2010 target article in issue 33 of *Behavioral and Brain Sciences*). We would expect few psychologists to disagree that more diverse and representative samples would be of great benefit to psychological research, and that most would advocate greater use of rigorous field studies (Paluck and Cialdini 2014). We believe this is of particular importance for psychology's contribution to the study of security, because many of the psychological questions that are most relevant to security concerns involve psychological processes and how those processes may differ among members of different groups in distinct national or international contexts.

In the sections that follow, we summarize research and theory on security from a psychological perspective.

What are security and insecurity from a psychological perspective?

Definitions of security in psychology can be applied to intrapersonal processes involving self-esteem (Marigold, McGregor, and Zanna 2010), feelings in close relationships (Clark and LeMay 2010), or understandings of relations between groups (e.g., Bar-Tal and Jacobson 1998; Huddy *et al.* 2007). In each case, psychological insecurity refers to a state of uncertainty or unease, which can motivate individuals to develop attitudes or engage in behaviors that seek to reestablish a sense of security.

Early models of human motivation identify security as a core psychological need. Maslow (1943) suggested that people are guided by a "safety-seeking mechanism" that leads to a "preference for familiar rather than unfamiliar ... or for the known rather than the unknown" (349). Thus, we tend to regard the unfamiliar and unknown as potentially threatening (Newcomb 1943), and encountering threatening situations provokes our needs for security (Arkin, Carroll, and Oleson 2010).

As we engage with others in our social worlds, we are especially likely to attend to and react to stimuli that could pose a threat to our well-being or that of our group (Fiske and Taylor 2013). These processes are especially problematic for relations between groups, as we develop negative expectations for how we will be treated by other groups (Kramer and Wei 1999), make stereotyped attributions to predict the future behavior of groups (Fiske and Taylor 2013), and blame other groups for actions committed by a mere few of their members (Lickel 2012; Lickel *et al.* 2006). Moreover, our emotional responses to potential threats can complicate relations between groups, as they may compel us to engage in defensive acts that antagonize members of other groups and worsen our relations with them (Stephan *et al.* 2009).

However, emotional processes are not necessarily destructive for reasoning and intergroup behavior. People can regulate their emotion using various strategies. For example, through the emotion regulation strategy of cognitive reappraisal, people can regulate how negative emotions affect them by reevaluating the situation in which they feel the negative emotion (Gross 2002). In a correlational study of Jewish Israelis' support for humanitarian aid in the Gaza war, researchers assessed the extent to which participants engaged in cognitive reappraisal of the emotions they felt during the war along with various other variables. Those who regulated their emotions through cognitive reappraisal felt more hope about resolving the conflict in the future and were more supportive of aid to Palestinians (Halperin and Gross 2011). Emotions may also be constructive for promoting more positive intergroup relations; when white Americans feel sympathy for the suffering of African Americans or angry about the relative advantage of white Americans, they are more supportive of reparatory policies to address racial inequality (Iyer, Leach, and Crosby 2006; Leach, Iyer, and Pedersen 2006).

What psychological factors predict feelings of security and insecurity between groups?

We organize our discussion of psychological factors predicting security around a limited number of relevant theoretical frameworks, including threat, social identity, contact between groups, and the reframing of group boundaries. Whereas much of the research we review is categorized into one framework, other research that we review builds onto understanding of the phenomena of interest – such as perceived threat – but is not necessarily part of the theory we discuss.

Difference and lack of familiarity can make people feel insecure, uncertain, and anxious regarding how members of other groups might perceive them (Stephan and Stephan 1985; Trawalter, Richeson, and Shelton 2009; Vorauer 2006). Consequently, people often approach cross-group relations with vigilance, as they are uncertain about, or threatened by, the possibility that members of other groups will regard or treat them negatively (Crocker and Garcia 2009; Kramer and Messick 1998: Kramer and Wei 1999).

Counteracting these tendencies, people often seek to align themselves with their own groups, in order to reduce feelings of uncertainty and threat and establish a greater sense of belonging and security in their social worlds (Hogg 2003, 2010). However, in some cases, enhancing affiliation with one's own groups can increase outgroup derogation (McGregor *et al.* 2008) and even intergroup violence (McGregor, Haji, and Kang 2008). In the sections that follow, we review how intergroup threat and group identification can contribute to security and insecurity in intergroup contexts, and how other psychological processes may offer constructive alternatives for engagement across groups.

Intergroup threat theory

Intergroup threat theory explains how people from different groups perceive and react to threats (Stephan *et al.* 2009). Extensive psychological research reveals that greater appraisals of intergroup threat typically predict more negative intergroup attitudes and behaviors (Riek, Mania, and Gaertner 2006; Stephan and Stephan 2000; Stephan *et al.* 2009). In particular, two primary types of perceived threats posed by other groups have been identified in this literature, realistic and symbolic threat (Stephan and Renfro 2002). Realistic threat refers to the perception that the presence of an outgroup endangers material resources that could support the welfare of one's own group, such as limiting access to jobs, housing, education, land, or the ingroup's security and existence. Symbolic threat refers to the perception that an outgroup endangers the worldview or way of life of one's own group, such as by introducing new customs, value systems, social standards, and attitudes (Stephan and Stephan 2000).

How people respond to intergroup threat can have profound consequences for intergroup relations and conflict (Stephan *et al.* 2009). Greater perceived threat typically predicts greater ethnocentrism, xenophobia, and prejudice (e.g., Marcus, Sullivan, Theiss-Morse, and Wood 1995; Levine and Campbell 1972), greater opposition to immigration and related policies (e.g., Pereira, Vala, and Costa-Lopes 2010; Zick, Pettigrew, and Wagner 2008), and greater support for aggressive, violent, and/or retaliatory policies against outgroups (e.g., Gordon and Arian 2001; Spanovic *et al.* 2010). For instance, studies have found that Jewish Israelis' perceptions of threat by Arabs predicted support for governmental violation of Israeli Arabs' civil rights (Shamir and Sagiv-Schifter 2006) and that the more Jewish Israelis perceived that Palestinians posed a threat to Israel, the more they supported exclusionist attitudes (Canetti-Nisim *et al.* 2009) and aggressive retaliatory policies (Maoz and McCauley 2008) against Palestinians.

Stephan and his colleagues (Stephan *et al.* 2009) describe intergroup threat as involving both affective and cognitive processes. Such responses may result from strong emotions such as anxiety and fear that people experience in the face of threat; they are not necessarily intentional, conscious, or rational. People often experience anxiety when interacting with members of other groups (Stephan and Stephan 1985). This anxiety can enhance prejudice, reliance on stereotypes, and a motivation to avoid future intergroup encounters (Amodio 2009; Plant and Devine 2003; Wilder 1993). More broadly, when people perceive an outgroup as threatening a valued group membership, people tend to report fear and engage in hostile reactions toward that outgroup (Bar-Tal 2009; Spanovic *et al.* 2010). For example, immediately after the September 11, 2001, attacks on the World Trade Center, Americans were especially likely to report strong emotions such as fear and anger in response to the attacks (Smith, Rasinski, and Toce 2001). In the wake of the 9/11 attacks, Americans' reports of fear predicted greater intolerance of Muslims and greater support for deportation of immigrants (Skitka *et al.* 2006); at threat predicted greater intolerance of both Arabs and Muslims and aggressive security policies (Huddy, Khatid, and Capelos 2002; Huddy *et al.* 2005). Fear can also predict support for intergroup violence and aggression, particularly when framed in terms of future threats that may arise from the other group in the conflict (e.g., Spanovic *et al.* 2010). Additionally, fear is not simply a result of threat, but may also enhance perceptions of threat (Lerner *et al.* 2003): As group members experience fear in response to an intergroup event or provocation, that fear can strengthen the view that the outgroup threatens one's own group. Taken together, these psychological approaches emphasize the need to interpret attitudes toward intergroup conflict and security policies in light of group members' threat perceptions and emotional responses to conflict.

Intergroup threat and emotions among advantaged and disadvantaged groups

How people perceive and respond to intergroup threat can depend upon the power and status of their own group. Emerging research in social and political psychology highlights the importance of understanding the divergent perspectives of groups based on their different levels of privilege, status, or power (e.g., Dovidio *et al.* 2012). We will use the terms "advantaged" and "disadvantaged" to refer to groups that differ in privilege, status, or power in their societal context, such as white and black Americans in the United States, Jewish Israelis and Palestinian citizens in Israel, and native-born and immigrant groups across many national contexts. By using these terms, we do not intend to imply that all members of one group are necessarily socially and economically advantaged, and that all members of the other group are socially and economically disadvantaged. Rather, we use these terms to represent the unequal and sociohistorical nature of relations between the groups, and the unique perceptions and motivations that typically correspond with their relative positions in the social structure (see Bobo 1999; Nadler and Shnabel 2008).

In part, members of advantaged and disadvantaged groups may differ in the forms of threat they perceive. For example, while members of advantaged groups tend to focus on realistic and symbolic threats as described previously, members of disadvantaged groups tend to be concerned about the ways in which their disadvantage affects their daily lives and how they may be subjected to discrimination and unjust treatment. Members of disadvantaged groups regularly experience threats associated with confirming negative stereotypes about their groups (Steele and Aronson 1995) and threats to their psychological sense of security and belonging in contexts where they are underrepresented (Brewer, Von Hippel, and Gooden 1999; Purdie Vaughns *et al.* 2008). Members of advantaged and disadvantaged groups also tend to have different emotional responses to intergroup encounters: Members of advantaged groups tend to feel anxious about being perceived as prejudiced, whereas members of disadvantaged groups tend to feel anxious about becoming the targets of prejudice (e.g., Devine and Vasquez 1998). Correspondingly, the intergroup attitudes of members of advantaged and disadvantaged groups are often predicted by different factors. For instance, white Americans' racial attitudes are predicted by antiegalitarian sentiments, whereas black Americans' racial attitudes are predicted by perceived racism and discrimination of whites (Monteith and Spicer 2000). Such trends parallel the divergent motivations of advantaged and disadvantaged group members in intergroup contexts; members of advantaged groups typically seek to preserve their moral integrity, whereas members of disadvantaged groups typically seek acknowledgment and discussion of the existing structural inequalities (Shnabel *et al.* 2009).

Group identity and social identity theory

One's identity as a member of social groups is a critical part of psychological security. Indeed, as Allport (1960) stated, "Security is found only within the ingroups – within the family, the church, the tribe, the nation. All else appears hazardous and unknown" (p. 344). Striving for a sense of belonging constitutes a core social motive (Fiske 2004).

Social identity theory explains the processes through which people identify with social groups, the functions that social identity serves, and the consequences for their attitudes and behavior. People's identities as group members may serve as important sources of esteem (Brown 2000; Tajfel and Turner 1986) and information about how to think and behave in their social worlds (Hogg and Abrams 1988; Smith and Louis 2008). Generally, when people identify with social groups, they take on the norms, behaviors, and attitudes of their groups and become increasingly motivated to promote their groups' welfare and serve as good representatives of their groups (see Hogg 2003).They tend to exaggerate differences between their own group and other groups, assuming that they are more similar to members of their own group and are more different from members of other groups (Wilder 1984). People also tend to evaluate their own groups more positively, and allocate more resources to their own groups compared to the way they evaluate and treat members of other groups (Bourhis, Sachdev, and Gagnon 1994; Tajfel, Billig, Bundy, and Flament 1971).

Potential consequences of uncertainty for group identity and security

Experiencing uncertainty motivates people to identify more with groups (Hogg 2003, 2007). In particular, uncertainty motivates people to identify with groups that have high entitativity, which means that the group has a clear structure, a coherent set of goals that its members agree upon, with clear lines demarcating ingroup from outgroup (Campbell 1957; Hamilton and Sherman 1996; Hogg and Adelman 2013).

Feelings of uncertainty can also make people more sensitive to perceptions of injustice, including not having a voice in procedures and not feeling as if they are given a fair chance (Van den Bos 2001; Van den Bos and Lind 2010). Perceiving that procedures authorities use are fair is important for a secure society; when people perceive that authorities use unfair procedures, they are less likely to cooperate with and help them (Tyler and Blader 2003).

People who identify more strongly with their groups are more likely to interpret intergroup situations as threatening and are more sensitive to intergroup threats they perceive. Once they interpret situations as threatening their ingroup they react more strongly to the threat (e.g., Riek *et al.* 2006). They also become more likely to justify violence and negative actions against outgroup members, and to view the acts of violence they commit against them merely as responses to threat and provocation posed by them (Bilali, Tropp, and Dasgupta 2012).

Different modes of identification

The concept of social identity has developed to explain how distinct modes of identification can have distinct consequences for attitudes and behavior. Certain aspects of group identification are especially likely to exacerbate threat responses and enhance ingroup-protective responses in the face of threat. Theoretical distinctions between patriotism and nationalism (e.g., Kosterman and Feshbach 1989) and constructive and blind patriotism (e.g., Staub 1997) suggest that there are at least two key dimensions of group identification: one that focuses on attachment to the ingroup, and one that refers to beliefs in the ingroup's superiority over other groups and deference to group norms and authorities (Roccas *et al.* 2008).

A growing body of research suggests that this latter aspect of group identification – or, *glorification* of the ingroup (Roccas *et al.* 2006, 2008) – is particularly likely to make group members prone to act aggressively in response to intergroup threat and to justify that aggression (Bandura 1999). For instance, among American respondents, a sense of ingroup superiority has been shown to predict greater support for military action against Iraq (Federico, Golec, and Dial 2005) and fewer demands for justice in response to torture committed by American and British forces against Iraqis (Leidner *et al.* 2010). Dutch Muslim youths who experienced greater uncertainty also viewed Muslims as superior to other groups, an attitude that predicted greater disconnection from Dutch society, and in turn, greater support for intergroup violence enacted by Muslims (Doosje, Loseman, and Van den Bos 2013). As evidenced by these examples, glorification of the ingroup reduces guilt about negative ingroup actions by increasing "exonerating cognitions" about the acts (Roccas, Klar, and Leviatan 2006). By justifying the transgressions of their own group, glorification helps group members to maintain a positive image of their own group, even after committing violence against other groups (Leidner and Castano 2012).

How responses to insecurity affect intergroup relations

Ironically, engaging in behaviors to protect the ingroup not only could enhance and justify aggression toward other groups, but may also inadvertently provoke vengeful and defensive responses among members of those other groups. Indeed, aggressive acts committed by ingroup members and justification of their aggression toward an outgroup can often provoke retaliatory efforts among members of that outgroup (Lickel *et al.* 2006; Lickel 2012). Perceiving that another group is apathetic to the mistreatment or injustice encountered by one's own disadvantaged group can also lead members of disadvantaged groups to endorse stronger retaliatory responses and greater efforts toward social change (Hawi *et al.* 2012; Saguy, Tropp, and Hawi 2013). As such, experiencing threat and a sense of insecurity can motivate intergroup attitudes and behaviors that have the potential to exacerbate intergroup conflict and enhance instability and uncertainty in relations between groups.

Yet, once our psychological needs for security are met, other psychological needs motivate us to grow (Molden, Lee, and Higgins 2008) and explore other interests and experiences (e.g., Maslow 1962; Wright, Aron, and Tropp 2002). Uncertainty could also be construed as a source of excitement as people seek out new experiences and if they see uncertainty as a challenge (Hogg 2010). People may also personally vary in the extent to which they feel comfortable with uncertainty and wish to learn new things about themselves and their abilities and to seek out new experiences (Szeto and Sorrentino 2010).

Taken together, these trends suggest that if we perceive or anticipate threat, or feel uncertain about whether we will be threatened by an outgroup, we are likely to desire safety and security and to become defensive and protective in intergroup encounters. However, to the extent that we are able to alleviate potential threats presented by other groups, we may feel more secure and more open to expressing interest, curiosity, and empathy in our relations with other groups.

Strategies to enhance security and improve relations between groups

In the sections that follow, we review a number of constructive strategies that may be considered to enhance feelings of security and positive relations between groups. These strategies have typically been regarded as approaches to prejudice reduction among members of advantaged groups. Relatively little attention has been granted to the perspectives and experiences of the disadvantaged (see Dixon *et al.* 2010; Hornsey and Hogg 2000). More work is needed to understand how these strategies may function differently for groups that vary in status, and how they may be used to promote fair and just relations between groups in addition to promoting intergroup harmony (Saguy et al. 2013).

Intergroup contact theory

Intergroup contact theory states that as members of different groups experience close, positive interactions with one another, their prejudice toward one another will decrease (Allport 1954; Pettigrew and Tropp 2011). Decades of research reveal that contact between members of different groups can reduce prejudice and promote a range of positive intergroup outcomes, including more positive intergroup attitudes, behavioral intentions, trust, and support for policies that would benefit members of other groups (Pettigrew and Tropp 2011). Indeed, many studies have shown positive effects of intergroup contact even among groups with legacies of violent or protracted intergroup conflict (see Wagner and Hewstone 2012, for a review). Although positive contact outcomes can occur across a broad range of settings and contexts, they are especially likely when the contact occurs under optimal conditions, such as when the interacting groups have equal status and cooperate in working together toward common goals, and when institutional norms and authorities support the positive nature of their contact (Allport 1954; Pettigrew 1998).

By "contact" we and other psychologists are referring to face-to-face interactions between members of different groups, rather than assessing contact in terms of proportional indices, such as percentages of different groups within a neighborhood or school setting. Proportional indices may provide opportunities for members of different groups to interact, yet are distinct from actual interactions between members of different groups (see Pettigrew and Tropp 2011). Proportional indices and face-to-face interactions may also predict intergroup attitudes in different ways; for example, in the absence of close contact experiences, greater proportions of immigrants in one's community may provoke greater perceptions of threat, whereas close contact with immigrants in one's community may lessen perceptions of threat (see Pettigrew, Wagner, and Christ 2010).

One of the primary ways contact reduces prejudice is by reducing the anxiety people feel and the threat they perceive when interacting with outgroup members (Pettigrew and Tropp 2008). Uncertainty and anxiety about cross-group interactions can increase feelings of insecurity, opening the door to hostile interactions and relations between groups (Stephan and Stephan 1985). Apprehensions about contact and expectations that one will be rejected can motivate people to avoid contact (Barlow, Louis, and Hewstone 2009; Plant and Devine 2003; Plant 2004). Perceiving that other groups pose threats to the livelihood of one's own group can further propel negative intergroup attitudes (Pettigrew et al. 2010).

Yet when members of different groups have positive contact experiences – particularly under optimal conditions – they experience less anxiety from intergroup encounters and have less bias favoring their ingroup over other groups (Levin, van Laar, and Sidanius 2003). Positive contact can also enhance the extent to which people trust members of other groups (Hewstone et al. 2006) and make favorable interpretations when outgroup members behave in ambiguous ways (Vollhardt 2010). Importantly, positive contact effects have been shown among groups with histories of conflict (see Wagner and Hewstone 2012), such as predicting trust among Catholics and Protestants in Northern Ireland (Hewstone et al. 2006), predicting the extent to which non-Jews helped Jews escape during World War II (Oliner and Oliner 1988), and predicting white South Africans' support of race-based policies that would benefit black South Africans (Dixon et al. 2010). Moreover, over time, upon reducing anxiety through intergroup contact, group members often become more inclined to adopt the perspectives of the other group and empathize with their concerns (Swart et al. 2011). Thus, encouraging positive contact between members of different groups is one strategy for promoting a psychological sense of security, through alleviating intergroup anxiety and threat, while enhancing the extent to which people are willing to engage and empathize with members of other groups.

Positive contact effects tend to be less pronounced among members of disadvantaged groups than among members of advantaged groups (e.g., Binder et al. 2009; Tropp and Pettigrew 2005). Moreover, focusing on positive experiences and commonalities when having contact can lead members of disadvantaged groups to become less inclined to perceive their group as disadvantaged (Dixon et al. 2010) or to challenge status inequalities (Tropp, Hawi, Van Laar, and Levin 2012) and more likely to have unrealistic expectations of fair treatment from the advantaged group (Saguy *et al.* 2009).

We believe it is generally useful for members of disadvantaged and advantaged groups to engage in contact with each other to increase intergroup trust and social harmony. Yet any effort to improve relations between groups must also take into account the different expectations and needs that groups of unequal power are likely to have in the contact situation (Bruneau and Saxe 2012; Dovidio *et al.* 2012). Intergroup harmony between groups of unequal status might be achieved in the short term, but persisting inequality and disparate treatment can threaten the prospects for intergroup harmony in the long term, as inequality leaves social conditions ripe for conflict between groups. Thus, contact approaches must ensure that the dual goals of intergroup harmony and social equality are addressed when members of disadvantaged and advantaged groups interact (Becker *et al.* 2013).

Reframing group boundaries and the common ingroup identity model

Growing from intergroup contact theory, the common ingroup identity model specifies that when members of two groups can think of themselves as one superordinate group with common goals, relations between the groups will improve (Gaertner and Dovidio 2000). For instance, beyond thinking of themselves solely as members of different racial and ethnic groups, black, white, Asian, and Latino Americans may identify as part of an inclusive American identity. When groups conceive of themselves and others as part of the same superordinate group, their attitudes toward former outgroup members become more positive and they begin to respond to former outgroup members in ways that they would typically reserve for ingroup members. These positive changes encourage more favorable evaluations and greater sharing of resources (Gaertner *et al.* 1989; Gaertner, Dovidio, and Bachman 1996).

However, reframing group categories at the superordinate level can be difficult to maintain or may not always be successfully achieved, particularly when there are group differences in status within the social structure (Hornsey and Hogg 2000; Dovidio, Gaertner, and Saguy 2009). In part, the groups may not always agree on how the superordinate category is or should be defined (Mummendey and Wenzel 1999). Advantaged groups may feel more "ownership" of the superordinate category than disadvantaged groups (see Sidanius, Feshbach, Levin, and Pratto 1997; Staerkle *et al.* 2010), while members of disadvantaged groups may also feel as if they are being subsumed within the broader social category (Hornsey and Hogg 2000). To the extent that they value their subgroup identities, they could interpret any attempt to diminish their loyalty to these subgroups as threatening (Branscombe *et al.* 1999; Hornsey and Hogg 2000). As such, encouraging members of advantaged and disadvantaged groups to identify only with the superordinate category may ultimately limit the extent to which all group members feel a sense of inclusion within the superordinate category.

A number of researchers have therefore proposed that both superordinate (e.g., national) and subgroup (e.g., racial or ethnic) identities be maintained as dual identities (see Gaertner and Dovidio 2000; Hewstone, Rubin, and Willis 2002; Hornsey and Hogg 2000). When valued subgroup identities are recognized in tandem with the superordinate identity, members of disadvantaged subgroups tend to experience this as validation and become less inclined to feel hostile toward the advantaged group (Hornsey and Hogg 2000). Furthermore, preserving valued dual identities may prevent the adverse effect that positive contact experiences can have on advocating just treatment in society (Glasford and Dovidio 2011).

Strengths and weaknesses of psychology's contribution to the study of security

The strength of psychology's contribution to the study of security is the potential to explain and predict how subjective perceptions of insecurity can create actual insecurity, by motivating people to respond to perceived threats in ways that create or exacerbate group conflict. Use of the scientific method, whether via laboratory or field studies, longitudinal or correlational survey designs, is essential to this contribution.

Psychology also has particular areas in which the discipline must grow to contribute to the study of security. Our views are in line with those of others who advocate broadening the scope of research participants and diversity of perspectives and using more field research

(Heinrich *et al.* 2010; Paluck and Cialdini 2014). As we have described throughout this chapter, psychologists must also continue to study relations between groups within communities, nations, and between nations, and to examine these processes at multiple levels to contribute more fully to a multidisciplinary understanding of security, threat, and identity in intergroup relations.

How can psychology connect to other disciplines in the study of security?

We see great potential in connecting with scholars in other disciplines to examine the origins and nature of human security, such as through links to studies of policy support in political science and the integration of qualitative and quantitative research approaches in sociology and anthropology. Both political scientists and social psychologists studying political psychology relevant to security use empirical approaches and develop theory. Some political scientists studying political psychology focus on applying psychological theory to explain political outcomes without collecting new data. For example, Jonathan Mercer has applied psychological research on emotion and cognition to study them in political contexts (Mercer 2005, 2010). Psychologists who have taught in political science or interdisciplinary departments led many of the empirical projects we refer to in this chapter, including the study by Huddy and her colleagues (Huddy *et al.* 2007) of US participants' feelings of security, threat, and support for policies, and the study by Halperin and Gross of Jewish Israelis' emotion regulation and support for aid to Palestinians (Halperin and Gross 2011).

We believe that greater integration of these disciplines would enable each to make a stronger contribution to the study of security. An integrative approach would combine the strength of the scientific methods used in different disciplines with an understanding of how psychological processes relevant to security manifest within particular social and political contexts.

Conclusions

In this chapter, we have reviewed theory and research concerning psychological motivations for security and the ways in which these motivations can affect relations between groups. People often reflexively turn to their groups to enhance feelings of security, yet such tendencies can lead to biases that provoke avoidance and rejection of other groups, which in turn may incite conflict and societal instability. Although seemingly counterintuitive, constructive long-term approaches to address insecurity may involve engagement with others and, at least initially, the experience of vulnerability (see Andersen, Saribay, and Thorpe 2008, for a related argument). Through forging ties and reframing relations between groups, people can become more inclined to express concern for the welfare of groups beyond their own and question ingroup aggression against those groups, thus curbing intergroup conflict and enhancing the prospect for greater security and stability within societies.

8 International political economy
Conceptual affinities and substantive differences with security studies

RONEN PALAN AND HANNAH PETERSEN

"Europeans concerned with matters of strategy and security," observed Susan Strange, "are usually not the same as those who write about structures affecting economic development, trade, and money, or with the prospects for particular regions or sectors" (Strange 1982, 481).* Of course, this is not a distinctly European predicament; globally, international security and international political economy (IPE) have evolved somewhat in isolation from one another. As Homolar notes, "The disciplinary fields of security studies and political economy too often maintain a deliberate distance from each other," often citing an "artificial division between foreign policy and security issues on one hand and domestic and economic issues on the other" (Homolar 2010, 411). True exceptions to this trend are few. She counts among the earlier studies that buck the trend those by Gilpin (1975), Knorr (1957, 1973, 1975, 1978), and Baldwin (1985) and recent books by Cooley (2008), Kirshner (1998, 2007), and Narizny (2007). The distinction of foreign policy and traditional security studies from political economy resurfaces sometimes in scholarly output even after it is bridged in official policy documents and briefings (Dombrowski 2005).

The separation between the two disciplinary trajectories is quite strange (forgive the pun) for two obvious reasons. First and foremost, economics and politics may be considered different analytical spheres, but they operate within the same single reality and both economic issues and political issues are interlinked, not only with each other but with security issues at so very many important junctures that analysis of these together is quintessential to sound analysis of each (Buzan 1994, 89ff.). A key argument of the relatively young discipline of IPE has always been that successful international economy cannot function without a stable political and legal international regime, and

* The authors are grateful to Amnon Aran, Philippe Bourbeau, and Daniel Goldstein for their advice and support in preparing this chapter.

vice versa, that stable security regimes are unlikely to survive for any length of time in volatile economic conditions.

Second and related, the theoretical foundations of all international relations theories are rooted in political economic theories, from mercantilism and realism, to standard economics and neorealism, to constructivism and evolutionary economics. One way or another, they all take for granted and imply linkages in the triad of concepts: security – stability – economy. The problem, however, is, first, that the relationship between economics and politics has tended to remain implicit in some cases, for example, classical realism, and second, that the relationship between economics and politics that these theories espouse is not subject to the sort of theoretical scrutiny and empirical verification that characterize internal debates within these schools of thought.

One of the fundamental questions orienting the research on security in IPE has historically been the causality or direction of the linkage between political and economic security. This is most plainly evident in core writings by the more traditional theories of neorealism and neo-liberalism. A further important question is that of the referent object: Who needs to be secured? Realists and proponents of a more traditional conception of security would argue that the state is the referent object; most liberalists and proponents of a more critical, modern conception of security would argue it is the individual; yet the scholarly debate is far from a conclusion at this point.

The relationship between IPE and security is complex and multifaceted and often remains somewhat implicit. Security is not traditionally an explicit element of theorizing within the field; it is treated as an epiphenomenon by the various subfields of IPE and some might say it remains undeveloped. Regardless, just as security is fundamental to, for example, the anthropological notions of culture, so is it centrally related to all matters of political and economic reality in contemporary nations. Security and political economy are evidently universal bedfellows, and this is as true today as it ever was. It simply does not make sense to consider them in isolation.

Here it is important to consider that IPE is a relatively young discipline within political science that was developed from the merging of international politics with economic studies and is very open to other interdisciplinary input. Hence, a large portion of the relevant debate about security rests upon issues and events that both occurred and were analyzed before the emergence of IPE as a field of study. For example, both the original traditional thoughts on state security as well as the interest in collective security after World War II long preceded the IPE debate that began in the 1970s.

In this chapter, while giving an overview of the different theoretical perspectives within international political economy that consider the concept of security more closely, we reach several conclusions, some of which are surprising. The first, perhaps better known argument is that neorealism despite characterizing economics as "low politics" is in fact at its core an economic theory or at least closely adapted from one to fit the political system. A second surprise discovery about contemporary international relations (IR) theory is that security concerns seem to be much less at the forefront than previously thought. A third result derived from analyzing the relationship between Marxist IPE theory and security studies further supports the original argument of this chapter, that security studies and political economy are the two sides of one coin (Homolar 2010, 410), and any attempt to separate them is ideologically motivated, and analytically false.

Despite such synergies, security concerns, and more broadly, the sort of discussions that could be subsumed under the label of security studies, remains undeveloped in the field of IPE. The relationship between IPE and security, as we will show in this chapter, is rather one-sided: The different schools of IPE treat security concerns as an epiphenomenon, a desired condition that will come about provided the necessary structural political economic conditions are fulfilled.

International political economy consists of a diverse set of theories and approaches, each of which draws on one of the core traditions in political economy: standard economics, Marxian economics, evolutionary theory, and even libidinal economy (see Palan 2013 for discussion). IPE tends to take these traditions to a new place and asks how their "units of analysis" and theoretical constructs would behave in a world that is divided among political communities of varied size and shape. The result is a diverse set of theories that mirror the complexity and diversity of political economy. Consequently, IPE has never developed around a single core set of orienting questions and/or subscribed to a set of methodologies. The different theories each both advance quantitative, qualitative, and interpretative methods and draw on case studies as well as general theoretical frameworks. This means that the relationship between IPE and security cannot be easily summarized and does not follow any of the predicted paths, other than the common path known as "economic imperialism."

Importantly, political economy as well as international political economy bring to the table something that is often ignored in foreign policy and security studies that are considered more isolated from it – the centrality of the policy-making process, including the balancing of interests and procedural biases (Adler 1997; Ruggie 1998), and a look at actors such as banks and multinational corporations (MNCs). Earlier well-known voices had already reminded us of the necessity of strong industry in case of war (Kennedy 1984; Knorr 1975; Morgenthau 1978; Strange 1988) and a need to have control over the industry important to security (Dombrowski 2005; Friedberg 1989; Kapstein 1990; Moran 1990; Ziegler 1991;) as well as a strong financial sector (Earle 1986; Gilpin 1987; Haglund 1986; Milward 1977; Rasler and Thompson 1983).

The purpose of this chapter is to introduce and subsequently compare the different perceptions and understandings of the concept of security, its precursors, its implications, and its importance within the main branches of international political economy schools of thought. As we will show, contrary to common perceptions, security studies and IPE have had a long, deep, and ongoing, if somewhat implicit and one-sided engagement that goes to the very core of the two sets of apparently different disciplines.

The political economic underpinning of realist theory

Most textbooks tell us that classical realism as well as neorealism are mainly concerned with the "security dilemma" (Herz 1951), that is, how strength or weakness of a state can both endanger another state's security as well as provoke other states and thereby endanger its own security (Aron 1966; Carr 1962). In that sense realism appears as far apart from IPE as possible. Yet, as we will show, under the guise of the new rationalist synthesis (Milner 1998), a silent revolution has taken place with the result that the neorealist field of security studies shares much in common with standard IPE. The rationalists achieved that incredible fit by simultaneously introducing marginalism to the study of politics and moving the deep political economic assumption of realism to the surface.

Three key assumptions form the basis for realist theory (Baylis 2011; Morgenthau 1978). The first noteworthy aspects are realism's consistent state-centric focus (Brooks 1997) on external and international relations and its treatment of the national state as a "black box": The nation state is considered the appropriate unit of analysis for realists (Dunne and Schmidt 2011, 87). The international system is irrevocably anarchical in nature; in it states must try to survive while they answer to no higher authority. Realist theory further assumes that states constantly try to maximize their power; therefore, politics is a zero-sum game and conflict-laden by force majeure (Kahler 1998). Its focus on military politics as high politics becomes particularly clear with the following observation by Mearsheimer:

The greater the military advantage one state has over other states, the more secure it is. Every state would like to be the most formidable military power in the system because it is the best way to guarantee survival in a world that can be very dangerous. (Mearsheimer 1994, 5)

While realism allows economic considerations to complement strategies of power and security, in realist theory economics as well as interior politics are generally considered as "low politics" (Jackson and Sørensen 2007; Morgenthau 1978; Stubbs and Underhill 1994) and always subordinate to political security although Morgenthau himself, a key author of realism, suggested that natural resources but also industry capacity are necessary in order to achieve or maintain power as a state (Morgenthau 1985, 130ff.; see also Fordham 1998; Trubowitz 1998). Traditional realists accept that the goal of states may be economic welfare; nonetheless, this goal is translated to political struggles among states in an anarchical state system. Realists allow, in addition, for situations in which economic gain or economic security as a whole is given up in order to concentrate on political security or specifically to weaken opponent states as well. Economic tools (including economic sanctions or other forms of boycotts and/or financial assets) may be used, in other words, to achieve security goals. For example, there is growing concern in the recent debates about the rise of sovereign Wealth Funds; these funds have in particular given rise to concerns about financial stability, about corporate governance methods, but also about political interference and, as a key example of such, economic protectionism (Blundell-Wignall, Hu, and Yermo 2008). Established Western economies seem especially concerned whether the funds are likely to be used by actors such as China or Dubai strategically, to gain control of certain important industries not for financial reasons but political goals. This issue has led the EU in particular to reconsider the possibility of its members using golden shares to prevent particular foreign acquisitions.

More modern ideas of realism still concern themselves with external threats to the states but have since adapted considerably to go beyond the "black box" and discuss more specifically how external threats are reacted to domestically, for example, through political disagreement on how to respond, hence downscaling the importance of the state as the sole entity of power (i.e., Schweller 2004). Notwithstanding, the focus on states and external threats to states as a whole can be seen to be in line with traditional security studies, which in essence focus exclusively on the security of a state against the outside and the state's survival, rather than concern themselves fundamentally with individual security or negative security from the state. Considering that this concept of security (or freedom) from the state was widely popularized by the likes of Rousseau, Montesquieu, Sieyes, and even earlier theorists, and strongly emphasized by and central to many statesmen in the period that followed – especially the American founding fathers – this does seem rather an obvious oversight by realist thought, yet does not hinder its continued appeal and popularity, particularly in the United States (i.e., Wohlforth 2011).

Case studies exist in support of this labeling of political stability as the independent variable and necessity for economic stability as the dependent variable, showcasing the strong negative impact political instability or even the collapse of national political systems has on the corresponding national economic system. For example, in a recent IMF working paper, Aisen and Veiga (2010, 24) find that "political instability significantly reduces economic growth, both statistically and economically". Using a data set covering almost 170 countries between 1960 and 2004, they are able to point out how "political instability is particularly harmful" in its negative effects on total factor productivity growth and its discouraging both human and physical capital accumulation. Other examples clearly illustrate situations in which political instability is the principal threat to welfare and economic growth. A good general case to be made for political stability leading to economic stability lies with foreign investment: Clearly, political security promises a degree of continuity as well as transparency that make a country's economy more secure and thus more attractive to foreign investment, which in turn can strongly support the economy and achieve economic security.[1] Where there is no political stability and security and the return on investments hence cannot be guaranteed, both foreign as well as domestic investment in economy or infrastructure supporting the economy are unlikely or at least greatly hindered. Nations that are battered by civil war for long periods tend to destroy their economies completely in the process; as in the case of Somalia and piracy, this not only affects their own but the global economy in a considerably harmful way.

Besides arguing the case for the directional correlation of political security determining economic stability, all of the preceding points support the generally accepted view of the strong intellectual links between realism and security studies compared to weaker links to IPE. That perception, however, can be highly misleading.

One of the purported key differences between classical realism and neorealism relates to the role of economic theory in the constitution of neorealist theory of security challenges. The American IR scholar Kenneth Waltz was a founder of neorealism and structural realism and is likely the author most associated with the latter – he is also quite renowned for suggesting that proliferation and spread of nuclear weapons would indeed increase world peace rather than threaten it (Waltz 1981). Revealingly, Waltz himself explains the development of neorealism by "looking at a theoretical breakthrough in a related field: economics" (Waltz 1990, 27). He notices that "Aron drew a sharp distinction between the study of economics and the study of international politics" (1990, 25) and that "like classical economists before them, realists were unable to account for a major anomaly" (1990, 33). He goes on then to describe the similarities between neoclassical theory and neorealism. For Russett, "boundaries are artificial constructs imposed on more or less continuous distributions in order to simplify ordering the relationships on either side." Indeed, he argues

---

[1] Obviously when talking about political security or stability in this context a very specific kind of stability is in mind: political power through strong, continuous institutions as well as upholding of the rule of law; effective administration and bureaucracy and manageable crime and corruption rates; anything that facilitates and attracts investment. Otherwise, military dictatorships and countries such as Eritrea or Gambia can be considered politically stable, and there is no sign of growth or economic stability in either.

that "economic theory is at heart a set of assumptions and deductions about rational choice on the part of individuals and organizations. It is relevant whenever actors have determinate goals but limited means of achieving those goals, and hence must allocate scarce resources" (Russett 1968, 5).

Gilpin (who believes that Waltz is essentially a sociologist) argues that "My *War and Change in World Politics* emphasizes ... that of economic or rational choice theory: I start with individual state actors and seek to explain the emergence and change of international systems" (Gilpin 1984, 288). In a similar vein, Powell argues that one of the key debates of neoliberalism, institutionalism, and structural realism is about the veracity of marginalism: "Neoliberal institutionalism assumes that states focus primarily on their individual absolute gains and are indifferent to the gains of others.... In terms of preferences, this focus on absolute gains is usually taken to mean that a state's utility is solely a function of its absolute gain. In contrast, neorealism, or structural realism assumes that states are largely concerned with relative rather than absolute gains" (Powell 1991, 1303).

We could go further: Barry Buzan says that methodological individualist theories of the state system (or neorealism) are entirely consistent with and, in fact, assume the embeddedness of the "system of states" in broader cultural habitus, which he calls the society of states (Buzan 1994, 90ff.). But the logical steps that Buzan takes in presenting this argument simply follow the same arguments that have led standard economics to develop in the direction of the new institutional economics (NIE) of Williamson (2000). The cultural habitus of the system of states that is described by the "English school" as an "international society" is the equivalent step taken by NIE to describe market embeddedness in an institutional environment. Individual units, whether they are the individual consumers and producers of neoclassical economics or the state-actor unit of realism, operate within an institutional environment that evolves in ways that cannot be reduced to methodological individualism.

Other modern schools of thought that count themselves as realist, such as quite prominently the realist theory on hegemony and hegemonic stability theory (Gilpin 1987; Krasner 1976), explicitly integrate aspects of liberal economic theory. In HST the hegemon is responsible for providing certain public goods, a clearly liberal idea, and while the hegemon guarantees political security to support the economic system, his role is also dependent on his economic performance. The HST is attributable to Kindleberger (2013) and is based on his study of the 1930s depression.

The evolution of realist theory presents, therefore, the first surprise in the study of the ongoing relationship between security studies and IPE. Far from treating economics as "low politics," as implied, neorealist theory is at its core an economic theory applied to the political sphere of the relationship between states – the latter assumed to have capabilities to act as discrete unities. Neorealism played an important role in what is otherwise known as "economic imperialism" and the capture of international relations theory by economic modeling and thought. Not only the core assumption of neoclassical theory invades other spheres of social life; its modeling and quantitative techniques are present in every sphere of security studies.

Utility, market economy, and security

There are a number of fundamental assumptions central to the liberal perspective. One of them is that humans are not inherently bad, as in Hobbes's early realist thought, but rather rational and utility maximizing. In addition, humans, or individuals, are considered to be the proper unit of analysis and thus the principal actors in political economy by liberals (Moravcsik 1997). Realist arguments about the importance of security and state survival are not neglected in the liberalist argument: Often enough it is pointed out that a stable, functioning economy is key to political security, especially in the traditional sense, as only a working economy guarantees the funding a state can then spend on defense, and so on. Further, the liberal perspective assumes that an important way of maximizing utility is by making trade-offs between goods and services.

Several conclusions regarding the relationship between political and economic security can already be drawn directly from these core assumptions. If the highest goal is to maximise utility and gains and the latter is generally achieved through trade-offs, then this can be translated into a desire for a productive, stable, and secure economy and market system. Unlike mercantilism and realist thought, liberalism supports the idea of a positive-sum game. As long as the majority of individuals and groups can realize their utility-seeking and gain-maximizing intentions within the economic system, they will want to preserve it, and interests in economic stability have political security as a direct consequence.

The focus on the individual is reminiscent of more modern critical security studies, which focus on individuals and groups and their safety from the state as well as certain positive rights, rather than a state's security from external threats.

Neorealism and liberalism both share core synergies with standard economics. Where they differ is in their treatment of the role of domestic politics in international affairs. Liberal theories tend to stress the importance of domestic political processes. Their argument is simple, but highly plausible: The state that interacts with other states in the international arena is not different from the state that interacts with domestic society. International relations theory must aim to draw upon and be consistent with empirical findings of "domestic" theories of state and government (Milner 1998). As the majority of political scientists do not recognize the unitary or volitional realist state model in a domestic setting, it stands to reason that the realist model of state must be either heavily modified or replaced altogether by a different theory.

The domestic source theories were developed during a period that saw the rise of behaviorism in political science (Dryzek 2006). In many ways, domestic source theories still bear the hallmark of behaviorism to this day. Behavioral political science centered on the concept of the political or governmental process (Easton 1953). The behaviorist research agenda was concerned primarily with the relationship between government and the governed. With their rather functionalist approach and strong focus on the individual as principal actors, modern liberals consider that the state in itself is not an actor but merely a "transmission belt," selecting and translating aggregated societal individual or group preferences regarding the economy that determine the political system. Assuming that the individuals within a state and thus the state as their representative gain more from economic interdependence and trade than they would from the economic costs of war on top of a loss of said economic relations, economic stability influences political security rather directly in a positive correlation.

Whereas Gilpin argues that the state is a variant on an organized interest group that evolved in conditions of scarcity, liberal theories of international relations consider individuals as the fundamental actors in the political sphere (Moravcsik 1997). States are denied volitional attributes and are viewed instead as stage vehicles in the transmission of needs and desires that emanate from society. In the words of Buchanan, states are "conceived as something that emerges from the choice processes of individual participants" (Buchanan 1966, 26). In contemporary populous states however, individuals have a limited capacity to influence the political process directly. They have no option but to join intermediate institutions and organizations that serve to transmit their choices and preferences in the political arena. The political process works through political parties, interest group associations, labor and business groups, and so on, which are treated as the "transmission belts" of individuals' needs and desires to the state.

When these theories are applied to the field of international relations, argues Moravcsik, they challenge many cherished assumptions of realism, for instance, the idea that states are able to sustain some fixed or pregiven set of goals (or "national interests") over a long period. As each state develops its own independent political process, we encounter diversity of behavior in the international arena. It follows, as Hendrik Spruyt argues, that "preferences are sometimes compatible or harmonious with the preferences of other states that are presumably going through similar "domestic" processes and sometime not." In such fluid situations, the resulting "realignments are essentially permutations and combinations of bargains based on material interests and shared belief systems.... Moreover, because powerful actors may have widely divergent preferences, second-best solutions and compromises abound. Furthermore, actors work with divergent discount rates" (Spruyt 1994, 25). One implication of such a theory is that "general" theories of the international system of the sort that Waltz advances cannot help to predict the likely state behavior.

More importantly, the diversity of states and political processes may not necessarily lead to a deleterious outcome – or to state it in realist terms, anarchy is not necessarily the source of conflict. Even if the "underlying state preferences are zero-sum or deadlocked, that is, where an attempt by dominant social groups in one country to realize their preferences through state action necessarily imposes costs (negative externalities) on dominant social groups in other countries, governments face a bargaining game with few mutual gains and a high potential for interstate tension and conflict" (Moravcsik 1997, 521). Even in instances of flagrant incompatibility in the aggregative preferences that emanate from different societies, this does not lead necessarily to an open conflict between states. Indeed, the sheer amount of permutations of outcomes that can be generated by such complexity of process renders systemic theories of IR less credible.

Liberal theory challenges, therefore, the conventional view of international relations as the science of the study of war and peace, and that is the second surprising discovery about contemporary international relations theory. Security concerns are not as much at the forefront of international relations as has been assumed. Within the liberal tradition there exist different trends with different focuses regarding the prerequisites for political stability and peace. Classic liberalism as well as most versions of neoliberalism advocate free markets, international trade, and economic growth and progress as supporting political security; neoliberal institutionalism and idealism acknowledge these but focus strongly on the role of international institutions and representative politics. Furthermore, an open trading system may be creating convergence of interests and institutions toward stability, yet lack of convergence may not necessarily and inevitably degenerate to conflict. Indeed, from a liberal perspective open military conflict is rarely, if ever, justifiable on economic grounds and tends to represent institutional failure of one kind or another. Contrary to realism, the security issues are not endemic to an international system as much as symptoms of institutional failure and structural economic malaise associated with countries such as "failed states."

As opposed to realist considerations about the relations between political and economic security or stability, liberal theory considers economic stability to be the driving force directly resulting in political security. This obviously is occurring on two different levels: Domestically, economic security and prosperity are thought to lead to political security; strong economic performance and economic well-being support the legitimacy of the political system and discourage political unrest. Internationally, trade and market exchange promote cooperation between states and make war economically undesirable, because of both the loss of the opportunity of economic trade-offs (discouraging market functions) as well as the economic costs of war.

Examples of economic turmoil resulting in political insecurity are readily available. The crisis of 1929, which began in the United States and engulfed the entire world shortly thereafter, within months led to a catastrophic collapse of international trade, and to the "Beggar thy neighbor" monetary policy, but it also immediately sparked great political instability, which saw the rise of the National Socialists in Germany (Schram and van Riel 1993) and subsequent appeasement politics that some suggest was also rooted in economic weakness (Ferris 1989); the formation of a British-led imperial trading block; the expansion of Japan into Manchuria in search of access to vital raw material to its industries; and, finally, the Second World War. A fairly current affair that at first glance seems to support the directional causal relation of economic stability leading to political stability is the most recent financial crisis. For example, in all the EU countries in which elections were held since, the political parties in power have changed (with the exception of Germany, and the German economy remains comparatively stable and secure to this point.) In Greece, arguably worst hit by the crisis within the EU, radical groups have dramatically gained in popularity, foremost the openly extremist party "Golden Dawn."

As liberalism concerns democracies (or at the time republics) where representatively elected governments are responsible for and accountable to their citizens, the latter's disinterest in and rejection of the economic costs of war should always be conveyable to the state. This is explored in most detail by the liberal theory of democratic peace, originally proposed by Immanuel Kant (Eberl and Niesen 2011), a theory not seeking to explain the root causes of war (like many other schools of thought at the time) but to establish common motives to avoid the latter (Doyle 1986; Macmillan 2004; Russett 1993). In his "Perpetual Peace," Kant dabbles in cosmopolitanism even as he suggests a form of cosmopolitan overarching guiding corpus of law to protect all people from the possibility of war, which is based on a principle of universal hospitality (which was much later developed further by Derrida to new conclusions). The democratic peace theory stipulates that democracies are reluctant to engage in a war with other democracies, making war increasingly unlikely the more democratic a region becomes. First off, in "Zum ewigen Frieden," Kant states insistently that nation states should under no circumstances interfere with other states' affairs (Baruzzi 2001, 96). This is again in direct contradiction of realism's insistence that (hostile) interference with another state is natural in the context of the anarchical world system. There exist several main motives for avoiding conflict that can be drawn from the democratic peace theory as Kant first stated it. First, it implies public accountability in a democracy and suggests that representative governments, naturally seeking reelection (Downs 1957), will try to avoid accepting responsibility for the costs of war; second, it assumes that it is unlikely for democracies to view other democracies with similar policies and regulatory philosophies as enemies; further, it assesses that democracies tend to possess much more of public goods (such as infrastructure) and public prosperity as a whole than autocracies, which they are therefore less willing to risk.

This can be followed up to modern times as well as, more importantly, to the economic realm: For example, Kirshner remarks that bankers are risk-averse and interested in security the more international integration there is financially, which serves as a "systemic disincentive to the initiation of war to an extent directly related to the size and significance of global financial markets" (Kirshner 2007, 20). Ripsman (2005) agrees that domestic interest groups with strong bilateral or international trade interests will lobby the government to avoid anything that could endanger the former (see also Abdelal and Kirshner 1999; Newnham 2002).

In this section it is further worth noting that not all theorists who subscribe to the view that the economic situation determines the political situation assume that the two have a positive correlation. Although supporters of the "good growth hypothesis," suggesting that economic growth and stability will lead to political stability and security, are more numerous, one cannot neglect supporters of the opposite position, the "destabilizing growth hypothesis" (Paldam 1998). The latter insists that the growth associated with stability also leads to complex social and societal changes and thereby creates political instability. Without going into detail or judging the extent of instability, strongly varying examples of growth leading to social change come readily to mind: in South Korea the change led to democracy, in Iran to theocracy.

Marxism and the problem of security

Marxist theory distinguishes between principles of market economy and capitalism. Traditional market economies, or rather economies that contained aspects of market exchanges, worked on the following principle: c–m–c (c = commodity, m = money), which Aristotle suggests is, among others, defined by the fact that it "has a limit" (Meikle 1996, 140). In such systems, markets are system of exchanges or forms of barter between individuals. Money has evolved as a "third commodity," typically rare and highly sought after material such as gold, silver, or copper, or other precious stones, to accommodate and simplify the system of barter. Markets, however, remain subordinate in such systems to political or traditional modes of exploitative extraction (such as feudalism or Asian societies).

Capitalism is completely different: The principles of capitalism are captured by the equation m–c–m' – or what Aristotle called "unnatural chrematistike" – the unnatural exchange where the end gain is the exchange value itself (Meikle 1996). In other words, it is a system whereby money (or capital) is invested (m) in commodity production (c) in order to make more money m. The pecuniary principle is therefore paramount, and production or manufactured product is simply a by-product of the system. Capitalism always values the "exchange value" of products over their "use value"; hence, paradoxically, some of the most valuable commodities, the air we breathe, the water we drink, and so on, are least valuable in a capitalist economy and are readily subject to pollution and destruction. The capitalist, the owner of the means of production, invests money in order to sell at higher prices than overall cost of production. His or her profits are determined by four conditions: the ability to reduce unit costs, including raw material and labor costs; the ability to reduce these by achieving higher productivity per unit of production; the ability to do this by increasing unit sale price; or the ability to do this by increasing unit sales. These four options combined are at the heart of the Marxist interpretation of the problem of security, which we will summarize in the following paragraphs.

Reduction in costs of all elements of production will ultimately put pressure on labor wages, whether directly on labor at the firm, or indirectly, on labor that is located elsewhere and is involved in the production of essential raw materials or the necessary machinery. Hence, capitalism is a violent process at the heart of which is the capitalist "extraction." Political stability, therefore, is more apparent than real and represents one of the following scenarios:

Secure dominance of one class or an alliance of classes of another in perpetrating an exploitative situation. In other words, stability cannot be equated with peace or lack of violence. On the contrary, a period of stability represents the stability of governance by one class or an alliance of classes over others, and in that sense, it is, ipso facto, a form of violence. And classes in the international realm can of course imply classes of countries. Roemer suggests categorizing these with reference to the use of the credit market (Roemer 1983, 54).

Conversely, episodes of open violence, in the form of either a "civil war" or a war between nations, are expressions of a breakdown in the relationships among the ruling classes and/or in the exploitative chains. It is not by accident that the most "insecure" regions in the world and those characterized as "failed states" tend to be home to some essential or lucrative raw materials. These countries are characterized by very low productivity, low wages, extremes of unequal wealth distribution, and a highly coercive system of extraction of those resources, which are then sold fairly cheaply in the world markets. Insecurity in these regions is a product of a brute exploitative situation combined with linkages to a capitalist world market.

Hence, following a Marxist understanding of IPE means assuming that periods of stability and security are by their very nature transitional only and represent an intermediate time of relative calm before capitalist contradictions are felt at full force.

The theory of capitalism as an m-c-m type of society suggests that capitalism is a self-expansionary system, always in search of new markets. The expansionary tendency of capitalism is another of the principal causes of conflict in the world. Typically the most advanced capitalist countries of their age, be they the Italian city-states of the Renaissance, the Dutch trading nation, England or the United States, and possibly China in the future, known as hegemonies, are the torch bearers of capitalist expansion. They maintain large armies or navies whose job it is to open up forcefully new lands for capitalist exploitation, ensure steady flow of necessary raw material, and maintain trade routes.

Imperialism and colonialism may take various guises: They can range from territorial capture of certain land for capitalist exploitation, to financial–industrial dependence or subtle forms of support for political elements in society that will ensure the same ultimate results – but they are all driven by the expansionary tendencies of capitalism (Dos Santos 1996). A well-known argument for the impact of economic considerations on political security was made by Lenin in his 1920 (1917) work *Imperialism, the Highest Stage of Capitalism*. In this book Lenin builds upon and alters Marx's economic theories as well as

Hobson's earlier work *Imperialism* (1988 [1902]) to fit his cause, and looks closely at the role of capital (generation) in imperialism (or colonialism). The book is partially inspired by and is concerned with World War I, which Lenin describes among others as "plunderous" and "predatory," discarding nationalism as the cause of the conflict and calling attention to the economic reasons behind the security disaster that was the full-blown war. Key to this is the accumulation of financial capital by monopolies to the point where they cannot find enough opportunities to invest it anymore in the industrialized world but need to expand to other regions to generate further profit.

IR [Imperialistic International Relations] emerge from differences in development and a competitive international capital market, in a stationary world with fully developed capitalist relations of production. Internal limits to accumulation and realisation problems are unnecessary to understand imperialism: IIR can be explained by capitalists' quest for profits. The existence of less developed countries provides profit-making opportunities to developed countries via competitive credit markets, which create exploitive relations. (Veneziani 2009, 207)

Lenin argued that capitalism had outgrown Marx's three laws of capitalism and avoided crisis by expanding to imperialism and exploiting an international workforce. As a result of the desire to expand economic profits beyond that which the home country's resources as well as markets can generate, the elites of strong states as well as large companies will divide the rest of the world up for economic exploitation and consequently engage in geopolitical conflict in their struggle to gain the largest possible share of both markets and resources (Dos Santos 1996, 166).[2]

Wars, therefore, serve a purpose, and the purpose is capitalist expansion or maintenance of existing exploitative situations.

An argument is made that the very specific relationship between research and the military in the post–World War II United States shaped and corrupted the development of contemporary political science more generally. Unlike the British or German armies, the US

---

[2] Interestingly, John A. Hobson considered that imperialism was only born out of the necessity of economic competition – until, for example, Germany and the United States began to be considered as earnest competition in the late nineteenth century, the United Kingdom according to Hobson had no need for imperialist politics as they had prime access to the entire world's important market secured regardless (Hobson 1988[1938], 72).

Army, Navy, and Air Force did not have their own in-house research units. Hence, the US Armed Forces commissioned research from private think tanks such as the RAND Corporation or Brookings. Those, in turn, oriented their research to the way the Armed Forces liked to "consume" such research, that is, quantitative analysis that would present security dilemmas in simple statistical equations. This notably oriented much of the output of mainstream American political science in the direction of "rationalism" and quantitative methods.

The relationship between mainstream security studies and liberal internationalism, an alliance of classes at the heart initially of the expansion of an Atlantic vision of capitalism, later also incorporating East Asia, gave rise to another theory of the role of the security services and security studies. Following World War II, the United States, with its allies, sought to create a new organization of the world based on liberal principles. In that they were opposed by a rising "communist" bloc. In other words, the communist bloc inhibited the expansion of the capitalist market. Rather than view the cold war as an inevitable outcome of incompatible ideologies and/or a classical realist interpretation, the cold war is viewed functionally by modern Marxist theorists in terms of the class interests it represents.

The "cold war" represented, first and foremost, the conflict that arises whenever capitalism is faced with a physical barrier to expansion. The war turned hot, inevitably, Marxists would say, at the frontiers of the two blocs, the territories that could swing either way. Korea, Cuba, Vietnam, and the Middle East were exactly those meeting points. The cold war could also ensure funds from the United States to its allies through the Marshall Plan and the NATO alliance, that is, funding to ensure compliance with and an expansion of the American vision of a market economy. The Cold War was used in addition as a tool of military Keynesianism, from legitimizing the emergence of a military-industrial complex that has shaped US economy since, expanding to include the aviation, IT, and even entertainment sectors. At the same time, it formed a core of a "planned economy" that sustained the development of the US economy through federal funding to the military-industrial complex.

From a Marxist perspective, therefore, security and political economy are so closely interrelated that studying one without the other leads to completely false interpretations of events; the division of such related disciplines is considered "arbitrary and unhelpful" (Hobden and Wyn Jones 2011, 132). Security studies or conventional "security discourses" represent the language of power and accommodation among the ruling classes. The security that is normally sought in conventional security studies is temporary stability predicated on violence. At the same time, societies that are violent reveal the inner contradiction of capitalism, whether they may appear on the surface economically successful or not. Finally, the fourth intriguing conclusion promised in the introduction is that security studies and political economy are two sides of the same coin, and any attempt to separate them is ideologically motivated, but analytically false.

The hen and egg conundrum of political and economic influence

As we have shown in this chapter, there are many points of contact between IPE and security studies. Indeed, all the major theories of international political economy implicitly assume a connection between economic and political security, where the term "security" is often used almost interchangeably with the term "stability."

But here lies the problem in the linkages between IPE and security studies. IPE never developed an extended discussion of the concept of security as such and did not concern itself with debates in security studies. IPE has tended to assume that political stability is an absolutely necessary condition for a successful economy, both nationally and internationally, but also that stability will ensure security, and vice versa. Yet, to the best of our knowledge, these are assumptions that are never subject to a deep or extended discussion.

The great debate truly lies elsewhere – it could almost be summarized as the hen and egg conundrum of political and economic influence – which comes first? All theories attribute an ever-influential cycle of subsequence between security and economics; however, the main theories argue as to whether political security or economic security needs to occur first in order to ensure the other. This is despite growing support for the view that the two are simply two parts of a system that are too interwoven with another to be adequately separated and assessed for all purposes. Surely it makes sense to divide the two for specific interests of study – however, considering that in today's world almost every single economic transaction occurring takes place within the realm of economic law and regulation, written by or at least overseen by elected political persons, really there is little left where one can take effect free of the influence of the other.

There are clear limits to the discussion of security in IPE – mainly that it largely happens implicitly. Security is not explicitly incorporated into most current debates within IPE, despite the fact that it is a key concept used as an axiom for many of the theoretical assumptions posed in IPE theory. And yet it is rarely discussed directly and rather left to other subfields of IR such as security studies.

One of the strength of IPE's treatment of security lies within a strict continuation of Susan Strange's original demands: with an insistence on the constant consideration of both economic and political factors, without mingling the two into an unintelligible megaconcept. As we have discussed in brief examples, there is little doubt that economic factors have influence on political stability such as security. All of the theories within IPE discussed agree on a strong connection between economic interests and political security strategy. Further, the idea that wars are begun partly or largely out of economic interests is a rather common notion in everyday discussions; for example, inside as well as outside academic forums, Iraqi oil is often cited as a strong reason for the recent military offensive in the region, rather than the official reasoning of suspected weapons of mass destruction. It therefore makes sense in every way to address these concerns, ideas, and examples by institutionalizing the study of a combination of economics and security: a key task within the field of international politics and economy and arguably one of its strong advantages. Perchance one could add that the various theories within IPE disagreeing on the directional connection between security and economy limit the explanatory power of IPE, but one could likewise argue that they force scholars, who study all of them, to change angle continuously and thus achieve a more reflective knowledge of the mechanisms at work.

Similarly, in its methods, IPE is considerate of divergent approaches: Much of the research in IPE is undertaken through mixed methods, allowing for both quantitative and qualitative data and analysis of the latter, as there is general respect for the value of both large N quantitative numerical data, common in economics, and qualitative, inductive, and in-depth case studies, often found in political science.

The relationship between IPE and security studies therefore follows the well-trodden path of "economic imperialism." IPE, or, more properly, political economy, has had a profound influence on the development of security studies, but the same cannot be said about the impact of security studies on IPE. There is certainly a niche of security studies concerned with resource economics and the impact of resource allocation diversity on security (Mildner 2011), or one fraction of the "greed versus grievance" debate, prominently pioneered by Paul Collier and Anke Hoeffler, that argues that greed and economic calculation are more often linked to violent conflict than grievances such as ethnic conflict or religion. Yet, political economic theories are by their nature comprehensive in outlook and self-referential; they each present a core set of concepts and ideas that in theory can be applied to the study of society at large, including issues of security, stability and violence.

In conclusion we stress that while the importance of economic factors and issues surrounding security has recently gained support, security remains something slightly outside the realm of actual IPE studies – it is an implicit consequence of or connection to many of the subjects studied (such as hegemony), but not a trending term in the writings of IPE scholars.

9 Criminology
Reimagining security

JAN FROESTAD, CLIFFORD SHEARING, AND MELANI VAN DER MERWE

My point is not that everything is bad, but that everything is dangerous.
(Foucault, in Rabinow 1984, 343)

Have you ever read any criminological texts? They are staggering. And I say this out of astonishment, not aggressiveness, because I fail to comprehend how the discourse of criminology has been able to go on at this level. One has the impression that it is of such utility, is needed so urgently and rendered so vital for the working of the system, that it does not even seek a theoretical justification for itself, or even simply a coherent framework. It is entirely utilitarian.
(Foucault 1980, 47)

The whole aim of practical politics is to keep the populace alarmed (and hence clamorous to be led to safety), by menacing it with an endless series of hobgoblins, all of them imaginary.
(Mencken 1918, 18)

Criminology's most fundamental topic has long been security, understood in Hobbesian terms (Hobbes 1651/1968, 185–186) as interpersonal safety – with the embedded implication of freedom from the fear of interpersonal harms – and the peaceful coexistence that this enables.[1] While the meaning of "security" has varied considerably over time and across disciplines (see the papers in this volume), this core meaning of interpersonal safety and peaceful coexistence, which has recently been the focus of the "new" "human security" (United Nations 1994; Wood and Shearing 2007), has been remarkably consistent within criminology, though, as we will see, the term "security"

---

[1] Hobbes (1651/1986) likens security to fine weather, which is said to be fine not only because it is not inclement at the moment but because it is likely to remain clear for some time.

has not been as prominent as it has been within other areas of inquiry, such as international relations.

Historically, criminology has explored security by focusing its attention on what one might think of as "hitting and taking" harms, typically thought of as "crimes," that threaten peaceful coexistence along with the governance processes, particularly criminal justice, that have been developed to respond to them. This focus has ensured that individuals have long been at the center of criminological analyses of security. Criminology's crime focus has meant that, while a concern with security, understood as safety, has long been central to criminology, it has been the term "crime," rather than "security," that has held pride of place on the criminological stage, as the term "criminology" itself makes clear.

In recent thinking that has sought to "decriminalize criminology" (Shearing 1989) – see, for example, Hillyard et al.'s (2004) use of the term "zemiology" and "harmology" and Ditton's (1979) earlier use of "controlology" – "security" as a term, has, for the most part, been eschewed as criminology has explored ways of moving beyond its self-definition as a crimeology.[2] Today, while the term "security" has gained greater currency within criminology, its synonym "safety" has emerged as a preferred term both within criminology and within its associated practical politics. For example, "safety" is being used increasingly to cushion the implications of "national security," within its state rather than individual focus, which criminologists sense remains embedded in the term "security" – for example, in the phrase "the safety and security web" used in the recently released report on the "Future of Canadian Policing Models" (Council of Canadian Academies 2014) commissioned by the Canadian government's Department of Public Safety.

In this chapter we explore the history of "crime" and "security" and how it is that "security" has begun to move closer to the center of the criminological stage. Central to these developments, we will argue, has been criminology's "utilitarian" character, which Foucault so caustically depreciates, and the way in which its "use-inspired" (Stokes 1997) nature, to use a less acerbic term, has coupled developments within criminology to the shifting priorities of practical politics.

---

[2] For an exception, see Wood and Shearing's (2007) and Johnston and Shearing's (2003) discussion of the "governance of security."

In developing our arguments, our focus will be on criminology within English-speaking contexts as it is here that contemporary criminology has been primarily shaped.

The emergence of a crime-centered criminology

A practical politics that proved to be particularly influential in constituting criminology's established crime focus, within English-speaking contexts, was the development of the New Police within the City of London at the beginning of the nineteenth century. These New Police emerged in London as a consequence of widespread concern about the inadequacy of the existing mechanisms for governing safety (Emsley 1986). The existing potpourri of arrangements, which had been developed previously within rural and feudal contexts, was proving to be inadequate within urban contexts (Beattie 2006; Critchley 1978; Radzinowicz 1956). A particular concern, at the time, were ad hoc initiatives, such as the businesses of thief taking, which involved private sector entrepreneurs offering the return of stolen goods for a fee, goods whose theft they had often arranged (Beattie 2006; Zedner 2006).

The long and the short of these concerns, and responses to them, was the development of a plan, by influential policing reformers (early criminologists), for policing arrangements that would eschew the backward-looking strategies that initiatives such as thief taking offered, which Leman-Langlois and Shearing (2004) have termed "repairing the past," to more forward-looking arrangements that would "repair the future." The core idea informing these plans for a New Police was the development of a police organization dedicated to preventing disturbances of "the peace" – "peace" was a term that Hobbes (1651/1968, 186) used in the mid-1600s to designate a state of interpersonal safety – within the City of London, which was then, as it is today, a relatively small geographic area, "a city within a city."

These New Police were to "keep the peace" by establishing conditions that would promote safety. The core of these conditions was to be the establishment of a pervasive system of surveillance – which Radzinowics (1968, 164) has termed "an unremitting watch" – across the City of London. This "watch" was to be accomplished by instituting a "beat" system that would distribute police officers across the City (Grimshaw and Jefferson 1987). This arrangement would, it was believed, establish a pervasive police gaze that would deter potential wrongdoers from committing crimes, because detection would be certain, a crucial condition for effective deterrence identified by Beccaria (1996).

So confident was Sir Robert Peel, the British home secretary, who instituted these arrangements, of the success of this venture that few provisions were made to enable these "Bobbies on the beat" (a term that derived from "Bob," the shortened version of "Robert") to respond to crimes after they had occurred – for example, there was no provision for police investigators who would investigate crimes (Beattie 2006, 31–32).

What transpired in practice deviated considerably from these plans. The "Peelers" (another nickname given to these New Police) found it exceedingly difficult in practice to establish the unremitting watch that they had been established to create. The flies in Peel's ointment were the "institutions of privacy" (Stinchcombe 1963), particularly those associated with private property.

These institutions established legal restrictions that kept Peel's New Police on public streets, and off private property, effectively restricting their watch to what transpired in public places. These restrictions placed Peel's "Bobbies" in a Catch-22 predicament – they were required to establish an unremitting watch within a context of a combination of physical and legal barriers that prevented them from realizing this objective.

The source of this difficulty was the model of Marine Police (also known as the Thames River Police), a policing arrangement that was thought to have been very successful, which had inspired the police reformers (Barrie 2008; Radzinowicz 1956; Reynolds 1998). What the architects of the New Police had not paid sufficient attention to, in their plans, was just how different the context within which the Marine Police operated was from the context within which their New Police would operate. Unlike Peel's police, the Marine Police was a private sector organization that operated primarily on private property, with authorized access to both public and private spaces.

The response of the New Police to their restrictive physical barriers, such as walls and doors, and to their restrictive legal context was to shift their role from one of preemptive and pervasive surveillance to that of postcrime responders who would go to the aid of victims of crime. At the heart of this postcrime response was the identification of offenders who had committed crimes so that they could be brought before courts where they would they would receive their "just deserts" (von Hirsch 1993) – ironically this meant that the New Police very quickly evolved into a form of "thief takers" (what the Canadian police chief James Harding has termed "bandit-catchers"), albeit ones who did not provide for the return of property but rather became the "front end" of an emerging criminal justice system. While this meant that the New Police did not realize their founding mission, this shift went a long way to ameliorating the considerable opposition to the possibility of an unremitting watch.

It is this role as bandit catchers, rather than as unremitting watchers, that has become the model that police organizations have followed in Britain and in many other countries – in part because of the reach that British colonialism enabled. Accordingly, these developments, though very space-time-specific, have been very influential in shaping the way in which the governance of safety has come to be understood within criminology. Indeed, they have proved to have had a very long tail, which has shaped criminology as a crimeology rather than as a safetyology or, if one accepts the "governance of security" language of Wood and Shearing (2007, 6) and Johnston and Shearing (2003, 9), as a securityology.

As a consequence of these developments in safety governance, criminology has fashioned for itself a conceptual box, focused on the governance of interpersonal hitting and taking that Brodeur (1983) has termed "low policing." This box has shaped criminology into an area of inquiry that has been concerned primarily, and at times almost exclusively, with bandit catching, blaming, and punishing and how these processes might be improved in terms of both effectiveness and propriety. With this use-inspired conceptual narrowing criminology has for many years firmly cemented itself into a crimeology frame that has shaped, and continues to shape, its research and thinking.

In developing its value for safety governors (largely governments), criminology has drawn primarily on sociology and psychology to develop theories of bandits, bandit catching, bandit catchers, blamers, and correctors (in particularly punishers) to assist these governors to "govern through crime" (Simon 2007) more effectively and legitimately. In developing its methods, criminology has drawn on the same disciplinary sources as it has for its theories. While there has been considerable interest in the use of qualitative methodologies of anthropology and sociology (Shearing and Marks 2011), criminology's primary methodological tools have been quantitative ones. This quantitative tendency, which has always been strong within American criminology, has become stronger over the past decade. This has led to the emergence of a particularly strong quantitative research culture within criminology that has been organized under signs such as "computational criminology" (Birks 2005), "experimental criminology" (Sherman 2009), and "crime science" (Laycock 2003).

This development is having a major impact on the way in which questions of effectiveness and propriety are being explored within criminology. Indeed, this stance has been steadily encroaching on the well-established and more legal and philosophical terrain of "critical criminology" (Taylor, Walton, and Young 1975/2011), which has focused in particular on issues of propriety and its relationship with effectiveness. An example of this can be found in the experimental criminology research that is currently being conducted under the sign "procedural justice" – a concept that was explored earlier by the philosopher John Rawls (1971) in his "Theory of Justice." Within criminology this term has become associated with the experimental work of the legal psychologist Tom Tyler (2006) and a growing body of work that is seeking to extend his ideas and findings (for example, Murphy 2004). These developments have done much to cement criminology as a crimeology that is in the process of becoming a "crime science" providing evidence-based guidance to governments.

This story points to several "strengths" (or "weaknesses," depending on one's perspective). These include a defining focus on after-the-fact crime control as the route to safety, which provides an integrating thread within criminology and constitutes a shared criminological identity. "Criminology," as one of our colleagues said to one of us recently, "is about crime and what to do about it." This identity has proved symbolically and financially beneficial. Criminology departments within universities often have among the highest undergraduate and diploma student enrollments and have often been able to persuade governments to be major supporters of their use-inspired research – for example, over the years the British Home Office has proved to be an extraordinarily lucrative source of research funding for British criminology.

From criminalities to securities

A variety of voices within criminology are beginning to argue – often implicitly – that if criminology remains within its established crime-focused framings it will not be in a position to recognize, let alone respond to the shifting landscape of insecurities, and their associated securities, that emerged in the twentieth century and are defining the current century. As we turn to examine these voices we, inevitably, encounter a language conundrum, something of a Gordian knot, that is difficult to untangle – for a recent discussion of the difficulties involved in surmounting established nomenclatures, and the framing they cement, see Albrecht and Moe (2014).

This challenge arises because the established criminological language – which we have relied upon to this point in the chapter, of "crime," "harms," "safety," "justice," "criminal justice," and so on – is the language of the terrain criminology is hesitantly moving beyond. It is difficult – as Hegel's (1967, 63) oft-quoted line "The owl of Minerva spreads its wings only with the falling of the dusk" reminds us – to develop a new language, while still embedded in the old. Faced with this conundrum we will use the new terms within an emerging new criminology, even though the meanings of these terms, as we will see, often remain vague and are contested.

A central theme that unites the emerging voices questioning established conceptions within criminology has been that criminology needs to lift its gaze beyond crime, and its management. Three subthemes, all of which are grounded in a practical politics to which criminology has responded, can also be detected. The first is the argument that the governance of both the old securities and new securities has become, and should become, more multilateral both within governments ("whole-of-government") and beyond government ("whole-of-society"). The second argues that the governance of security, again both old and new, has shifted, and should shift, away from its traditional backward-looking approach to a more forward-looking, preemptive approach that seeks to mitigate harms before they occur. A third argument is that criminology should include within its gaze thing-to-human and human-to-thing engagements and not simply human-to-human ones.

A conceptual event that has proved to be remarkably influential in shifting criminology away from its established framing was the publication of Ulrich Beck's *The Risk Society* (Beck 1992). While not a criminological text, Beck's work has had a significant impact on criminological thinking, especially in regard to the second and third of these subthemes. At the heart of Beck's thesis was the argument that there has been a significant change in the nature of harms that humans have had to contend with since the nineteenth century European state-building era that proved to be so important in shaping criminology. For Beck, at the heart of this change has been a fundamental shift in the nature of the harms that humans face. Contemporary harms, he argued, have shifted from harms with relatively limited impacts, for which a backward-looking harm governance is appropriate, to harms with consequences that are much more dangerous and for which the emerging (and appropriate) stance is to act to prevent them before they occur. What this has meant, Beck argued, is that managing harms after they have occurred has given way to managing risks – that is, to managing the possibilities of harm before they are realized (Beck 1992).

Two criminologists who have been at the forefront of exploring the implications of these developments for security and its governance have been Jonathan Simon (2007) and Pat O'Malley (2004, 2008), both of whom have explored the various and often contesting ways that risks are identified and managed and their implications for harm governance.

Another enormously influential criminologist who actively explored the implications of this shift for criminology was Richard Ericson (1994, 2007), who, shortly before his untimely death, turned his attention to the insurance industry – a risk-managing industry that he (and his collaborators) described as "*the* institution of governance beyond the state" (Ericson, Doyle, and Barry 2003, 45, original emphasis). As Ericson and other insurance scholars have noted, insurance seeks, on the one hand, to enable its clients to recognize risks before they materialize and become members of risk pools who collectively put aside resources that will enhance their resilience in the face of harms and, on the other, to act to manage in ways that will reduce the likelihood of their realization (Ewald 1991; Heimer 1989). Together, these and other risk-focused criminological scholars have been actively reshaping criminology in ways that are establishing it as a riskology, and a securityology, as well as a crimeology.

To return to the first of our subthemes: A development that predates Beck's writing, that is firmly grounded in a practical politics, has been the study of "private security" (see Abrahamsen and Williams 2011; White 2011 for discussions of the extent and financial worth of this industry). Both the industry itself and scholars who have studied it have used the term "security" as a way of distinguishing this set of institutions from those of the public police. A key distinguishing feature of this industry, which many scholars have identified, is its concern with managing risk – a role that is reminiscent of the intended role of Peel's New Police. While, this industry does sometimes engage in services that are similar to those of police (Rigakos 2002) – for example, when they provide clients with emergency assistance – for the most part the focus of private security has been, and is, preventative.

The tactics used by private security are very often intended to produce an "unremitting watch" – for example, the widespread use of surveillance cameras in a wide variety of settings. An instructive example, referred to by Shearing and Stenning (1980) some years ago, is the widespread use of surveillance, not to identify wrongdoing but rather to identify opportunities for wrongdoing, that, if left unattended, might lead to wrongdoing – see also Shearing and Stenning's (1987) analysis of embedded risk managing ordering in Disney World. Yet another example of embedded ordering intended to maintain order, rather than respond to breaches of order, can be found in tactics that have been developed to maintain desired orders within cyberspace (Lessig 1996; Dupont 2013) that have been developed largely under private "auspices" and by "providers" of security governance (Bayley and Shearing 2001).

As these and similar developments have emerged, so too has the term "security" emerged as a preferred nomenclature for referencing forward-looking, risk-focused forms of security governance and for the auspices and providers who engage in this form of security governance. An analytic outcome of thinking about the emergence of a diversity of auspices and providers of safety across public, private, and community sectors has been discussion around the notion of "nodal governance" (Burris *et al.* 2005) as an approach that enables criminologists to theorize the emergence of security governance as a multilateral and plural domain of governance (Bayley and Shearing 2001).

Although these proactive, forward-looking developments have been, to a large extent, pioneered by auspices and providers of security within the private sector, a discernable shift in this direction can be detected within public sector ordering initiatives within the realm of low policing. Together these developments have began significantly to loosen the hold that the established backward-looking crime focus has had on the institutions of criminal justice and, accordingly, on criminology. There are several established domains within public sector low policing where this is becoming evident.

One of the most significant developments has been the emergence of what has been termed "environmental criminology" – a criminology that has drawn inspiration from architectural thinkers such as Jane Jacobs (1970) and Oscar Newman (1972). A number of criminological scholars – for example, Clarke (1997), Felson and Boba (2010), Cornish (1994), and the Brantinghams (1981) – have sought to encourage governments to pay greater attention to the shaping of opportunities, especially through redesigning the physical environments that enable crimes, so as to make criminal wrongdoing less likely. There are strong resonances here with the preventative activities of private security, except that the focus here has tended to be state-centric and has, for this reason, continued to be crime-focused. A common thread, however, is the forward-looking, anticipatory and risk-focused approach to this preventative crime governance – a focus that it shares with broader crime prevention initiatives (Waller and Sansfacon 2000). An important and influential line of thinking and research within environmental criminology, which resonates with Peel's unremitting watch, has focused attention on the presence (and absence) of "capable guardians" who can, and do, limit opportunities for crime (Eck 1995; Eck and Eck 2012; Felson 1995; Reynald 2011).

As developments such as these have focused attention on anticipating and avoiding harms, so too have the terms "security" and "security governance" increasingly been used to refer to what was thought of as "peace" and "peacekeeping." Further these older terms themselves have interestingly been resurrected and put to use in postconflict contexts where the terms "peacekeeping" and "peace building" have become ubiquitous. As these developments have taken place there has been a growing disinclination among scholars, and practitioners, to use terms such as "crime fighting," "war on crime," "law enforcement," and so on. It is not that the word "crime" and its related terms are no longer being used; rather they are being used to designate a particular form of security governance – namely, Simon's "governing through crime" (2007) – rather than security governance more generally. This shift in understanding and its expression in language is nicely illustrated by some of the titles being used to label criminological programs, for example, University College London's Department of "Security and Crime Science" and the University of Liverpool's Singapore campus's program in "Criminology and Security."

This shift to "security," as a descriptor, is also evident within institutions of security governance across both the private and public sectors. A recent example of this has been the establishment, by the US government, of the Department of Homeland Security. This department, created in the aftermath of the 9/11 terrorist attacks, reflects a Beck-like understanding of the shifting nature of contemporary harms that extend significantly beyond crime. In line with this broad ambit the department consolidated twenty-two existing agencies only some of which were policing and justice agencies, for example, the government's "Energy Security" and "Assurance Program."

While a broad security focus is certainly not new to governments, – as the US Central Intelligence Agency makes clear – what is now emerging is a blurring of lines that have traditionally been used to separate the security governance of high policing and the crime governance of low policing. This is at once redefining low policing and creating a host of new domains that "security" is being used to describe – for example, food security, water security, and energy security. This is not the only evidence of this sort of an explicit reframing by governments of the way in which they understand the governance of security and how it should be practiced. Another example, found in the United States' northern neighbor, is the recent adoption of the name Department of Public Safety by the Government of Canada for the federal department responsible for the Royal Canadian Mounted Police.

This move to "security" and the associated shift away from "crime" across both the private and public sectors has been enabled by, and is enabling, a broadening of criminology's domain beyond Hobbes's hitting and taking harms. As noted, this shift has been accompanied by a growing concern with risks of harms and how these might be mitigated. As this broadening has occurred, the term "security" has been increasingly drawn upon to give expression to these new framings (Valverde and Wood 2001). Similarly, as this has happened, criminology has been tentatively exploring a new life for itself as a riskology and securityology.

In the next section we explore further the link between security and risk within criminological thinking.

Security and risk

As we have suggested, the changes that have been taking place with respect to security governance can in part be accounted for by a broadening of the notion of safety beyond the hitting and taking harms that Hobbes conceived of as a foundational order. Understandings of safety have been, and are being, broadened to include a wider array of social, economic, and environmental conditions (Lynch and Stretesky 2014; Neocleous 2008; Wood and Shearing 2007).

By the end of the nineteenth century the developmental boom in most of the Western world (in terms of economy, science, and technology) was accompanied by two important risk related changes (Foucault 1978, 15). First, as a result of wage earning workers and the complexities of ownership and service delivery, third-party liability, as opposed to individual liability, became a necessary transformation in civil law structures. This is simply because there were now a number of harms that had no clear harm doer, and thus could be described as accidents. Second, because no existing civil claims fit the bill for this type of harm, forms of "no fault" protection were created. This signaled the start of social insurance, accident insurance, and a new era for risk governance. Prior to this development, risk was understood as a simple zero sum equation between the harmed and the harmer. The idea of objective risks, unrelated to the moral character of individuals, encountered by all who participated in the modern economy was a view forwarded by a range of intellectual experts including sociologists, criminologists, historians, and economists.

What the idea of risk brought to the table was a calculable predicting arm to security analyses. As a consequence of this academic work, by criminologists and others, the exploration of risk and security took many different directions. At the Symposium of the Future of Risk, held in 2012 at the Chicago Center for Contemporary Theory, Bernard Harcourt listed five different directions, which the theory of risk has since taken.

One is the "re-individualization of risks" (Harcourt 2012). In the welfare state, risks were shared among the members of solidarity groups, while neoliberalism, it has been argued, has tended to disaggregate these collectives, arguing that individuals should manage their risks themselves both rationally and proactively (Harcourt 2012). As suggested by O'Malley (2004), rational risk management came to be associated with the market and with entrepreneurial individuals, rather than with the regulatory institutions of the state compensating for market failures.

With these neoliberal developments risk began to emerge as a tool for exclusion as well as inclusion. With the identification of risk groups was the second splinter, the responsibilization of risk (Harcourt 2012). By way of example, within the insurance industry, social profiles are constructed (age, gender, residential suburb) and are then used to label persons and organizations as forming part of a risk group. This categorization, together with statistical and actuarial knowledge, is used to price risks and assess premiums of risk bearers who wish to join, and gain the protection of, the risk pools that insurance companies establish and manage (Ericson *et al.* 2003; Harcourt 2012; Heimer 1989).

Another direction that the risk conversation has taken has been to consider practices that embrace risk rather than simply fear it (Baker and Simon 2002). These practices view uncertainty as a challenge to be mastered, not simply as the source of potential harms to be avoided. The works of Pat O'Malley (2004), in particular, provide instructive examples of how risk can be imagined, reimagined, and portrayed in both negative and positive ways. As a way of illustrating his analysis of the system that has emerged to govern responsible driving, O'Malley (2009) pictures a governmental system that works efficiently with very limited disciplinary and individualizing elements. This enables him to develop an analysis of risk-related practices as constituting governmental technologies that require, and can benefit from, criminological analysis and critique. Similarly scholars have explored how nonstate forms of security governance, such as the international movement for restorative justice, may benefit from future-focused risk management developments (Froestad and Shearing 2013; Johnston and Shearing 2003).

Today so much is being done and governed in the name of risk and security that it is difficult to identify a single set of goals or ethical foundations that underlie these risk governance practices. O'Malley suggests, in the face of this diversity, that it is more appropriate to view risk as an abstract theoretical construct that is fundamentally shaped by its social, political, and other space-time environments. In developing his arguments for a risk-focused criminology, O'Malley (2008) proposes building on a governmentality approach that will focus attention on how different categories of risks are governed.

Another direction is that of risk avoidance through risk management (Harcourt 2012). Neocleous (2008), echoing Wildavsky's (1988, 1) observation that risk is so often treated as "a bad thing," "rather than as an inevitably mixed phenomenon from which considerable good, as well as harm, is derived," warns against the assumption, inherent in the notion of security, that safety is by definition a good thing (see also Baker and Simon 2002; Loader 2009). He cautions that accepting this assumption binds criminology too tightly to the utilitarian motivations of traditional security studies, where the goal becomes doing "security" better rather than gaining a better understanding of security and its governance as social practices. As an alternative, as do both O'Malley (2004) and Valverde (2001), Neocleous (2008, 4), following Foucault, proposes that security should be viewed not as a value or an aspiration, but rather as a mode of governing.

What these, and similar, risk scholars argue is that not only has what is done in the name of security shaped society, but this shaping has taken and continues to take place through a particular ideological lens. For Neocleous, central to this shaping is a state-centric ideology. He argues that it is important that scholars "get beyond security politics, not add yet more 'sectors' in a way that simply expands the scope of the state and legitimizes state intervention in yet more and more areas of our lives" (2008, 185). For Neocleous it is important to consider "desecuritisation" as a possible pathway – this is an old theme within the practical politics of criminology, where there have long been arguments to decriminalize harms. An example are the arguments by Schur and Maher for a policy of "radical non-intervention" (Schur and Maher 1973) for some crimes as a way of preventing the escalation of harms, which labeling theorists such as Howard Becker (1963) and Edwin Lemert (2010) argue are all too often a consequence of crimeizing harms.

Finally, a major direction of risk studies has been the management of risks (Harcourt 2012). Technologies for managing risk have often involved relying on the calculations, or the research, of some designated expert authority regarding a specific risk and then making adjustments to one's actions in light of their technical specifications.

An example would be the directions that are offered with respect to seat belt use to prevent injury or death in automobile accidents, which have persuaded many people to wear these belts. Another example would be the high walls and electric gates that have become so ubiquitous in many parts of the world to safeguard the security of persons and property from unwanted intrusion.

These habitual practices that follow from expert knowledge and the "expert systems" (Giddens 1990) to which this knowledge gives rise have become a ubiquitous part of the governance of security. Beck (1992, 2000), in seeking to understand the governance of security, views risks, and the harms associated with them, in terms of three periods: premodernization, modernization, and reflexive modernization. In these periods, risk is framed differently and this framing shapes the governance of security.

Risk in the premodern period was seen as something that we could not control, something caused by gods or demons or simply an act of nature. Risk in the modernized world was viewed as a probability to be calculated (Bernstein 1996). According to Beck, modernized societies have reached a point of reflexivity that arises from the trajectory of their development. This has introduced a third period, of reflexive modernization, that is forming the basis for the way risk is viewed and security governed today. Today risks are a consequence of the risk governance processes of yesteryear. They reflect "the hazards and insecurities of modernisation itself" (Beck 1992, 21). This idea is captured by the notion that we are now living within a new geological era, the "Anthropocene" (a terms proposed by Steffen *et al.* 2007; see also Steffen *et al.* 2011), in which human activity has become a very influential driver of earth systems. Within this era, as Beck has argued, many of the most fundamental risks that humans face today are ones that they have created though their engagements with earth systems. These new risks, it is argued, require very different processes of risk management from, for example, the actuarial practices that lie at the heart of commercial insurance, as a security governance enterprise that assumes stable systems that have not been, and that cannot be, affected by human engagements with them.

The central thrust of the work of these scholars has not simply been to move beyond crime, but to shift the focus of criminology to risks and risk management. In doing so they have not argued that conventional crimes and criminal justice processes are not important, but rather that criminology should broaden its focus beyond its established, nineteenth century-based, conception of harms and responses to them.

Security and the Anthropocene

At the heart of Beck's analysis, as we have noted, was his argument that the nature of the risks humans face has recently changed dramatically and that this shift was ushering in different understandings of security and its governance. The emblematic example of this change for Beck was the earth's shift from the Holocene era to the Anthropocene – although Beck did not use these terms.

During the Holocene era humans took for granted, and treated as unproblematic, the largely benign patterns of outputs from earth systems – they treated these outputs as simply the way things are. Humans, in Heidegger's (1977) words, treated the earth as a "standing reserve" – as a warehouse of goods that would never be, and could never be, emptied, and so would always be available for their use. This "reserve" required no maintenance and would quite simply be there for humans to draw upon for whatever they required for their biophysical well-being. Certainly, humans had many concerns about how best to tap into these resources and how best to make things from them, but the extraction and waste processes of this take, make, and waste paradigm were not of concern to them.

What Beck identified, and what the term "Anthropocene" signals, is a dramatic shift in an understanding of earth systems and the location of humans in relation to them. This emerging understanding of humans – as not only integral to biophysical systems but hugely influential drivers of these processes and their outcomes – goes against the grain of well-established understandings (both popular and social science) of humans as essentially "social" and "spiritual" beings rather than as fundamentally biophysical beings who have had, and are having, profound impacts on biophysical systems as "geological agents" (Chakrabarty 2009). This includes the ecological support systems (Heidegger's "standing reserve") that humans rely upon for their well-being and the functioning of the social systems that they have, as biophysical beings, created. With this shift has arisen a new awareness of the "environmental security" that has long been provided by earth systems – see Le Billon, this volume, for a discussion in the context of the notion of "securitization" (see Neocleous 2008; Waever 1993).

As criminology begins increasingly to view itself as a "riskology" it is beginning, following Beck (1992), to rethink its understandings of the risks, and associated securities, that it should explore. One consequence of this, which is beginning to be visible, is the emergence of "green criminology" (White 2009) – also termed "conservation criminology" (Gibbs *et al.* 2010). As this happens, an additional and deeper foundational order – in addition to the Hobbesian interpersonal foundational order – is beginning to be identified by criminologists (Ngoc and Wyatt 2012; South and Brisman 2013; White 2009), namely, the biophysical order of ecological services and related earth system boundaries that cannot be breached if human well-being is to be safeguarded – see, for example, Rockström *et al.* (2009) on planetary boundaries and the associated idea developed by Raworth (2012, 7) of a "safe and just space for humanity." This conception of a safe space for human existence provides an ecological basis for concepts such as "environmental security" (see Lynch and Stretesky 2011) – a term that has been used within the international relations literature since the late 1970s and 1980s and has since been deployed by the Copenhagen school (Buzan *et al.* 1998; see also Dalby 2002).

It is to this emerging idea of a foundational order of ecological services that terms such as "food security," "water security," "energy security,",and so on, have been pointing. As criminology begins to recognize the importance of a biophysical foundational order, this has given impetus to the shift toward the forward-looking risk focus that the term "security" has come to signify. What is emerging, within practical politics and criminology, is both a return to the Hobbesian forward-looking focus on security and its governance and a broadening of his conception of order from a foundational order of interpersonal peace to one that includes a biophysical "peace."

Cybersecurity

Before bringing this chapter to a close we turn to yet another shift in focus within criminology that we have already alluded to, namely, the emergence of what has come to be termed cyberspace (Dupont 2013). This space is a digital, electronic space populated by digital entities.

As humans enter this space they find themselves transformed into such entities. As with the biophysical world of the Anthropocene, here too a distinct shift in conception and language has been taking place. The emergence of cyberspace, as a focus of attention within security studies, has given birth to yet another security, namely, "cybersecurity" and the emergence of "cybersecurity strategies" (Bayuk et al. 2012; O'Connell 2012). The language of governance in relation to this world that has emerged is very clearly the language of "security" and the "risks" that threaten it. What is sought here, as with the New Police, is the absence of harm, and the emerging governance strategies are focused on how to realize such an absence.

Benoit Dupont (2013), a leading criminologist who has concerned himself with cyberspace, recently undertook an analysis of the language employed, using automated text analysis software, in eleven government reports (totalling 46,403 words) from around the world, setting out their governments' cybersecurity strategy. This analysis revealed thirty-three main concepts that were used in these reports, and these were then ranked in terms of their prominence within the reports. At the top of this list was "security"; "crime" was ranked twenty-fourth.

Interestingly in this article Dupont, although a criminologist, does not use the term "crime" or "cybercrime" in his analysis to identify the insecurities of cyberspace. While "cybercrime" has become a common term within criminology (Yar 2013), Dupont in his analysis is careful to articulate a broader understanding of cyberharms and to demonstrate how governments, in their attempts to respond to these harms, are taking a distinctly forward–looking approach and are very deliberately signifying this through the use of the term "security" rather than "crime." Throughout Dupont refers to these harms as risks, which governments are seeking to govern through "cybersecurity solutions" designed to reduce the likelihood of the realization of these risks as harms. Within his analysis Dupont, implicitly rather than explicitly, recognizes yet another foundational order, namely, the order of cyberspace, which governing authorities are seeking to secure in support of human well-being, in this case, a digital well-being. He also in his work recognizes, again implicitly rather than explicitly, that the governance of cybersecurity displays clear resonances with the notions of the unremitting watch that shaped Peel's vision of policing (Dupont 2008).

Conclusion

In this chapter we have traced the way criminology, and the practical politics it mirrors, has been redefining its understanding of security and its governance. We have conceived of these developments in terms of two related themes. The first has been a broadening of the way in which safety, as a desirable governance objective, has been understood. The second has been a shift in governance strategies from a focus on realized harms (past-focused) to a focus on the risks of harms (future-focused).

Criminology finds itself in the midst of a rapidly shifting practical politics that is redefining its understanding of and approach to safety. Within this context criminology has been engaged in an uneven game of catch-up that has created different, and often inconsistent, pockets of criminological thinking about security. Much of the emerging thinking in criminology, and within practical politics, is focusing attention on the risks of a broad range of harms. Within this thinking the term "security" is being used to identify this focus – a focus that is actively reimagining criminology as being as much a riskology and a securityology, as it is a crimeology.

Contemporary criminologists find themselves at a consequential crossroad. If they choose their established crimeology path they will limit themselves, both descriptively and normatively, to the study of the threats to security, and the responses to them, that were prevalent at the end of the eighteenth century. If this is to be the fate of criminology, its practitioners will have chosen to trap themselves within a conceptual framing that will significantly limit their ability to remain as relevant as they might be within a twenty-first century context.

10 International law
Between legalism and securitization
WOUTER WERNER

Among international lawyers, questions about theory and research method tend to generate awkward silences. After all, for scholars of international law, "what passes as method ... has to do with what counts as persuasive argument" because "international law is an argumentative practice" (Koskenniemi 2010). This is reflected in the dominant approaches to "security" in international law. While the concept is omnipresent in both positive international law and international legal scholarship, reflection on theories and research methods is only marginally developed. More theoretically oriented work on security in international law can mainly be found within specific "schools" that identify themselves as different from mainstream international legal scholarship, such as neo-Kelsenian approaches, critical legal studies, or third world approaches to international law.[1]

In what may loosely be called "mainstream" international law scholarship, however, "security" is approached without much reflection on theory or method. Most books and articles on security in international law published in the past few decades focus almost exclusively on interpreting and applying existing law, sketching developments in

---

[1] For an example of a neo-Kelsenian approach in the field of security see, inter alia, Jorg Kammerhofer (2009). One of the core articles of faith in neo-Kelsenian approaches is the possibility of separating the categories of is and ought. This is translated into a search for methodological purity, understood as the need to keep legal analysis strictly separated from both empirical studies of law and moral considerations of how law ought to be. The classical works in critical legal studies in international law are by David Kennedy (1987) and Martti Koskenniemi (2005). As will be set out in more detail, both works showed the instability or "ungroundedness" of the methods used in mainstream international law and thereby the openness of international law to politics. Third world approaches in international law have built on the insights of critical theory, showing how foundational categories and accepted methods of international law have structurally disadvantaged colonized peoples. One of the classical studies in this respect is Anthony Anghie (2007). A very interesting and readable example is Fleur Johns (2013).

international law, or suggesting how existing legal arrangements can be improved. Questions regarding epistemology, ontology, or the methods through which arguments obtain validity are largely left unconsidered.

Take, for example, the recent debates on the use of armed drones by the United States. Their use has been the topic of several reports of expert committees and special rapporteurs and given rise to a great number of articles and blog posts by legal scholars.[2] So far, arguments about drone warfare and international law have predominantly revolved around the (in)compatibility of the use of armed drones with existing provisions of international law, combined with calls for more transparency to make such assessments possible. Leading questions are framed in terms of preexisting legal categories such as state consent, self-defense, armed conflict, legitimate military targets, and human rights protections. Practically no explicit consideration is given to questions regarding method or theory, apart from the invocation of the sources of international law. The international legal debate on armed drones is illustrative of the kind of knowledge questions that dominate the field of international law in general. In the vast majority of cases, the purposes of international legal research are to make sense of the world in terms of existing legal categories, to interpret and apply legal norms, and to suggest improvements or make policy recommendations.[3] Despite the existence of more reflexive approaches at the edges of the discipline, international law remains most of all an argumentative practice in which persuasion is more important than recourse to explicitly spelled-out theories and research methodologies.

And yet, method and theory do fulfill a crucial function in the practices of international law, both academically and in different legal

---

[2] The list of publications on the topic is long and I will make no attempt at providing an exhaustive overview. By way of examples see: Melina Sterio (2012); Mary Ellen O'Connell (2013), Report of the Special Rapporteur on the Promotion and Protection of Human Rights and Fundamental Freedoms while Countering Terrorism (2013); Dutch Advisory Committee on Issues of Public International Law (2013). A notable exception to the atheoretical approach to drones is the excellent book by Fleur Johns on "nonlegality" (2013).

[3] In terms of Habermas's sociology of knowledge, one could say that the interest of knowledge (*Erkenntisinteresse*) revolves around problem solving and systematizing, an interest that is closest to what Habermas has identified as the historical-hermeneutic approach. However, where Habermas links hermeneutical sciences to communicative action, my reading of legal discourse would be a combination of strategic and communicative action. See also the second section for a more elaborate account of the legal method; Jürgen Habermas (1968).

professions. It would be quite a mistake to infer from the lack of explicit reflections that mainstream international legal discourse proceeds without theory or method. Debates on international law take place on the basis of rather well-developed assumptions how legal arguments can be produced. These assumptions structure international law as a disciplinary practice that allows certain forms of argumentation and excludes others. While the basic assumptions underlying the practice of international law evolve over time,[4] they do possess stickiness and provide for relative stability. What is more, the basic assumptions and generative rules are shared across academic and professional practices. By and large, mainstream academic arguments are produced with the same methodological toolbox that is available to, say, a legal counsel for the International Court of Justice. This makes academic legal research a somewhat peculiar practice: The same legal sources that supposedly define what counts as international law are used as methods to research international law.

In this chapter I will make an attempt to reconstruct the methods used in what may loosely be called "mainstream" international legal writings on security. Of course, I can only sketch a partial picture, as my focus on the dominant approaches to security includes an exclusion of more historical and critical approaches that deliberately distance themselves from mainstream writings on security. To compensate for this bias, I will make use of some of the critical tools developed in critical writings to reconstruct mainstream international law understandings of "security" and revisit some of the alternative approaches briefly at the end of my chapter.

The chapter will proceed as follows. The first section sketches a more elaborate picture of the methods and disciplinary self-understanding in international law that structure the majority of publications on international law and security. I will illustrate my reconstruction by means of the recently published *Tallin Manual on Cyberwarfare*, written by an international group of experts on conflict and security law.

---

[4] In this context it is illustrative to contrast the writings of Grotius, often labeled as one of the founding fathers of modern international law, with the writings in the twentieth and twenty-first centuries. Grotius construed his arguments on the basis of a rather loose set of criteria, mixing natural law, historical precedent, theology, and the practice of states. In post-1945 international legal scholarship, it would be difficult to be taken seriously if one invoked ancient Israeli practice or precedents from Greece and Rome to underpin an argument on international law.

The second section then moves from the more general discussion on methods in international law to the specific problems that need to be tackled when international legal methods are applied in the field of security. More in particular, I will focus on a tension that has structured many writings on the topic of international law and security, the tension between a logic of legalism and a logic of securitization. I will illustrate this point by means of an analysis of some key publications on the program of targeted sanctions as adopted by the Security Council.

Deep structures of international legal argumentation

Before I move to the topic of research in conflict and security law specifically, it is necessary to delve into the methods, assumptions, and paradoxes that structure research in international law generally. For those in other disciplines, this may appear to be a detour – why not start out by analyzing the central topic of this volume, the methods and approaches used in the specific field of security? As I will set out, however, what seems to be a detour is actually a necessary exercise simply because there are no specific legal methods for researching issues of security. What are available are the more general foundations that structure (mainstream) research across international law. This section will therefore start out with an attempt to articulate some of the boundaries that structure mainstream international legal research, albeit illustrated by means of examples drawn from the field of security law. In the third section I will then return to research in conflict and security law more specifically and explicate some of the driving rationalities in this field.

Between state consent and sources of law

For outsiders, international law may appear to be a field that is difficult to penetrate and understand. International legal arguments often appear as formal, technical points made by people who have learned how to produce arguments according to a specific deeper-lying generative structure. Political issues such as the 2001 intervention in Afghanistan are translated by lawyers in technical terms such as modes of liability, the *Nicaragua* versus the *Tadic* test, due diligence, self-defense, and definitions of combatants and civilians. Moreover, they are read through a particular historical lens, which selects and reorders past events as legally relevant and defines other events as legally insignificant. International legal argumentation, in other words, often comes across as a language game that can only be played by those who master its specific rules, vocabulary, and argumentative strategies. At the same time, international legal arguments often look highly political, indeterminate, or reversible. If it comes to contentious issues such as the war against Iraq, targeted killing, or self-defense against cyber attacks, one can easily find international lawyers producing opposing arguments on the basis of the same legal provisions and the same historical precedents.

As critical scholarship has pointed out, the combination of formality and indeterminacy to a considerable extent follows from the structure of modern international law.[5] Modern international law rests on the assumption that legal rules are to a significant degree rooted in the will and behavior of states. Although today one would be hard-pressed to find international lawyers who deny the importance of nonstate actors or the existence of some minimum core of pregiven norms altogether, there is still a widely shared assumption that international law is ultimately rooted in the consent and practice of states. Higgens, for example, states that "we have in international law a system in which norms emerge either through express consent or because there is no opposition ... to obligations being imposed in the absence of such specific consent" (Higgins 1994, 16). In similar fashion, Sweetser regards consent "as constitutive of the international legal order; treaties and even customary international law are based on norms of state consent, whether explicit or tacit" (Sweester 2009, 10). Even when authors readily admit the limits of the consensual paradigm, they often fall back on consent as the sine qua non for the existence of international law. Shaw, for example, while admitting the existence of some legal obligations that do not rest on state consent, still contends,

---

[5] The link between indeterminacy and the deep structure of international law was made in the 1980s by David Kennedy (1987) and Martti Koskenniemi (2005, originally published in 1989). Lack of determinacy in law also follows from factors such as the inherent dynamic nature of meaning, which makes it impossible to predict possible future uses of words. The problem of the lack of determinacy of (legal) language is a classical topic in legal theory and has been discussed by, inter alia, Herbert Hart (1961). The point made by critical legal studies, however, goes beyond the ever-recurring issue of the dynamic and underdetermined nature of language, as it deals with tensions within the foundational assumptions underlying modern international law.

"In a broad sense, states accept or consent to the general system of international law, for in reality without that no such system could possibly operate" (Shaw 2003, 10). In similar terms, Weil argues, "Absent voluntarisrn, international law would no longer be performing its functions" (Weil 1983, 420). The constitutive value or functional necessity of consent is reaffirmed in several general introductions to international law.[6]

However, as many scholars have pointed out, the will or behavior of states cannot as such be the basis of a system of law. For one this would imply that norms could be based on facts (acts of will) alone-a logical fallacy.[7] Second, if norms flow from the will of states alone, their validity and meaning would completely depend on what a state wants at a particular time; the moment a state changed its will, a new norm or a new interpretation would arise. This of course would make the creation of a (stable) legal order, which stabilizes expectations among its subjects, impossible. The will and behavior of states, therefore, are translated into – and supplemented by – a set of *sources of law*, that provide anchor points for legal argumentation. By now there is consensus that these sources at least comprise treaty law, customary law, general principles of law, and – subsidiary sources – judicial decisions and the teachings of the "most highly qualified publicists of the various nations."[8] Another aspect of the deep structure of international legal argumentation is the canon of interpretation, as codified in the Vienna Convention on the Law of Treaties. Articles 31 and 32 of the convention set out how treaty provisions are to be interpreted,

---

[6] For an overview see Andrew Guzman (2012). O. A. Elias and C. L. Lim (1998, xi), while acknowledging the paradoxical nature of state consent, still hold on to consensualism: "seeking to impose some conception of the law as being distinct from the actual claims of states fails for a number of reasons ... [because] there is no better evidence of international law doctrine than that which is expressed by States as a reflection of their legal expectations."

[7] In analytical positivism this point was made by Herbert Hart (1961, 225): "For, in order that words, spoken or written, should in certain circumstances function as a promise, agreement, or treaty, and so give rise to obligations and confer rights which others may claim, rules must already exist providing that a state is bound to do whatever it undertakes by appropriate words to do." See also Hans Kelsen (1960) and for a historical contextualization Christian Reus-Smit (2003).

[8] These five sources are enumerated in article 38 of the Statute of the International Court of Justice. Note, however, that the list in the ICJ Statute was never meant to be exhaustive. Currently, there are ongoing debates about the importance of other possible sources, such as resolutions and decisions by international organizations, soft law, and the rules produced by private actors.

emphasizing the importance of factors such as the intention of the parties, agreements relating to the treaty concerned, the object and purpose of a treaty as a whole, and the subsequent practice of application of the treaty.

At its core, international law is thus grounded on an uneasy combination of, on the one hand, state consent and, on the other, the existence of sources and canons of interpretation. Legal norms derived from the established sources of international law obtain independent validity, need to be interpreted by others, and can also be held against the state that has consented to them, even if that state has changed its mind since the creation of the norms in question. For international law to be possible at all, processes of norm finding cannot therefore be made wholly dependent on the whims of states. It should, in principle, be possible that someone else successfully claims that she knows better what a state has consented to than that state itself. In other words, state consent can only function as basis for international obligation if "the movement is from consent into something more, or other than that" (Koskennimi 2005, 309).[9]

Many debates in international law are thus structured by the tension between consensualism and nonconsensualism; between the idea that law should be grounded in the will, interest, and behavior of states and the idea that the validity of norms derives from preexisting sources and can be held against the states that have created them through their own free will. In the field of security, this tension plays out at several levels. Take, for example, the recently published *Tallinn Manual on the International Law Applicable to Cyber Warfare* (hereafter: the *Tallinn Manual*).[10] The manual was written by an international group of experts in (inter alia) conflict and security law and chaired by probably the most influential author on issues of international law and cyberwar, Michael Schmitt. The core question of the commission was to determine how existing international law applies to the relatively new issue of cyberwar.

The Tallinn Manual takes great pains to argue that it remains within the international rules as created by states. This attitude is not

---

[9] See also Lim and Elias (1998, 241): "The logic of consensually-derived law entails the 'objectivation' of the law and its consequent detachment from the subsequent claims of a State as to what it had 'actually' or 'in fact' willed."

[10] The Tallinn Manual has recently been published by Cambridge University Press (2013).

surprising in a manual produced by a group of experts assembled by invitation of a NATO Centre of Excellence. However, the emphasis on the need to base international law on the will, interests, and behavior of states is shared more broadly in conflict and security law. It is also a basic assumption in one of the classical textbooks in conflict and security law and fits in earlier academic writings of the Tallinn group chair, confirming his belief that international law is ultimately made, applied, and enforced by states.[11] This statement is echoed in the Tallinn Manual's repeated assurances that experts by no means create new rules of international law, but only state and clarify what states have already agreed. At the same time, however, the Tallinn Manual seeks to develop normative guidelines on the basis of rules that were created long before states could even imagine the possibility of cyberspace, let alone cyberwar. The manual establishes the meaning of provisions from, inter alia, the UN Charter or the Geneva Conventions even though it is impossible to trace this meaning back to what states had originally willed when they signed and ratified these treaties. When it comes to the existence and application of rules of customary law, the Tallinn Manual even explicitly claims that it is the superior expertise of its members that legitimizes the conclusions of the report: "Ultimately, the professional knowledge, experience, and expertise of the Experts form the basis for the Tallinn Manual's conclusions as to the customary status of a Rule or its extension into non-international armed conflict" (Tallinn Manua 20, 21). The manual thus moves around state consent, independent sources, and the authority of the interpreter in ways that are illustrative of much scholarship in international law.

International law as a vocation

International law as an academic discipline is not only structured around some basic assumptions *how* international legal arguments can be produced; it also contains some core assumptions setting out *why* scholars should produce legal arguments and thus *what type of questions* are regarded as relevant within legal discourse. Although these assumptions are difficult to pin down and subject to contestation, it is still possible to identify particular types of research questions that

---

[11] For an example see Michael Schmitt (2010, 7).

are generally regarded as more relevant to the discipline than others. For example, when at a mainstream international law conference a scholar presents a paper deconstructing a particular legal regime, almost invariably someone will comment: "So what is the alternative?" "What is left of the rule of law if we only deconstruct law?" or "Don't we all know that law is underdetermined; the question is how lawyers can productively deal with that." The underlying assumption of such comments is that international lawyers are bound to have a commitment to international law, not merely as an object of study, but as a body of rules that is in need of further explication and development. This is also visible in the officially declared aims of the European and American Societies of International Law, "to contribute to the rule of law in international relations and to promote the study of public international law" (ESIL Web site) and "foster the study of international law and to promote the establishment and maintenance of international relations on the basis of law and justice" (ASIL Web site). Similar aims can be found at the Australian and New Zealand Society, aiming to develop and promote the discipline of international law,[12] and the Asian Society of International Law, seeking to promote international law (supplemented by the aim of encouraging specific Asian perspectives on international law). While the African Society focuses even more explicitly on regional perspectives (fostering the dissemination of African perspectives on international law), it does remain committed to the "development of international law," albeit with a recognition of "the special needs of Africa" (Web site African Society).

Admittedly, this is all anecdotal evidence that is unable to capture international legal research in its diversity. Yet, it remains important to notice that four of the continental societies officially commit themselves to the promotion and development of international law and one (Australia/New Zealand) to the promotion of the discipline of international law. Once again, this shows that being an academic lawyer is widely regarded as implying a belief in the beneficial effects of the international rule of law. Researching international law is often regarded as both an academic enterprise and an act of faith; a combination of impersonal analysis of the rules of international law and a

---

[12] It is interesting to note that unlike the other societies, the Australian and New Zealand Society speaks of the *discipline* of international law and not international law as such (Website ANZIL).

personal, normative vocation to improve and develop the international legal system. As Paulus has characterized it, international lawyers have a responsibility to use the paradoxes of their discipline to build an international legal community further: "In their permanent search for the space between consent and justice, sovereignty and community, apology and utopia, international lawyers should both use the potentiality and accept the limits of their task. Only then they may become able to fulfil their share of responsibility in building a way for what we have got used to call, maybe prematurely, an international community" (Paulus 2001, 755).

Another illustration of international law's oscillation between analysis and prescription is the by now classical study of Schwarzenberger (Schwarzenberger 1965). Although Schwarzenberger's book is some fifty-plus years old and subjected to much criticism, his combination of objectivism and subjectivism, distance and commitment, description and prescription still captures much of what goes on in contemporary international legal research. Schwarzenberger starts out from the list of sources as enumerated in article 38 of the Statute of International Law (discussed in the previous section). Through recourse to sources, he seeks to ensure international law's objectivity and by separation of personal normative preferences from the requirements of law (Schwarzenberger 1965). For Schwarzenberger, explicating the law as it is on the basis of existing sources is the main task of international lawyers. However, the alleged objectivity of international law as derived from its sources is immediately coupled to a mission of international lawyers that *cannot* be grounded on any of the sources of international law. According to Schwarzenberger, international lawyers are bound by a normative agenda of (a) systematizing the legal system, (b) determining the social functions served by the legal system, and (c) criticizing existing law and making proposals for better legal arrangements in the future (Schwarzenberger 1965).

International lawyers, in other words, are supposed to believe in the existence of law as a system, to be able to identify social purposes behind that system, to believe that the world can and should be improved through better legal rules, and to be able to prescribe how these rules should look. It goes without saying that methodological tools available to international lawyers hardly equip them for all these difficult tasks. Recourse to legal sources and existing canons of interpretation helps to produce legal arguments and may contribute to a systemization of law but does not tell you why it would be important to believe in the coherence or system of law. Nor does it provide much assistance when it comes to political functions such as identifying social purposes or making suggestions for the improvement of law. And yet, combining analyses of law as it is with setting out how law ought to be systemized and developed is what many international lawyers constantly do and expect others to do. While not many international lawyers today would subscribe to Schwarzenberger's limited reading of the sources of international law, the idea that it is possible to separate legal from nonlegal argument through the use of predefined sources is still quite dominant. It allows international lawyers to make claims about the law as it is, based on existing legal materials and accepted methods of interpretation. At the same time, international lawyers engage in normative debates about the proper ways to organize legal materials, about the prioritization of basic values within the legal system, and about the social functions of law. In addition, observations about the law as it is are often accompanied by suggestions how law is to be improved or how states ought to behave, suggestions that generally are not derived from academic research, but from the expertise, intuitions, and normative preferences of the researcher in question.

An apt illustration of the preceding points is provided by one of the earliest responses o the 9/11 attacks in international legal scholarship. The article, entitled "Terrorism Is Also Disrupting Some Crucial Categories of International Law," was written by one of the most influential international lawyers since the 1980s or so, Antonio Cassese (Cassese 2001).[13] The article contains the combination of assessment of existing law, systematization of law, identification of social purposes, and normative prescription that can be found in much scholarship in the field. The self-proclaimed aim of Cassese's article is to define terrorism under international criminal law and to delineate the scope of forcible action available to the

---

[13] Published in *European Journal of International* Law (2001), 12 (5), 993–1001. Antonio Cassese (1937–2011) not only held prestigious chairs in international law, but also fulfilled many professional functions, including presidencies of the International Criminal Tribunal for the Former Yugoslavia and the Special Tribunal for Lebanon. For his full cv see: www.antoniocassese.com/english/curriculum.html (accessed July 22, 2013).

United States under international law generally. It soon turns out that these tasks require a going back and forth between existing legal sources and new practices that emerged so quickly after 9/11. Under international law as it stood at the time, terrorism was not considered as an international crime, as Cassese argues on the basis of available legal sources. In the same fashion, Cassese interprets past state behavior and *opinion iuris* as speaking out against a right to self-defense against attacks by nonstate actors. Yet, directly after 9/11 the attack was labeled a crime against humanity and states seemed to accept the right of self-defense of the United States, despite the fact that the attack was carried out by a nonstate actor. Existing law was thus called into question by the responses to the 9/11 attacks, creating uncertainty as to the legal qualification of both the attack and the response by the United States and its allies. However, the article does not stop short of identifying the possible challenges to existing law. It makes a deliberate attempt to locate the possible legal qualifications of terrorism and counterterrorism in the broader *system* of international law, for example, by explaining how crimes against humanity relate to jurisdictional issues of the International Criminal Court or how the right of self-defense is situated in the structure of the UN Charter as a whole. What is more, the article takes great pains to identify the basic principles "constituting the foundation of the international community" (Cassese 2001, 998) and sets out what it perceives to be the sociopolitical function of international law today: preserving international peace and security.[14] Finally, the article contains several normative evaluations and prescriptions that do not follow from the sources of international law. A possible broadening of the scope of self-defense, for example, is termed "unsettling," "conspicuous," and a potential "Pandora's box" (Cassese 2001, 997, 998); a case is made for prosecution of terrorist suspects before the International Criminal Court instead of a national court (although legally speaking domestic US courts would have jurisdiction, of course); and the United States is called to struggle for social justice instead of solely focusing on repressive methods.

---

[14] According to Cassese, preserving international peace and security is "the supreme goal of the UN (and indeed of the whole international community)" (Cassese 2001, 1000).

Legalism and securitization

The meanings of security in international law

The assumptions, methods, and knowledge interests of international law scholarship in general also structure the production of arguments in the field of international conflict and security law. As the illustrations in the previous section have indicated, international conflict and security law is argued on the basis of more general presumptions about the nature and sources of international law, the accepted canons of interpretation, and ideas about what counts as responsible legal scholarship. So far, however, I have not said much about the specific characteristics of the study of *security* in international law. What is typical about the study of security by contrast to, say, the study of human dignity or maritime delimitation law? Is it best to regard "security" as a separate functional field or as a problem that cuts across different functional fields? I will turn to these issues now.

A first methodological problem that arises in this context is the proliferation of the concept of "security" across international law and international legal scholarship. The term "security" has been used in many different ways, varying from the name of a whole body of law (conflict and security law) to a label to capture the nature of institutions (as in collective security), a shorthand for general ideas (as in human security), a ground to take exceptional measures (as in national security and collective security), a label for specific fields that are in need of protection (e.g., energy security or environmental security), and so forth. If it is true that "the meaning of a word is its use in the language" (Wittgenstein 1953, 43),[15] then the meaning of "security" is scattered around international law in different usages and different practices. And indeed, it would be quite unproductive to enter the field of international law with a pregiven, clear-cut definition of what security "really" means. As a matter of fact, security "really" means different things in different contexts across international law.

Having said that, it is still possible to identify some typical contexts in which the concept of security is employed in international legal

---

[15] Note that Wittgenstein is more cautious than the phrase "meaning is use" suggests. Wittgenstein held that "for a *large* class of cases – though not for all – in which we employ the word 'meaning' it can be defined thus: the meaning of a word is its use in the language."

reasoning. In the first place, "security" is generally used to refer to the (perceived) need to protect and maintain a valued object. The term "security" is then coupled to different adjectives, as in "national security," "collective security," and "human security" – adjectives that inform the audience which object is apparently in need of protection. Secondy, and for the purposes of this chapter more interesting, the concept of security is invoked across international law to justify measures that deviate from rules that would otherwise apply. In human rights law, for example, states can deviate from several obligations to respect the freedom of individuals if this is necessary for their national security.[16] In addition, they are allowed to deviate from substantive parts of human rights conventions in cases of declared states of emergency, which are necessary because something "threatens the life of the nation" (art. 4 ICCPR). National security exceptions allowing for deviations from specific provisions in treaties can also be found in other fields of international law including trade law,[17] investment law,[18] and environmental law. The exceptional nature of "security" is embodied in the form of the highest political organ of the United Nations, the Security Council. Under the UN Charter, the Security Council is empowered to set aside rules of international law if it deems it so necessary in order to stop acts of aggression or to maintain or restore international peace and security (articles 25, 42, 103 of the UN Charter). States are held to accept and carry out decisions by the Security Council, and decisions by the council take precedence over conflicting obligations states may have. Where in times of normalcy states are held to respect their international legal obligations, the picture changes dramatically when the Security Council adopts resolutions under chapter VII. In the name of collective security states are now required to set aside their normal legal obligations if these would hinder the effectuation of decisions by the council.

---

[16] To mention just a few examples of such deviations provided for in international human rights treaties: Articles 12, 19, 22 of the International Covenant on Civil and Political Rights allow for national security exceptions; the same applies to articles 8, 10, and 11of the European Convention on Human Rights; articles 13, 15, 16 of the American Convention on Human Rights; articles 11 and 12 of the African Charter on Human and Peoples' Rights.

[17] For a discussion see inter alia Dominik Eisenhut (2010), Roger Alford (2011).

[18] Essential Security Interests under International Investment Law, report published by the OECD (2007), available at www.oecd.org/daf/inv/investment-policy/40243411.pdf

In many cases, the concept of "security" in international law thus works as a trump card that allows competent actors to deviate from rules that would otherwise apply. This is not to say that the logic of exception precludes the involvement of experts and bureaucrats, nor the development of routines.[19] It does indicate, however, that issues have been moved out of legal regimes that would apply in situations not labeled as falling under the rubric of "security." In the following section, I will delve deeper in this understanding of security, with a specific focus on the role of the Security Council in international law.

Opposite rationalities in law

The idea of "security" as a trump card that enables agents to deviate from rules that would otherwise apply closely approaches the understanding of security as developed in the so-called Copenhagen school. As the approach of the Copenhagen school will be discussed extensively in a separate chapter of this volume,[20] I will limit myself to a brief sketch of those aspects that are most relevant for the analysis of international law. As may be recalled, the concern of the Copenhagen school is not what security essentially *is*, but rather what a successful invocation of security *does*: what is brought about when an agent manages to convince an audience that measures need to be taken because a valued object is existentially threatened. The main focus of analysis thus moves toward the process through which objects are presented as matters of security as well as to the consequences of the successful performance of such speech acts. The consequences of a successful "securitization" of an object are then described in terms of normalcy and exception. Successful securitization moves allow agents to go beyond or break rules that apply in times of normalcy.

Following the Copenhagen school, *any* object can thus become securitized, depending on how intensely a political community feels about it.[21]

---

[19] For an analysis along these lines see also Philippe Bourbeau (2014) "Moving Forward Together: Logics of the Securitisation Process, *Millennium: Journal of International Studies*, 43(1): 187–206.

[20] See Chapter 6.

[21] In this sense there is a resemblance between the Copenhagen conception of security and the conception of the political in the writings of Hans Morgenthau and Carl Schmitt (who revised his concept of the political after reading Morgenthau's critique on his earlier work). Morgenthau critiqued the idea that the political could be set apart as a separate sphere. Instead, he argued, the

This may indeed lead to breaking rules that would normally apply. However, in (international) law, it is quite often not necessary to *break* rules in the name of security, because the legal system itself contains metarules that determine how existing rules can be *set aside or suspended*. Examples are the previously mentioned clauses in international treaties that allow for suspension of rules when national security is at stake or the power of the Security Council to set aside almost all rules that would normally apply if this were deemed necessary to protect international security. The example of the Security Council is especially interesting, because the UN Charter does not contain any substantive criteria on what counts as a threat to international peace and security.[22] The determination of such a threat and what needs to be done about it is left to the Security Council itself. In line with the securitization approach, the Security Council can thus label practically any issue as a security issue and take measures that go beyond rules that normally apply. However, in doing so the Security Council does not break existing rules, but rather sets aside the application of other rules of international law insofar as they conflict with the measures taken by the council.

The logic of securitization is thus not foreign to international law, but part and parcel of one of its core documents, the United Nations Charter. However, the logic of securitization sits uneasily with what Judith Shklar has called the "ethos of legalism," an ethos that is still predominant among (international) lawyers today. Legalism, in Skhlar's account, is an attitude made up of four interrelated elements:[23] (a) It views social relationships in terms of rights and duties as determined by more general rules; (b) is treats law as something "out there," as a body of preexisting rules; (c) it believes in the possibility to separate law from nonlaw (morality, politics, esthetics, etc.); and (d) it fears and fights arbitrariness. To underscore the latter point, Shklar affirmatively quoted De Tocqueville's observation that

political should be regarded as an "intensity relation" that could cover any conceivable topic. Hans J. Morgenthau (1929). See also the discussion on the political in the works of Morgenthau and Schmitt in: Martti Koskenniemi (2004).

[22] There have been attempts to suggest a (nonexhaustive) list of criteria to define an act of aggression. In 1974 the General Assembly adopted Resolution 3314 (XXIX) on the Definition of Aggression, which was meant to guide the Security Council when it has to determine whether an act counts as an act of aggression.

[23] I have reconstructed these four elements on the basis of Shklar's account of legalism in (Shklar 1986, 1–28).

lawyers, "if they prize freedom much, they generally value legality still more: they are less afraid of tyranny than of arbitrary power."[24]

All four elements are still predominant in contemporary international law and legal scholarship (as could alre ady be inferred from the analysis in the second section of this chapter). By training, lawyers tend to conceptualize social relations in terms of rights and duties as determined by a preexisting legal order that can be set apart from rules of morality or political expediency. In addition, international law tends to define itself in opposition to international politics, where law is portrayed as the domain of the orderly and politics as the domain of power struggles and the arbitrary. Take, for example, the way in which one of the classical textbooks on international law sketches the differences between international law and international politics. After it has acknowledged that international law and international politics are intertwined, the textbook continues: "Power politics stresses competition, conflict and supremacy and adopts as its core the struggle for survival and influence. International law aims for harmony and the regulation of disputes. It attempts to create a framework, no matter how rudimentary, which can act as a kind of shock-absorber clarifying and moderating claims and endeavouring to balance interests. In addition, it sets out a series of principles declaring how states should behave" (Shaw 2003, 12).

Given the dominance of the ethos of legalism in international law, it is not surprising that international lawyers often have a quite ambivalent attitude toward the Security Council. On the one hand, the primacy of the Security Council and the priority of UN Charter obligations over competing obligations provide hierarchy and order to the international legal system.[25] On the other hand, the work of the Security Council is characterized by a logic of securitization that stands in sharp contrast to the spirit of legalism. The Security Council enjoys exceptional powers to respond in almost every way it sees fit to perceived threats to international security. Its responses are political and contextual, often ad hoc and selective; they take into account prudence and realpolitik; they are often based on classified information.

Recent debates on targeted sanctions attest to the ambivalence of international lawyers toward the Security Council. Since the late

[24] Shklar (1986, 15).
[25] For some, the UN Charter and the exceptional powers of the Security Council are even indications of a constitutional international order. For the most radical defense of this position see Bardo Fassbender (2009).

International law: Between legalism and securitisation 213

1990s the UN Security Council has started to list specific individuals and entities, on the basis of intelligence information that allegedly links them to terrorist activities. The Security Council puts all member states under an obligation to take measures against these individuals, in particular to freeze their assets, to restrict their freedom of movement, and to prevent arms trade. The measures adopted by the Security Council follow a logic of security, rather than one of criminal law enforcement. There is no formal determination of guilt by a court of law, according to principles of fair trial. Instead, individuals are put on the list on the basis of information obtained from secret services, and the sanctions against them are meant to preserve international peace and security, not to do justice. Under the strictures of the UN Charter, states are, at least prima facie, obliged to carry out the decisions of the Security Council, even if this would conflict with other international obligations, for example, stemming from human rights law.

However, for lawyers schooled with the idea that international relations are subjected to the rule of law, it is hard to swallow that international law would contain provisions that prioritize a logic of securitzation over a logic of legalism. This issue is all the more pressing for those who are professionally bound to uphold standards of human rights and the rule of law, for instance, in their capacity as judges of the European Court of Human Rights. Not surprisingly, therefore, the turn to targeted sanctions has spurred a huge debate on the possible limits on the Security Council and the importance of including human rights in matters of international security. Both scholars and courts have made several attempts to subject the Security Council to preexisting, independent legal standards. Let me briefly discuss a few of these attempts. The point of this brief discussion is neither to be exhaustive nor to assess the quality of the arguments involved; neither is the point to determine the effects of the interpretations on world politics. The point is merely to illustrate some of the ways in which international lawyers have sought to contain the logic of securitization through recourse to preexisting legal sources and accepted canons of interpretation.[26]

---

[26] For an extensive discussion of the different arguments put forward in debates on the legality and judicial review of Security Council resolutions see Stephan Hollenberg (2013). The examples discussed later are taken from this book, although my discussion differs in several respects from that by Hollenberg.

First, it has been argued that the Security Council cannot transgress so-called peremptory norms of international law (also called *ius cogens*).[27] Peremptory norms consist of a small group of core norms of the international order that are considered to be so important that all conflicting norms are rendered null and void. There is much controversy and uncertainty as to the emergence and scope of peremptory norms. For some these norms have an a priori character, not unlike norms of natural law; for others they originate in the will of the international community; for a third group peremptory norms eventually flow from the consent of sovereign states.[28] Yet, the existence of peremptory norms as such has been accepted by many scholars and courts – and there seems to be consensus around at least a small group of norms such as the prohibitions on genocide, slavery, torture, and aggression. If one accepts the existence of a group of superior core norms, this has direct consequences for the scope of the powers of the Security Council. The council would then be bound by a set of higher norms, and decisions that conflict with norms of *ius cogens* would be without legal effect. In practice, European courts have indeed found that the Security Council cannot transgress the boundaries of *ius cogens*.[29] Through recourse to *ius cogens* norms it is thus possible to identify some minimum limitations on the powers of the Security Council. In practice, however, it is quite unlikely that the Security Council would adopt decisions that contradict norms such as the prohibition of aggression, slavery, or torture. As the European Court confirmed, decisions that bypass the right to fair trial may be problematic from a human rights perspective; yet they do not constitute a violation of peremptory norms. Invoking *ius cogens* thus remains a principled, but also rather limited way to set limits to the powers of the council.

Second, and much more radically, it has been argued that the UN Charter itself puts the Security Council under an obligation to "discharge its duties in accordance with the Purposes and Principles

---

[27] See, for example, Erika de Wet (2004).
[28] For a discussion of the indeterminate foundations of *ius cogens* see Koskenniemi (2005).
[29] Case T-315/01 *Yassin Abdullah Kadi v Council of the European Union and Commission of the European Communities* [2005] ECR II-3649; *Youssef Mustapha Nada v Staatssekretariat für Wirtschaft* [2007] 1 A.45/2007.

of the United Nations" (as article 24 of the UN Charter states).[30] The principles and purposes of the UN, the argument continues, include human rights obligations as they have been further developed in global and regional human rights treaties. Since article 25 places states under an obligation to carry out decisions by the Security Council in accordance with the UN Charter, states would not be bound to carry out obligations that violate the provisions of those treaties. This argument fundamentally challenges the special position of the Security Council and the primacy of the logic of securtization as set out in chapter VII of the UN Charter. According to advocates of this position, the Security Council is no longer privileged to set aside rules that apply in times of normalcy; it would be turned into a body that can only bind states insofar as it respects their human rights obligations under international law.

The third argument I would like to discuss is put forward by the European Court of Human Rights in its function of guardian of the Convention on Human Rights. In the cases of *Al Jedda* and *Nada*, the European Court formulated the so-called presumption of compliance. According to this presumption, the Court is to work under the assumption that the Security Council does not intend to impose obligations upon states that are in violation of the fundamental principles of human rights. If the Security Council seeks to bypass existing human rights provisions, it should frankly acknowledge so and indicate this to the member states. The presumption of compliance thus raises the political stakes of bypassing human rights and requires the Security Council to identify itself as the body that privileges security considerations over the rights of individual citizens.

As said, the three positions discussed previously are by no means exhaustive. Several other arguments have been put forward in the debate on the legal limits and judicial review of Security Council resolutions. However, the three positions do indicate some of the typical ways in which lawyers and courts tend to counter a logic of securitization through a logic of legalism; insisting on *ius cogens*, putting states in a position where they have to review Security Council decisions for their compatibility with human rights, and introducing a presumption of compliance are all ways to structure social relations in accordance with pregiven rules, in terms of rights and duties and with

---

[30] For this argument see, inter alia, Andre Nollkaemper (2002).

legal limits to curtail the arbitrariness of political decision making. Whether such attempts are successful remains to be seen. They may very well push the Security Council to show more respect for legal limits and preexisting rights. However, they may also induce actors to bypass existing rules; to forgo legal obligations in the name of what they believe is an urgent issue of security. For those whose professional ethos is one of legalism, such speculations on conceivable effects may not be decisive; for them what counts is their fidelity to the international legal system.

The importance of the internal dimension

One of the main purposes of this edited volume is to spur interdisciplinary dialogue on the use of methods in security studies. This raises the question of what law has to offer to other disciplines in this respect. At first sight, this question seems problematic since it is very difficult for other disciplines to adopt what counts as a method in (international) law. As I have set out, international law is characterized by a relative lack of interest in reflection on method and theory, combined with a broad agreement that international legal arguments should be based on the sources of international law and the accepted canons of interpretation. None of these methodological tools have any place in other disciplines studying security. Moreover, international law is very much geared toward the production of normative statements within the system of law, an orientation that sets it apart from both empirical sciences and moral and political theory.

It will not be surprising, therefore, that much interdisciplinary scholarship involving international law has in effect been a hegemonic enterprise that defines away the internal, normative dimension of law.[31] This is done through a reformulation of the language of law into the language of, for example, game theory or rational choice. Normative validity then becomes "rational expectation," binding force becomes "chance of sanctions," the system of law becomes the "strategic environment," and so on.[32] Often, what passes as "interdisciplinarity" is in fact a takeover by political science, economics, or

---

[31] For critiques along these lines see, inter alia, Jan Klabbers (2009); Martti Koskenniemi (2004).

[32] An example of such reformulation can be found in: Jack L. Goldsmith and Eric A. Posner (2006).

sociology, to the detriment of the internal perspective on law. Now in and of itself there is nothing wrong with the application of external theories to law. It may (or may not) be very helpful to search for patterns, to lay bare power relations, to determine dominant cultural patterns etc.

What is problematic, however, is to claim that external perspectives on law are somehow superior to the way in which lawyers themselves understand and practice law. What is problematic is the belief that the turn to "scientific language" counts as emancipation from mystifying notions such as legal validity or normativity. In effect such approaches "take law out of international law," as Michael Byers has characterized it (Byers 1997, 201). This leads to sometimes naïve understandings of issues such as compliance, as if it is possible somehow to freeze the meaning of a legal provision and then to check objectively whether states have lived up to their obligations.[33] Moreover, it leads to a flattened idea of what international law does, as if international law only regulates relations between preexistent agents and has no role in *creating* the world we inhabit.[34] Finally, the attempt to denounce the internal and critical dimension of law is problematic from a normative point of view. It presents international law as primarily a management tool for those in power, as something that has instrumental value only. While it cannot be denied that legal provisions have often been used instrumentally by the powerful, this is not the whole story.[35] International legal provisions have also frequently been used to critique those in power, to open up spaces for contestation, and to redirect politics. This is only possible because international law is an interpretative practice, and not a state of affairs that can be measured and mobilized in an objective fashion.

This takes me back to the awkward silence mentioned at the beginning of this chapter. Most of all, this silence indicates an anxiety of international lawyers about the nature of their own field, based as it is on unstable foundations, and a mixture of normativity and facticity. And yet, it is only through these unstable foundations that

---

[33] For similar critiques see Jeffrey Dunoff and Mark Pollack (2012).
[34] Wouter Werner (2010).
[35] It is even possible to maintain that this *cannot* be the whole story. If law were simply an instrument for those in power, it would lose its capacity to generate legitimacy and thus cease to be useful as an instrument for those in power in the first place.

international law becomes intelligible as an ongoing argumentative practice in the first place. Attempts at normative closure or attempts to define away core notions such as "legal validity" simply miss the point of the practice of international law. If one wants to understand the ever-growing role of law in matters of international security, the way forward is not to purge international law from its internal perspective. On the contrary, it is to engage with the way the field of security is construed through the constant production and contestation of legal arguments.

References

Abdelal, R., and Kirshner, J. (1999) "Strategy, Economic Relations, and the Definition of National Interests." In Blanchard, J.-M. F., Mansfield, E. D. and Ripsman, N. M. (eds.) *Power and the Purse: The Political Economy of National Security*. London: Frank Cass, 119–156.

Abrahamsen, R., and Williams, M. C. (2011) *Security beyond the State: Private Security in International Politics*. Cambridge: Cambridge University Press.

Achen, C., and Snidal, D. (1989) "Rational Deterrence Theory and Comparative Case Studies." *World Politics* 41(2): 143–169.

Ackerly, B. A., Stern, M., and True, J. (eds.) (2006) *Feminist Methodologies for International Relations*. Cambridge: Cambridge University Press.

Adams, R. E., and Serpe, R. T. (2000) "Social Integration, Fear of Crime, and Life Satisfaction." *Sociological Perspectives* 43(4): 605–629.

Adler, E., and Pouliot, V. (eds.) (2011) *International Practices*. Cambridge: Cambridge University Press.

Adler-Nissen, R. (2012) *Bourdieu in International Relations*. London: Routledge.

Adler, E. (1997) "Seizing the Middle Ground: Constructivism in World Politics." *European Journal of International Relations* 3(3): 319–363.

(2012) "Constructivism and International Relations: Sources, Contributions, and Debates." In Carlsnaes, W., Risse, T., and Simmons, B. A. (eds.) *Handbook of International Relations*. London: Sage, 112–144.

Agamben, G. (2005) *State of Exception*. Chicago: University of Chicago Press.

Agnew, J. (1994) "The Territorial Trap: The Geographical Assumptions of International Relations Theory." *Review of International Political Economy* 1(1): 53–80.

Ahmad, M. (2002) "Homeland Insecurity: Racial Violence the Day after September 11." *Social Text* 20: 101–115.

Aisen, A., and Veiga, F. J. (2010) "How Does Political Instability Affect Economic Growth?" *IMF Working Paper*, No 11/12.

Albrecht P., and Moe L. W. (2014) "The Simultaneity of Authority in Hybrid Orders." *Peacebuilding* 11: 1–16.
Albro, R., Marcus, G., McNamara, L. A. *et al.* (2011) *Anthropologists in the Securityscape: Ethics, Practice, and Professional Identity*. Walnut Creek, CA: Left Coast Press.
Alford, R. (2011) "The Self-Judging WTO Security Exception." *Utah Law Review* (3): 697–759.
Alker, H. (2006) "On Securitization Politics As Contexted Texts and Talk." *Journal of International Relations and Development* 9(1): 70–80.
Alkire, S. (2003) "A Conceptual Framework for Human Security: Working Paper 2." *CRISE Working Paper. Centre for Research on Inequality*. Oxford: Human Security and Ethnicity.
Allhoff, F. (2012) *Terrorism, Ticking Time-Bombs, and Torture*. Chicago: University of Chicago Press.
Allport, G. W. (1960) "The Ego in Contemporary Psychology." In *Personality and Social Encounter: Selected Essays*. Boston: Beacon Press, 71–93.
(1954) *The Nature of Prejudice*. Oxford: Addison-Wesley.
Altheide, D. L. (1975) "The Irony of Security." *Urban Life* (now *Journal of Contemporary Ethnography*) 4: 179–196.
(2004) "Consuming Terrorism." *Symbolic Interactionism* 27: 289–308.
(2009) "Moral Panic: From Sociological Concept to Public Discourse." *Crime, Media, Culture: An International Journal* 5(1): 79–99.
Amenta, E. (2006) *When Movements Matter: The Townsend Plan and the Rise of Social Security*. Princeton, NJ: Princeton University Press.
Amodio, D. M. (2009) "Intergroup Anxiety Effects on the Control of Racial Stereotypes: A Psychoneuroendocrine Analysis." *Journal of Experimental Social Psychology* 45(1): 60–67.
Andersen, S. M., Saribay, A., and Thorpe, J. S. (2008) "Simple Kindness Can Go a Long Way: Relationships, Social Identity, and Engagement." *Social Psychology* 39(1): 59–69.
Anderson, B. (1983) *Imagined Communities: Reflections on the Origin and Spread of Nationalism*. London: Verso.
Anderson, E. S. (1999) "What Is the Point of Equality?" *Ethics* 109: 287–337.
Andreas, P. (2008) *Policing the Globe: Criminalisation and Crime Control in International Relations*. Oxford: Oxford University Press.
(2009) *Border Games: Policing the U.S.-Mexico divide*, 2nd ed. Ithaca, NY: Cornell University Press.
Anghie, A. (2007) *Imperialism, Sovereignty and the Making of International Law*. Cambridge: Cambridge University Press.

References

Appelbaum, E., Bernhardt, A. D., and Murnane, R. J. (eds.) (2006) *Low-Wage America: How Employers Are Reshaping Opportunity in the Workplace*. New York: Russell Sage Foundation.

Aradau, C., and van Munster, R. (2007) "Governing Terrorism through Risk: Taking Precautions (Un)Knowing the Future." *European Journal of International Relations* 13(1): 89–115.

Arends, J. F. M. (2008) "From Homer to Hobbes and Beyond – Aspects of "Security" in the European Tradition." In Brauch, H. G., Spring, Ú. O., Mesjasz, C. et al. (eds.) *Globalization and Environmental Challenges: Reconceptualizing Security in the 21st Century*. New York: Springer.

Arkin, R. M., Carroll, P. J., and Oleson, K. C. (2010) "Commentary: The End of the Beginning." In R. M. Arkin, K. C. Oleson, and P. J. Carroll (eds.) *Handbook of the Uncertain Self*. New York: Psychology Press, 444–448.

Aron, R. (1966) *Peace and War: A Theory of International Relations*. Weudenfield: Weudenfield and Nicholson.

Ashley, R., and Walker, R. B. J. (1990a) "Special Issue: Speaking the Language of Exile: Dissidence in International Studies." *International Studies Quarterly* 34(3): 259–417.

— (1990b) "Introduction: Speaking the Language of Exile: Dissident Thought in International Studies." *International Studies Quarterly* 34(3): 259–268.

Ayoob, M. (1995) *Third World Security Predicament: State Making, Regional Conflict and the International System*. Boulder, CO: Lynne Rienner.

Baechler, G., and Spillman, K. R. (eds.) (1996) *Environmental Degradation as a Cause of War: Regional and Country Studies*, Vols. 2 and 3. Bern: Swiss Peace Foundation/Swiss Federal Institute of Technology.

Baechler, G., Boege, V., Kloetzli, S. et al. (1996) *Environmental Degradation as a Cause of War: Environmental Conflicts in the Third World and Ways for Their Peaceful Resolution*, Vol. 1. Bern: Swiss Peace Foundation/Swiss Federal Institute of Technology.

Bail, C. A. (2012) "The Fringe Effect: Civil Society Organizations and the Evolution of Media Discourse about Islam since the September 11th Attacks." *American Sociological Review* 77: 855–879.

Bajc, V. (2013) "Sociological Reflections on Security through Surveillance." *Sociological Forum* 28: 615–23.

Baker, J. C., Lachman, B. E., Frelinger, D. R. et al. (2004) *Mapping the Risks: Assessing the Homeland Security Implications of Publicly Available Geospatial Information*. Santa Monica: Rand Corporation.

Baker, T., and Simon, J. (eds.) (2002) *Embracing Risk: The Changing Culture of Insurance and Responsibility*. Chicago: University of Chicago Press.

Bakker, K. and Bridge, G. (2006) "Material Worlds? Resource Geographies and the Matter of Nature." *Progress in Human Geography* 30(1): 5–27.

Bakker, K. (2012) "Water Security: Research Challenges and Opportunities." *Science* 337(6097): 914–915.

Baldwin, D. (1985) *Economic Statecraft*. Princeton, NJ: Princeton University Press.

(1995) "Security Studies and the End of the Cold War." *World Politics* 48 (1): 117–141.

(1997) "The Concept of Security." *Review of International Studies* 23(1): 5–26.

Baldwin, E. R. (2003) "Staking Claim to Employment Law Remedies for Undocumented Immigrant Workers After Hoffman Plastic Compounds, Inc. v. NLRB." *Seattle University Law Review* 27: 233–271.

Balzacq, T. (2005) "The Three Faces of Securitization: Political Agency, Audience and Context." *European Journal of International Relations* 11(2): 171–201.

(2011) "Enquiries into Methods: A New Framework for Securitization Analysis." In Balzacq, T. (ed.) *Securitization Theory: How Security Problems and Dissolve*. London: Routledge, 31–54.

(2014) "Discourse Analysis and Process-Tracing: The Significance of Triangulation to Critical Security Studies." *Critical Studies on Security* 2(3): 377–381.

Bandura, A. (1999) "Moral Disengagement in the Perpetration of Inhumanities." *Personality and Social Psychology Review* 3(3): 193–209.

Bankston, III, C. L., Barnshaw, J., Bevc, C. et al. (2010) *The Sociology of Katrina: Perspectives on a Modern Catastrophe*, 2nd ed. Lanham, MD: Rowman & Littlefield.

Bar-Tal, D. (2007) "Sociopsychological Foundations of Intractable Conflicts." *American Behavioral Scientist* 50(11): 1430–1453.

(2009) "Reconciliation As a Foundation of Culture of Peace." In de Rivera J. (ed.) *Handbook on Building Cultures of Peace*. New York: Springer, 363–377.

Bar-Tal, D., and Jacobson, D. (1998) "A Psychological Perspective on Security." *Applied Psychology: An International Review* 47(1): 59–71.

Barlow, F., Louis, W. R., and Hewstone, M. (2009) "Rejected! Cognitions of Rejection and Intergroup Anxiety As Mediators of the Impact of Cross-Group Friendships on Prejudice." *British Journal of Social Psychology* 48(3): 389–405.

Barnes, T. J., and Minca, C. (2013) "Nazi Spatial Theory: the Dark Geographies of Carl Schmitt and Walter Christaller." *Annals of the Association of American Geographers* 103(3): 669–687.

Barnes, T. J., and Farish, M. (2006) "Between Regions: Science, Militarism, and American Geography from World War to Cold War." *Annals of the Association of American Geographers* 96(4): 807–826.

Barnes, T. J. (2008) "Geography's Underworld: The Military-Industrial Complex, Mathematical Modelling and the Quantitative Revolution." *Geoforum* 39(1): 3–16.

Barnett, J., and Adger, W. N. (2007) "Climate Change, Human Security and Violent Conflict." *Political Geography* 26(6): 639–655.

Barnett, J. (2001) *The Meaning of Environmental Security: Ecological Politics and Policy in the New Security Era*. London: Zed Books.

Barnett, M., and Duvall, R. (eds.) (2005) *Power in Global Governance*. Cambridge: Cambridge University Press.

Barrie, D. G. (2008) "Patrick Colquhoun, the Scottish Enlightenment and Police Reform in Glasgow in the Late Eighteenth Century." *Crime, Histoire and Sociétés/Crime, History and Societies* 12(2): 59–79.

Baruzzi, A. (2001) "Immanuel Kant 1712–1778." In Denzer, H. and Maier, H. (eds.) *Klassiker des Politischen Denkens*. Nördlingen: C. H. Beck.

Bayley, D., and Shearing, C. (2001) *The New Structure of Policing*. Washington, DC: National Institute of Justice.

Baylis, J., Smith, S., and Owens, P. (2011) *The Globalization of World Politics*. Oxford: Oxford University Press.

Bayuk, J. L., Haeley, J., Rohmeyer, P. et al. (2012) *Cyber Security Policy Guidebook*. Hoboken, NJ: John Wiley & Sons.

Beattie, J. M. (2006) "Early Detection: The Bow Street Runners in Late Eighteenth-Century London." In Emsley, C. and Shpayer-Makov, H. (eds.) *Police Detectives in History*, 1750–1950. Aldershot: Ashgate, 15–32.

Beccaria, C. (1995) *On Crimes and Punishments and Other Writings*, Cambridge: Cambridge University Press.

(1996) "On Crimes and Punishments." In Muncie, J., and McLaughlin, E. (eds.) *Criminological Perspectives: A Reader*. London: Thousand Oaks, 15–24.

Beck, C., and Miner, E. (2013) "Who Gets Designated a Terrorist and Why?" *Social Forces* 91: 837–872.

Beck, C. J. (2008) "The Contribution of Social Movement Theory to Understanding Terrorism." *Sociology Compass* 2(5): 1565–1581.

Beck, U. (1992) *Risk Society: Towards a New Modernity*. New York: Sage.

(2000) "Risk Society Revisited: Theory, Politics and Research Programmes." In Adams, B., Beck, U., and Van Loon, J. (eds.) *The Risk Society and Beyond: Critical Issues for Social Theory*. London: Sage, 211–229.

Becker, H. S. (1963) *Outsiders*. New York: Free Press of Glencoe.

Becker, J. C., Wright, S. C., Lubensky, M. E. *et al.* (2013) "Friend or Ally: Whether Cross-Group Contact Undermines Collective Action Depends on What Advantaged Group Members Say (or Don't Say)." *Personality and Social Psychology Bulletin* 39(4): 442–455.

Beckett, K., and Herbert, S. (2009) *Banished: The New Social Control in Urban America.* Oxford: Oxford University Press.

Béland, D. (2005) *Social Security: History and Politics from the New Deal to the Privatization Debate.* Lawrence: University Press of Kansas.

Bender, D. E., and Greenwald, R. A. (eds.) (2003) *Sweatshop USA: The American Sweatshop in Historical and Global Perspective.* New York: Routledge.

Bennett, D. S., and Stam, A. C. (2004) *The Behavioral Origins of War*, Ann Arbor: University of Michigan Press.

Bentham, J. (1843) "Principles of the Civil Code." In Hildreth, R. (ed.) *The Theory of Legislation.* London: Trubner.

Benyshek, D. C., and Watson, J. T. (2006) "Exploring the Thrifty Genotype's Food-Shortage Assumptions: A Cross-Cultural Comparison of Ethnographic Accounts of Food Security among Foraging and Agricultural Societies." *American Journal of Physical Anthropology* 131: 120–126.

Bergesen, A. H., and Han, Yi (2006) "New Directions for Terrorism Research." *International Journal of Comparative Sociology* 46: 133–151.

Berkes, F., Colding, J., and Folke, C. (eds.) (2003) *Navigating Social-Ecological Systems: Building Resilience for Complexity and Change.* Cambridge: Cambridge University Press.

Bernazzoli, R. M., and Flint, C. (2009) "From Militarization to Securitization: Finding a Concept That Works." *Political Geography* 28(8): 449–450.

Bernstein, P. L. (1996) *Against the Gods: The Remarkable Story of Risk.* New York: John Wiley & Sons.

Bevir, M., and Rhodes, R. A. W. (2002) "Interpretive Theory." In Marsh D. and Stoker G. (eds.) *Theory and Methods in Political Science.* Basingstoke: Palgrave Macmillan, 131–152.

Bhambra, G. K. (2007) *Rethinking Modernity: Postcolonialism and the Sociological Imagination.* Basingstoke: Palgrave Macmillan.

Bialasiewicz, L., Campbell, D., Elden, S. *et al.* (2007) "Performing Security: The Imaginative Geographies of Current US Strategy." *Political Geography* 26(4): 405–422.

Bigo, D. (2002) "Security and Immigration: Toward a Critique of the Governmentality of Unease." *Alternatives* 27(2): 63–92.

(1996) *Polices en Réseaux: L'expérience europeenne.* Paris: Presses de Sciences Po.

Bilali, R., Tropp, L. R., and Dasgupta, N. (2012) "Attributions of Responsibility and Perceived Harm in the Aftermath of Mass Violence." *Peace and Conflict: Journal of Peace Psychology* 18(1): 21–39.

Binder, J., Zagefka, H., Brown, R. *et al.* (2009) "Does Contact Reduce Prejudice or Does Prejudice Reduce Contact? A Longitudinal Test of the Contact Hypothesis among Majority and Minority Groups in Three European Countries." *Journal of Personality and Social Psychology* 96 (4): 843–856.

Birks, D. J. (2005) "Computational Criminology: A Multi-Agent Simulation of Volume Crime Activity." *British Society of Criminology Conference*, July 4, 2005, University of Leeds, UK.

Bittner, E. (1973) *The Functions of the Police in Modern Society*. Brandeis University, National Institute of Mental Health, Center for Studies of Crime and Delinquency.

Blanchard, J.-M. F., Mansfield, E. D., and Ripsman, N. M. (eds.) (1999) *Power and the Purse: The Political Economy of National Security*. London: Frank Cass.

Bloch, A., Sigona, N., and Zetter, R. (2011) "Migration Routes and Strategies of Young Undocumented Migrants in England: A Qualitative Perspective." *Ethnic and Racial Studies* 34(8): 1286–1302.

Blundell-Wignall, A., Hu, Y., and Yermo, J. (2008) "Sovereign Wealth and Pension Fund Issues." *OECD Working Papers on Insurance and Private Pensions*, No. 14, OECD.

Bobo, L. D. (1999) "Prejudice as Group Position: Microfoundations of a Sociological Approach to Racism and Race Relations." *Journal of Social Issues* 55(3): 445–472.

Bohle, H. G., Downing, T. E., and Watts, M. J. (1994) "Climate Change and Social Vulnerability: Toward a Sociology and Geography of Food Insecurity." *Global Environmental Change* 4(1): 37–48.

Booth, K., and Wheeler, N. J. (2008) *The Security Dilemma: Fear, Cooperation and Trust in World Politics*. London: Palgrave.

Booth, K. (1991) "Security and Emancipation." *Review of International Studies* 17(4): 313–327.

(2005) "Beyond Critical Security Studies." In Booth, K. (ed.) *Critical Security Studies and World Politics*. London: Lynne Rienner, 259–278.

(2007) *Theory of World Security*. Cambridge: Cambridge University Press.

Bosniak, L. (1998) "The Citizenship of Aliens." *Social Text* 16(3): 29–35.

(2006) *The Citizen and the Alien: Dilemmas of Contemporary Membership*. Princeton, NJ: Princeton University Press.

Bourbeau, P. (2011) *The Securitization of Migration: A Study of Movement and Order*. London: Routledge.

(2013) "Resiliencism: Premises and Promises in Securitization Research." *Resilience: International Policies, Practices and Discourses* 1(1): 3–17.

(2014) "Moving Forward Together: Logics of the Securitization Process." *Millennium: Journal of International Studies* 43(1): 187–206.

(2015a) "Resiliencism and Security Studies: Initiating a dialogue." In Balzacq, T. (ed.) *Contesting Security: Strategies and Logics*. London: Routledge, 173–188.

(2015b) "Resilience and International Politics: Premises, Debates and Agenda." *International Studies Review*, 17(3): early-view.

Bourhis, R. Y., Sachdev, I., and Gagnon, A. (1994) "Intergroup Research with the Tajfel Matrices: Methodological Notes." In Zanna, M. P. and Olson, J. M. (eds.) *The Psychology of Prejudice: The Ontario Symposium*. Hillsdale, NJ: Erlbaum, 209–232.

Bowles, P., and MacPhail, F. (2008) "Introduction to the Special Issue on Pathways from Casual Work to Economic Security: Canadian and International Perspectives." *Social Indicators Research* 88(1): 1–13.

Boyce, J. K., and O'Donnell, M. (eds.) (2007) *Peace and the Public Purse: Economic Policies for Postwar Statebuilding*. Boulder, CO: Lynne Rienner.

Brady, D. (2005) "The Welfare State and Relative Poverty in Rich Western Democracies, 1967–1997." *Social Forces* 83(4): 1329–1364.

Branscombe, N. R., Ellemers, N., Spears, R. *et al.* (1999) "The Context and Content of Social Identity Threat." In Ellemers, N., Spears, R., and Doosje B. (eds.) *Social Identity: Context, Commitment, Content*. Oxford: Blackwell Science, 35–58.

Brantingham, P. J., and Brantingham P. L. (1981) *Environmental Criminology*. Beverly Hills, CA: Sage.

Brauch, H. G. (2008) "Securitization of Space and Referent Objects." In Brauch, H. G., Spring, Ú. O., Mesjasz, C. *et al.* (eds.) *Globalization and Environmental Challenges: Reconceptualizing Security in the 21st Century*. New York: Springer, 323–344.

Braudel, F. (1979) *Civilization and Capitalism 15th–18th Century*. Vol. III. *The Perspective of the World* (translated by S. Reynolds). Berkeley: University of California Press.

Brecher, R. (2007) *Torture and the Ticking Bomb*. Oxford: Blackwell.

Brewer, M. B. (1999) "The Psychology of Prejudice: Ingroup Love or Outgroup Hate?" *Journal of Social Issues* 55(3): 429–444.

Brewer, M. B., von Hippel, W., and Gooden, M. P. (1999) "Diversity and Organizational Identity: the Problem of Entrée after Entry." In Prentice, D. A., and Miller, D. T. (eds.) *Cultural Divides: Understanding and*

Overcoming Group Conflict. New York: Russell Sage Foundation, 337–363.

Brock, G. (2009) *Global Justice: a Cosmopolitan Account*. Oxford: Oxford University Press.

Brodeur, J. P. (1983) "High and Low Policing: Remarks about the Policing of Political Activities." *Social Problems* 30(5): 507–520.

Brooks, S. G. (1997) "Dueling Realisms (Realism in International Relations)." *International Organization* 51(3): 445–477.

Brooks, S. G., and Wohlforth, W. C. (2008) *World Out of Balance: International Relations and the Challenge of American Primacy*. Princeton, NJ: Princeton University Press.

Brotherton, D., and Kretsedemas, P. (2008) *Keeping Out the Other: A Critical Introduction to Immigration Enforcement Today*. New York: Columbia University Press.

Brown, R. (2000) "Social Identity Theory: Past Achievements, Current Problems and Future Challenges." *European Journal of Social Psychology* 30(6): 745–778.

Brown, T. (2011) "'Vulnerability Is Universal': Considering the Place of 'Security' and 'Vulnerability' within Contemporary Global Health Discourse." *Social Science and Medicine* 72(3): 319–326.

Browning, C. S., and McDonald, M. (2013) "The Future of Critical Security Studies: Ethics and the Politics of Security." *European Journal of International Relations* 19(2): 235–255.

De Bruin, B. (2010) "The Liberal Value of Privacy." *Law and Philos* 29: 505–534.

Bruneau, E. G., and Saxe, R. (2012) "The Power of Being Heard: The Benefits of 'Perspective-Giving' in the Context of Intergroup Conflict." *Journal of Experimental Social Psychology* 48(4): 855–866.

Bryan, J. (2010) "Force Multipliers: Geography, Militarism, and the Bowman Expeditions." *Political Geography* 29(8): 414–416.

Bubandt, N. (2005) "Vernacular Security: The Politics of Feeling Safe in Global, National and Local Worlds." *Security Dialogue* 36(3): 275–296.

Buchanan, J. M. (1966) "An Individualistic Theory of Political Process." In Easton, David (ed.) *Varieties in Political Theory*. Englewood Cliffs, NJ: Prentice-Hall, 25–37.

Bueno de Mesquita, B., Smith, A., Siverson, R. M. *et al.* (2003) *The Logic of Political Survival*. Cambridge, MA: MIT Press.

Buhaug, H., and Gates, S. (2002) "The Geography of Civil War." *Journal of Peace Research* 39(4): 417–433.

Buonfino, A. (2004) "Between Unity and Plurality: The Politicization and Securitization of the Discourse of Immigration in Europe." *New Political Science* 26: 23–49.

Burke, A. (2007) *Beyond Security, Ethics and Violence: War against the Other*. London: Routledge.

Burrell, J. (2010) "In and Out of Rights: Security, Migration, and Human Rights Talk in Postwar Guatemala." *Journal of Latin American and Caribbean Anthropology* 15(l): 90–115.

Burris, S., Drahos, P. and Shearing, C. (2005) "Nodal Governance." *Australian Journal of Legal Philosophy* 30: 30–58.

Burton, I., Kates, R. W., and White, G. F. (eds.) (1978) *The Environment as Hazard*. New York: Guilford Press.

Butler, J. (2011) *Bodies That Matter: On the Discursive Limits of Sex*. London: Taylor & Francis.

Buzan, B. (1991) *People, States and Fear: An Agenda for International Security Studies in the Post-Cold War Era*. Harvester Wheatsheaf: Lynne Reinner.

(1994) "The Interdependence of Security and Economic Issues in the 'New World Order.'" In Stubbs, R., and Underhill, G. R. D. (eds.) *Political Economy and the Changing Global Order*. New York: St Martin's Press, 89–102.

Buzan, B., and Hansen, L. (2009) *The Evolution of International Security Studies*. Cambridge: Cambridge University Press.

Buzan, B., and Little, R. (2000) *International Systems in World History: Remaking the Study of International Relations*. Oxford: Oxford University Press.

Buzan, B., Waever, O., and De Wilde, J. (1998) *Security: A New Framework for Analysis*. Boulder, CO: Lynne Reiner.

Byers, M. (1997) "Taking the Law Out of International Law: A Critique of the 'Iterative Perspective.'" *Harvard International Law Journal* 38: 201–206.

c.a.s.e. collective (2006) "Critical Approaches to Security in Europe: A Networked Manifesto." *Security Dialogue* 37(4): 443–487.

Caduff, C. (2012) "The Semiotics of Security: Infectious Disease Research and the Biopolitics of Informational Bodies in the United States." *Cultural Anthropology* 27: 333–357.

Cainkar, L. (2004) "Post 9/11 Domestic Policies Affecting US Arabs and Muslims: A Brief Review." *Comparative Studies of South Asia, Africa and the Middle East* 24: 245–248.

Calavita, K. (2005) *Immigrants at the Margins: Law, Race, and Exclusion in Southern Europe*. Cambridge: Cambridge University Press.

Caldeira, T. P. R. (1996) "Fortified Enclaves: The New Urban Segregation." *Public Culture* 8: 303–328.

Caldeira, T. (2000) *City of Walls: Crime, Segregation, and Citizenship in São Paulo*. Berkeley: University of California Press.

Campbell, D. (1998) *Writing Security: United States Foreign Policy and the Politics of Identity*. Minneapolis: University of Minnesota Press.

Campbell, D. T. (1957) "Factors Relevant to the Validity of Experiments in Social Settings." *Psychological Bulletin* 54(4): 297–312.

Canetti-Nisim, D., Halperin, E., Sharvit, K. *et al.* (2009) "A New Stress-Based Model of Political Extremism: Personal Exposure to Terrorism, Psychological Distress, and Exclusionist Political Attitudes." *Journal of Conflict Resolution* 53(3): 363–389.

Carlsnaes, W. (1992) "The Agency-Structure Problem in Foreign Policy Analysis." *International Studies Quarterly* 36(3): 245–270.

Carr, E. H. (1962) *The Twenty Years Crisis, 1919–1939: An Introduction to the Study of International Relations*, 2nd ed. London: Macmillan.

Carroll, P. J., Wichman, A. L., and Arkin, R. M. (2006) "Security in the Aftermath of 9/11." *Basic and Applied Social Psychology*, 28(4): 289–290.

Cassese, A. (2001) "Terrorism Is Also Disrupting Some Crucial Legal Categories of International Law." *European Journal of International Law* 12(5): 993–1001.

Caton, S. C., and Zacka, B. (2010) "Abu Ghraib, the Security Apparatus, and the Performativity of Power." *American Ethnologist* 37(2): 203–211.

Chakrabarty, D. (2009) "The Climate of History: Four Theses." *Critical Inquiry* 35(2): 197–222.

Chavez, L. (2008) *The Latino Threat: Constructing Immigrants, Citizens and the Nation*. Stanford, CA: Stanford University Press.

Checkel, J. T. (2008) Process Tracing. In Klotz, A. and Prakash, D., (eds.) *Qualitative Methods in International Relations*. Basingstoke: Palgrave Macmillan: 114–130.

  (2012) "Theoretical Pluralism in IR: Possibilities and Limits." In Carlsnaes, W., Risse, T., and Simmons, B. A. (eds.) *Handbook of International Relations*, 2nd ed. London: Sage, 220–242.

Chernoff, F. (2007) *Theory and Metatheory in International Relations: Concepts and Contending Accounts*. Basingstoke: Palgrave Macmillan.

Clark, J. H. (2013) "'My Life Is Like a Novel': Embodied Geographies of Security in Southeast Turkey." *Geopolitics* 18(4): 835–855.

Clark, M. S., and Lemay, E. R. (2010) "Close Relationships." In Fiske, S. T., Gilbert, D. T., and Lindzey, G. (eds.) *Handbook of Social Psychology*, Vol. 2, 5th ed. Hoboken, NJ: John Wiley & Sons, 898–940.

Clarke, L. (1999) *Mission Improbable: Using Fantasy Documents to Tame Disaster*. Chicago: University of Chicago Press.

Clarke, R. V. G. (1997) *Situational Crime Prevention*. Monsey, NY: Criminal Justice Press.

Cohen, S. (2001) *States of Denial: Knowing about Atrocities and Suffering.* Cambridge: Polity.

Cohn, C. (ed.). (2012) *Women and Wars: Contested Histories, Uncertain Futures.* Cambridge: Polity.

Coleman, M., and Grove, K. (2009) "Biopolitics, Biopower, and the Return of Sovereignty." *Environment and Planning. D, Society and Space* 27(3): 489–507.

Collier, P., and Hoeffler, A. (2002) "On the Incidence of Civil War in Africa." *Journal of Conflict Resolution* 46(1): 13–28.

(2004) "Greed and Grievance in Cicil War." *Oxford Economic Papers* 56: 563–595.

Collier, S. J., and Lakoff, A. (2008) "The Vulnerability of Vital Systems: How 'Critical Infrastructure' Became a Security Problem." In Dunn, M. and Kristensen, K. S. (eds.) *Securing 'the Homeland': Critical Infrastructure, Risk and (In)Security.* London: Routledge.

Collier, S. J., Lakoff, A., and Rabinow, P. (2004) "Biosecurity: Towards an Anthropology of the Contemporary." *Anthropology Today* 20: 3–7.

Collins, A. (2013) *Contemporary Security Studies*, 3rd ed. Oxford: Oxford University Press.

Collins, R. (2008) *Violence: A Micro-Sociological Theory.* Princeton, NJ: Princeton University Press.

Cooley, A. (2008) *Base Politics: Democratic Change and the US Military Overseas.* Ithaca, NY: Cornell University Press.

Cooper, M., and Walker, J. (2011) "Genealogies of Resilience: From Systems Ecology to the Political Economy of Crisis Adaptation." *Security Dialogue* 41.

Cooper, M. (2010) "Turbulence: Between Financial and Environmental Crisis." *Theory, Culture, and Society* 27: 1–24.

Cornelius, W. A. (2004) *"Controlling "Unwanted" Immigration: Lessons from the United States, 1993–2004."* Working Paper Number 92, Center for Comparative Immigration Studies. San Diego: University of California.

Cornish, D. B. (1994) "The Procedural Analysis of Offending and Its Relevance for Institutional Prevention." *Crime Prevention Studies* 3: 151–196.

Coutin, S. B. (1995) "Smugglers or Samaritans in Tucson, Arizona: Producing and Contesting Legal Truth." *American Ethnologist* 22(3): 549–571.

(1999) "Citizenship and Clandestiny among Salvadoran Immigrants." *Political and Legal Anthropology Review* 22(2): 53–63.

(2000) *Legalizing Moves: Salvadoran Immigrants' Struggle for U.S. Residency*. Ann Arbor: University of Michigan Press.

(2003) "Borderlands, Illegality and the Spaces of Non-Existence." In Perry, R., and Maurer, B. (eds.) *Globalization and Governmentalities*. Minneapolis: University of Minnesota Press, 171–202.

(2007) *Nations of Emigrants: Shifting Boundaries of Citizenship in El Salvador and the United States*. Ithaca, NY: Cornell University Press.

Cowen, D. and Smith, N. (2009) "After Geopolitics? From the Geopolitical Social to Geoeconomics." *Antipode* 41(1): 22–48.

Cox, R. W. (1986) "Social Forces, States and World Orders: Beyond International Relations Theory." In Keohane, R. O. (ed.) *Neorealism and Its Critics*. New York: Columbia University Press, 204–253.

Crampton, J. W., Roberts, S. M., and Poorthuis, A. (2014) "The New Political Economy of Geographical Intelligence." *Annals of the Association of American Geographers* 104(1): 196–214.

Crang, M., and Graham, S. (2007) "Sentient Cities: Ambient Intelligence and the Politics of Urban Space." *Information, Communication and Society* 10(6): 789–817.

Critchley, T. A. (1978) *A History of Police in England and Wales*. London: Constable.

Crocker, J., and Garcia, J. A. (2009) "Downward and Upward Spirals in Intergroup Interactions: The Role of Egosystem and Ecosystem Goals." In Nelson, T. D. (ed.) *Handbook of Prejudice, Stereotyping, and Discrimination*. New York: Psychology Press, 229–245.

Cuomo, D. (2013) "Security and Fear: The Geopolitics of Intimate Partner Violence Policing." *Geopolitics* 18(4): 856–874.

Curley, M. G., and Wong, S.-l. (eds.) (2008) *Security and Migration in Asia: The Dynamics of Securitisation*. London: Routledge.

Cutter, S., Richardson, D. B., and Wilbanks, T. J. (2003) *The Geographic Dimension of Terrorism*. London: Routledge.

Dalby, S. (1988) "Geopolitical Discourse: The Soviet Union as Other." *Alternatives* 13(4): 415–442.

(2002) *Environmental Security*. Minneapolis: University of Minnesota Press.

(2009) *Security and Environmental Change*. Cambridge: Polity.

Dalby, S., and O'Tuathail, G. (2002) *Rethinking Geopolitics*, Routledge.

Davis, R. C., and Erez, E. (1998) *Immigrant Populations as Victims: Toward a Multicultural Criminal Justice System*. National Institute of Justice: Research in Brief.

De Genova, N. (2002) "Migrant 'Illegality' and Deportability in Everyday Life." *Annual Review of Anthropology* 31: 419–447.

(2005) *Working the Boundaries: Race, Space and "Illegality" in Mexican Chicago.* Durham, NC: Duke University Press.

(2007) "The Production of Culprits: From Deportability to Detainability in the Aftermath of 'Homeland Security.'" *Citizenship Studies* 11: 421–448.

(2009) "Conflicts of Mobility, and the Mobility of Conflict: Rightlessness, Presence, Subjectivity, Freedom." *Subjectivity* 29: 445–466.

(2010) "The Queer Politics of Migration: Reflections on 'Illegality' and Incorrigibility." *Studies in Social Justice* 4(2): 101–126.

de Goede, M. (2008) "Beyond Risk: Premediation and the Post 9/11 Security Imagination." *Security Dialogue* 39(2–3): 155–176.

Deal, J. L. (2010) "Torture by Cieng: Ethical Theory Meets Social Practice among the Dinka Agaar of South Sudan." *American Anthropologist* 112(4): 563–575.

Debrix, F., and Barder, A. (2011) *Beyond Biopolitics: Theory, Violence, and Horror in World Politics.* London: Routledge.

Déclaration des droits de l'homme et du citoyen, 1789.

Del Rosso, J. (2011) "The Textual Mediation of Denial: Congress, Abu Ghraib, and the Construction of an Isolated Incident." *Social Problems* 58: 165–188.

(2014) "Textuality and the Social Organization of Denial: Abu Ghraib, Guantanamo, and the Meanings of U.S. Interrogation Policies." *Sociological Forum* 29: 52–74.

Der Derian, J., and Shapiro, M. J. (1989) *International/Intertextual Relations: Postmodern Readings of World Politics.* Lexington, MA: Lexington Books.

Der Derian, J. (1995) "The Value of Security: Hobbes, Marx, Nietzsche, and Baudrillard." In Lipschultz, R. D. (ed.) *On Security.* New York: Columbia University Press, 24–45.

Dershowitz, A. (2004) "Tortured Reasoning." In Levinson, S. *Torture: A Collection.* Oxford: Oxford University Press, 257–280.

Deudney, D. (1990) "The Case against Linking Environmental Degradation and National Security." *Millennium: Journal of International Studies* 19(3): 461–476.

(2007) *Bounding Power: Republican Security Theory from the Polis to the Global Village.* Princeton, NJ: Princeton University Press.

Devine, P. G., and Vasquez, K. A. (1998) "The Rocky Road to Positive Intergroup Relations." In Eberhardt, J., and Fiske, S. T. (eds.) *Confronting Racism: the Problem and the Response.* Thousand Oaks, CA: Sage, 234–262.

de Wet, E. (2004) *The Chapter VII Powers of the United Nations Security Council.* Oxford: Hart.

Diener, A. C., and Hagen, J. (2009) "Theorizing Borders in a 'Borderless World': Globalization, Territory and Identity." *Geography Compass* 3(3): 1196–1216.

Dillon, M., and Reid, J. (2009) *The Liberal Way of War: Killing to Make Life Live*. London: Routledge.

Dittmer, J., and Dodds, K. (2008) "Popular Geopolitics Past and Future: Fandom, Identities and Audiences." *Geopolitics* 13(3): 437–457.

Ditton, J. (1979) *Controlology: Beyond the New Criminology*. London: MacMillan.

Dixon, J., Durrheim, K., Tredoux, C. G. et al. (2010) "Challenging the Stubborn Core of Opposition to Equality: Racial Contact and Policy Attitudes." *Political Psychology* 31(6): 831–855.

Dixon, J., Durrheim, K., Tredoux, C. et al. (2010) "A Paradox of Integration, Interracial Contact, Prejudice Reduction, and Perceptions of Racial Discrimination." *Journal of Social Issues* 66(2): 401–416.

Dixon, J., Tropp, L. R., Durrheim, K. et al. (2010) "'Let Them Eat Harmony': Prejudice-Reduction Strategies and Attitudes of Historically Disadvantaged Groups." *Current Directions in Psychological Science* 19(2): 76–80.

Dombrowski, P. (2005) *Guns and Butter – the Political Economy of International Security*. London: Lynne Rienner.

Donnan, H., and Wilson, T. M. (eds.) (2010) *Borderlands: Ethnographic Approaches to Security, Power, and Identity*. Lanham, MD: University Press of America.

Doosje, B., Loseman, A., and Van den Bos, K. (2013) "Determinants of Radicalization of Islamic Youth in the Netherlands: Personal Uncertainty, Perceived Injustice, and Perceived Group Threat." *Journal of Social Issues* 69(3): 586–604.

Dos Santos, T. (1996) "The Structure of Dependence." In Goddard, C. R., Passé-Smith, J. T., and Conklin, J. (eds.) *International Political Economy: State-Market Relations in the Changing Global Order*. Boulder, CO: Lynne Rienner, 149–165.

Doty, R. L. (2007) "States of Exception on the Mexico–U.S. Border: Security, "Decisions" and Civilian Border Patrols." *International Political Sociology* 1(2): 113–137.

Dovidio, J. F., Gaertner, S. L., and Saguy, T. (2009) "Commonality and the Complexity of 'We': Social Attitudes and Social Change." *Personality and Social Psychology Review* 13(1): 3–20.

Dovidio, J. F., Saguy, T., West, T. V. et al. (2012) "Divergent Intergroup Perspectives." In Tropp, L. R. (ed.) *The Oxford Handbook of Intergroup Conflict*. New York: Oxford University Press, 158–175.

Dowler, L., and Sharp, J. (2001) "A Feminist Geopolitics?" *Space and Polity* 5(3): 165–176.

Downs, A. (1957) "An Economic Theory of Political Action in a Democracy." *The Journal of Political Economy* 65(2): 135–150.

Doyle, M. (1986) "Liberalism and World Politics." *American Political Science Review* 80(4): 1151–1163.

Dryzek, J. S. (2006) "Revolutions without Enemies: Key Transformations in Political Science." *American Political Science Review* 100(4): 487–492.

Dubartell, D. (2006) "Computer-Mediated Communication: Human-to-Human Communication across the Internet." *Journal of Linguistic Anthropology* 16(2): 284–285.

Dunn Cavelty, M. (2013) "From Cyber-Bombs to Political-Fallout: Threat Representations with an Impact." *International Studies Review* 15(1): 105–122.

Dunne, T., and Schmidt, B. C. (2011) "Realism." In Baylis, J., Smith, S., and Owens, P. et al. (eds.) *The Globalization of World Politics*. Oxford: Oxford University Press, 84–99.

Dunoff, J., and Pollack M. (2012) *What Can International Relations Learn from International Law?* Temple University Legal Studies Research Paper No. 2012-14: http://papers.ssrn.com/sol3/papers.cfm?abstract_id=2037299.

Dupont, B. (2008) "Hacking the Panopticon: Distributed Online Surveillance and Resistance." *Sociology of Crime Law and Deviance* 10: 259–280.

(2013) "The Proliferation of Cyber Security Strategies and Their Implications for Privacy." In Benyekhlef, K., and Mitjans E. (eds.) *Circulation international de l'information et securitie*. Montreal: Les Editions Themis, 67–80.

Elcioglu, E. F. (2010) "Producing Precarity: The Temporary Staffing in the Labor Market." *Qualitative Sociology* 33(1): 117–136.

Earle, E. M. (1986) "Adam Smith, Alexander Hamilton, Friedrich List: The Economic Foundations of Military Power." In Paret, P. (ed.) *Makers of Modern Strategy*. Oxford: Clarendon, 217–261.

Easton, D. (1953) *The Political System*. Chicago: University of Chicago Press.

Eberl, O., and Niesen, P. (2011) *Zum ewigen Frieden. Mit den Passagen zum Völkerrecht und Weltbürgerrecht aus Kants Rechtslehre* (To Perpetual Peace, with Commentary). Frankfurt: Suhrkamp.

Eck, J. E., and Eck, E. B. (2012) "Crime Place and Pollution." *Criminology and Public Policy* 11(2): 281–316.

Eck, J. E. (1995) "Examining Routine Activity Theory: A Review of Two Books." *Justice Quarterly* 12(4): 783–797.

Eden, L. (2004) *Whole World On Fire: Organizations, Knowledge, and Nuclear Weapons Devastation.* Ithaca, NY: Cornell University Press.

Eilstrup-Sangiovanni, M. (2009) "The End of Balance-of-Power Theory? A Comment on Wohlforth et al.'s 'Testing Balance-of-Power Theory in World History.'" *European Journal of International Relations* 15(2): 347–380.

Eisenhut, D. (2010) "Sovereignty, National Security and International Treaty Law: The Standard of Review of International Courts and Tribunals with Regard to 'Security Exceptions.'" *Archiv des Völkerreechts* 48(4): 431–466.

Elbe, S. (2006) "Should HIV/AIDS Be Securitized? The Ethical Dilemmas of Linking HIV/AIDS and Security." *International Studies Quarterly* 50: 119–144.

Elchardus, M., De Groof, S., and Smits, W. (2008) "Rational Fear or Represented Malaise: A Crucial Test of Two Paradigms Explaining Fear of Crime." *Sociological Perspectives* 51(3): 453–471.

Elden, S. (2009) *Terror and Territory: The Spatial Extent of Sovereignty.* Minneapolis: University of Minnesota Press.

(2013) "Secure the Volume: Vertical Geopolitics and the Depth of Power." *Political Geography* 34: 35–51.

Elliott, A. (2002) "Beck's Sociology of Risk: A Critical Assessment." *Sociology* 36(2): 293–315.

Emsley, C. (1986) "Detection and Prevention: The Old English Police and the New 1750–1900." *Historical Social Research/Historische Sozialforschung,* 37: 69–88.

Enloe, C. (1989) *Bananas, Bases and Beaches: Making Feminist Sense of International Politics.* London: Pinter.

(2000) *Maneuvers: The International Politics of Militarizing Women's Lives.* Berkeley: University of California Press.

Erickson, K. (1976) *Everything in Its Path: Destruction of Community in the Buffalo Creek Flood.* New York: Simon & Schuster.

Ericson, R. V., Doyle, A., and Barry, D. (2003) *Insurance as Governance.* Toronto: University of Toronto Press.

Ericson, R. V. (1994) "The Division of Expert Knowledge in Policing and Security." *British Journal of Sociology* 45(2): 149–175.

(2007) *Crime in An Insecure World.* Cambridge: Polity.

Eriksen, T. H., Bal, E., and Salemink, O. (eds.) (2010) *A World of Insecurity: Anthropological Perspectives on Human Security.* New York: Pluto Press.

Evans-Pritchard, E. E. (1937) *Witchcraft, Oracles and Magic among the Azande.* Oxford: Clarendon.

Ewald, F. (1991) "Insurance and Risk." In Burchell, G., Gordon, C., and Miller, P. (eds.) *The Foucault Effect: Studies in Governmentality.* Chicago: University of Chicago Press, 197–210.

Eyal, G., and Pok, G. (2015) "What is security expertise? From the sociology of professions to an analysis of networks of expertise." In Berling, T. V., and Bueger, C. (eds.) *Security Expertise: Practice, Power and Responsibility.* London: Routledge, 37–59.

Eyal, G. (2006) *The Disenchantment of the Orient: Expertise in Arab Affairs and the Israeli State.* Stanford, CA: Stanford University Press.

Faist, T. (2002) "Extension du Domaine de la Lutte: International Migration and Security before and after September 11, 2001." *International Migration Review* 36: 7–14.

Fassbender, B. (2009) *The United Nations Charter as the Constitution of the International Community.* Leiden: Martinus Nijhoff, Koninklijke Brill NV.

Fassin, D. (2013) *Enforcing Order: An Ethnography of Urban Policing.* Cambridge: Polity.

Fazal, T. M. (2014) "Dead Wrong? Battle Deaths, Military Medicine, and Exaggerated Reports of War's Demise." *International Security* 39(1): 95–125.

Fearon, J. D., and Wendt, A. (2002) "Rationalism v. Constructivism: A Skeptical View." In Carlsnaes, W., Risse, T., and Simmons, B. A. (eds.) *Handbook of International Relations.* London: Sage, 52–72.

Fearon, J. D., and Laitin, D. D. (2008) "Integrating Qualitative and Quantitative Methods." In Box-Steffensmeier, J. M., Brady, H. E., and Collier, D. (eds.) *Oxford Handbook of Political Methodology.* Oxford: Oxford University Press, 756–778.

Feaver, P. D., Hellmann, G., Schweller, R. L. et al. (2000) "Brother, Can You Spare a Paradigm? (or Was Anybody Ever a Realist?): Correspondence." *International Security* 25(1): 165–193.

Federico, C. M., Golec, A., and Dial, J. L. (2005) "The Relationship between the Need for Closure and Support for Military Action against Iraq: Moderating Effects of National Attachment." *Personality and Social Psychology Bulletin* 31(5): 621–632.

Feldman, G. (2011) *The Migration Apparatus: Security, Labor, and Policymaking in the European Union.* Stanford, CA: Stanford University Press.

Feldman, I. (2010) "Ad Hoc Humanity: UN Peacekeeping and the Limits of International Community in Gaza." *American Anthropologist* 112(3): 416–429.

Felson, M. (1995) "Those Who Discourage Crime." *Crime and Place* 4: 53–66.

Felson, M., and Boba, R. L. (2010) *Crime and Every Day Life*. London: Sage.

Ferris, J. R. (1989) *Money, Men and Diplomacy*. Ithaca, NY: Cornell University Press.

Fierke, K. (2007) *Critical Approaches to International Security*. London: Polity.

Fine, J. (2006) *Worker Centers: Organizing Communities at the Edge of the Dream*. Ithaca, NY: Cornell University Press.

Finnemore, M. (2003) *The Purpose of Intervention: Changing Beliefs about the Use of Force*. Ithaca, NY: Cornell University Press.

Fischer, C. S., and Mattson, G. (2009) "Is America Fragmenting?" *Annual Review of Sociology* 35(1): 435–455.

Fiske, S. T. (2004) *Social Beings: A Core Motives Approach to Social Psychology*. New York: Wiley.

Fiske, S. T., and Taylor, S. E. (2013) *Social Cognition: From Brains to Culture*, 2nd ed. London: Sage.

Flint, C. (2003) "Terrorism and Counterterrorism: Geographic Research Questions and Agendas." *The Professional Geographer* 55(2): 161–169.

Floyd, R. (2010) *Security and the Environment: Securitisation Theory and US Environmental Security Policy*. Cambridge: Cambridge University Press.

(2011) "Can Securitization Be Used in Normative Analysis? Towards Just Securitization Theory." *Security Dialogue* 42(4–5): 427–439.

(2015) "Just and Unjust Desecuritizations." In Balzacq, Thierry (ed.) *Contesting Security: Strategies and logics*. London: Routledge, 122–138.

Fluri, J. (2011) "Armored Peacocks and Proxy Bodies: Gender Geopolitics in Aid/Development Spaces of Afghanistan." *Gender, Place and Culture* 18(4): 519–536.

Fordham, B. (1998) *Building the Cold War Consensus: The Political Economy of U.S. National Security Policy*. Ann Arbor, MI: University of Michigan Press.

Fosher, K. B. (2009) *Under Construction: Making Homeland Security at the Local Level*. Chicago: University of Chicago Press.

Fouberg, E. H., Murphy, A. B., and De Blij, H. J. (2012) *Human Geography: People, Place, and Culture*. Hoboken, NJ: Wiley.

Foucault, M. (1978) "About the Concept of the "Dangerous Individual" in 19th Century Legal Psychiatry." *International Journal of Law and Psychiatry* 1: 1–18.

(1980) *Power/Knowledge: Selected Interviews and Other Writings, 1972–1977*. New York: Random House.

(2004) *Security, Territory, Population*. New York: Picador.

Freedman, L. (2012) "Does Strategic Studies Have a Future?" In Baylis, J., Wirtz, J. J., and Gray, C. S. (eds.) *Strategy in the Contemporary World*, 4th ed. Oxford: Oxford University Press, 378–391.

Freudenburg, W. R., Gramling, R., Laska, S. *et al.* (2012) *Catastrophe in the Making: The Engineering of Katrina and the Disasters of Tomorrow*. Washington, DC: Island Press.

Friedberg, A. (1989) "The Political Economy of American Strategy." *World Politics* 41(3): 381–406.

Froehling, O. (1997) "The Cyberspace 'War of Ink and Internet' in Chiapas, Mexico." *Geographical Review* 87(2): 291–307.

Froestad, J., and Shearing, C. (2013) *Security Governance, Policing, and Local Capacity: Advances in Police Theory and Practice Series*. Boca Raton, FL: CRC Press.

Frois, C. (2013) *Peripheral Vision: Politics, Technology, and Surveillance*. New York: Berghahn Books.

Gaertner, S. L., and Dovidio, J. F. (2000) *Reducing Intergroup Bias: The Common Ingroup Identity Model*. New York: Psychology Press.

Gaertner, S. L., Dovidio, J. F., and Bachman, B. A. (1996) "Revisiting the Contact Hypothesis: The Induction of a Common Ingroup Identity." *International Journal of Intercultural Relations* 20(3–4): 271–290.

Gaertner, S. L., Mann, J., Murrell, A. *et al.* (1989) "Reducing Intergroup Bias: The Benefits of Recategorization." *Journal of Personality and Social Psychology*, 57(2): 239–249.

Gallie, W. B. (1955) "Essentially Contested Concepts." *Proceedings of the Aristotelian Society* 56: 167–198.

Gambetti, Z., and Godoy-Anativia, M. (eds.) (2013) *Rhetorics of Insecurity: Belonging and Violence in the Neoliberal Era*. New York: NYU Press and the Social Science Research Council.

Gartner, S. S. (2008) "The Multiple Effects of Casualties on Public Support for War: An Experimental Approach." *American Political Science Review* 102(1): 95–106.

Gartzke, E. (2007) "The Capitalist Peace." *American Journal of Political Science* 51(1): 166–91.

Gasper, D. (2005) "Securing Humanity: Situating 'Human Security' as Concept and Discourse." *Journal of Human Development* 6(2): 221–245.

Schwarzenberger, G. (1965) *The Inductive Method in International Law*. London: Stevens and Sons.

George, A. L., and Bennett, A. (2005) *Case Studies and Theory Development in the Social Sciences*. Cambridge, MA: MIT Press.

Gheciu, A. (2005) *NATO in the "New Europe": The Politics of International Socialization after the Cold War*. Stanford, CA: Stanford University Press.

Gibbard, A., and Blackburn, S. (1992) "Morality and Thick Concepts." *Proceedings of the Aristotelian Society,* Supplementary Vol. 66: 267–299.

Gibbons, F. X., and McCoy, S. B. (1991) "Self-Esteem, Similarity, and Reactions to Active Versus Passive Downward Comparison." *Journal of Personality and Social Psychology* 60(3): 414–424.

Gibbs, C. M., Gore, E., McGarrell, E. F. et al. (2010) "Introducing Conservation Criminology." *British Journal of Criminology* 50(1): 124–144.

Giddens, A. (1990) *The Consequences of Modernity.* Cambridge: Polity.

—— (1991) *Modernity and Self-Identity.* Cambridge: Polity.

Gilpin, R. (1975) *US Power and the Multinational Corporation: The Political Economy of Foreign Direct Investment.* New York: Basic Books.

—— (1981) *War and Change in World Politics.* Cambridge: Cambridge University Press.

—— (1984) "The Richness of the Tradition of Political Realism." *International Organization* 38(2): 287–304.

—— (1987) *The Political Economy of International Relations.* Princeton, NJ: Princeton University Press.

Glaser, C. L. (1994–1995) "Realists as Optimists: Cooperation as Self-Help." *International Security* 19(3): 50–90.

—— (1997) "The Security Dilemma Revisited." *World Politics* 50(1): 171–201.

—— (2003) "Structural Realism in a More Complex World." *Review of International Studies* 29(3): 403–414.

—— (2010) *Rational Theory of International Politics: The Logic of Competition and Cooperation.* Princeton, NJ: Princeton University Press.

Glasford, D. E., and Dovidio, J. F. (2011) "E Pluribus Unum: Dual Identity and Minority Group Members' Motivation to Engage in Contact, as Well as Social Change." *Journal of Experimental Social Psychology* 47(5): 1021–1024.

Glassner, B. (1999) *The Culture of Fear.* New York: Basic Books.

—— (2010) *The Culture of Fear: Why Americans Are Afraid of the Wrong Things,* rev. ed. New York: Basic Books.

Gleeson, S. (2009) "From Rights to Claims: The Role of Civil Society in Making Rights Real for Vulnerable Workers." *Law and Society Review* 43(3): 699–700.

Glick Schiller, N., and Caglar, A. (2010) *Locating Migration: Rescaling Cities and Migrants.* Ithaca, NY: Cornell University Press.

Go, J. (2012) *Patterns of Empire: The British and American Empires, 1688 to the Present.* Cambridge: Cambridge University Press.

Gold, J. R., and Revill, G. (2000) *Landscapes of Defense.* Don Mills, Canada: Pearson Education.

Goldsmith, J. L., and Posner, E. A. (2006) *The Limits of International Law.* Oxford: Oxford University Press.

Goldstein, D. M. (2003) "'In Our Own Hands': Lynching, Justice, and the Law in Bolivia." *American Ethnologist* 30(l): 22–43.

(2004) *The Spectacular City: Violence and Performance in Urban Bolivia.* Durham, NC: Duke University Press.

(2007) "Human Rights as Culprit, Human Rights as Victim: Rights and Security in the State of Exception." In Goodale, M., and Merry, S. E. (eds.) *The Practice of Human Rights: Tracking Law between the Global and the Local.* Cambridge: Cambridge University Press, 49–77.

(2010a) "Toward a Critical Anthropology of Security." *Current Anthropology* 51(4): 487–517.

(2010b) "Security and the Culture Expert: Dilemmas of an Engaged Anthropology." *Political and Legal Anthropology Review (PoLAR)* 33(1): 126–142.

(2012a) *Outlawed: Between Security and Rights in a Bolivian City.* Durham, NC: Duke University Press.

(2012b) *"Securitized Immigration in a New Jersey Town."* Russell Sage Foundation: www.russellsage.org/blog/contributor/Daniel%20Goldstein (accessed November 4, 2013).

(2014) "Qualitative Research in Dangerous Places: Becoming an "Ethnographer" of Violence and Personal Safety" Social Science Research Council, Drugs, Security and Democracy Program, DSD Working Papers on Research Security: no. 1: www.ssrc.org/pages/qualitative-research-in-dangerous-places-becoming-an-ethnographer-of-violence-and-personal-safety/ (accessed September 30, 2014).

Gomberg-Muñoz, R., and Nussbaum-Barberena, L. (2011) "Is U.S. Immigration Policy Labor Policy? Immigration Enforcement, Undocumented Workers, and the State." *Human Organization* 70(4): 366–337.

González, R. J. (2007) "Towards Mercenary Anthroplogy? The New US Army Counterinsurgency Manual FM 3-24 and the Military-Anthropology Complex." *Anthropology Today* 23: 14–19.

Goodin, R. E., and Jackson, F. (2007) "Freedom from Fear." *Philosophy and Public Affairs* 35: 249–265.

Goodwin, J. (2006a) "A Theory of Categorical Terrorism." *Social Forces* 84: 2027–2047.

(2006b) "What Do We Really Know about (Suicide) Terrorism?" *Sociological Forum* 21: 315–330.

Gorard, S., and Taylor, C. (2004) "What Is 'Triangulation'?" *Building Research Capacity* 7: 7–9.

Gordon, C., and Arian, A. (2001) "Threat and Decision Making." *Journal of Conflict Resolution* 45(2): 196–215.

Gordon, J. (2007) *Suburban Sweatshops: The Fight for Immigrant Rights*. Cambridge, MA: Belknap Press.

Graham, S. (2008) *Cities, War, and Terrorism: Towards an Urban Geopolitics*. Oxford: John Wiley & Sons.

(2011) *Cities under Siege: The New Military Urbanism*. New York: Verso Books.

Graham, S., and Gregory, D. (2009) "Security." In Johnston, R., Gregory, D., Pratt, G. et al. (eds.) *Dictionary of Human Geography*. Chischester: Wiley.

Gray, J. N. (1977) "On the Contestability of Social and Political Concepts." *Political Theory* 5: 331–348.

Grayson, K. (2008) "Human Security as Power/Knowledge: The Biopolitics of a Definitional Debate." *Cambridge Review of International Affairs* 21(3): 384–401.

Greenwald, A. G., Pratkanis, A. R., Leippe, M. R. et al. (1986) "Under What Conditions Does a Theory Obstruct Research Progress?" *Psychological Review* 95(4): 216–229.

Gregory, D. J., and Pred, A. R. (2007) *Violent Geographies: Fear, Terror, and Political Violence*. New York: CRC Press.

Gregory, D. (2003) "Defiled Cities." *Singapore Journal of Tropical Geography* 24(3): 307–326.

(2004) *The Colonial Present: Afghanistan, Palestine, Iraq*, London: Wiley-Blackwell.

(2006) "The Black Flag: Guantanamo Bay and the Space of Exception." *Geografiska Annaler: Series B, Human Geography* 88(4): 405–427.

(2011) "The Everywhere War." *The Geographical Journal* 177(3): 238–250.

Gregory, D., and Graham, S. (2009) "Militarism." In Johnston, R., Gregory, D., Pratt, G. et al. (eds.) *Dictionary of Human Geography*. Chischester: Wiley, 464–465.

Griffin, J. (1986) *Well-Being: Its Meaning, Measurement and Moral Importance*. Oxford: Clarendon Press.

(2008) *On Human Rights*. Oxford: Oxford University Press.

Grimshaw, R., and Jefferson, T. (1987) *Interpreting Policework: Policy and Practice in Forms of Beat Policing*. London: Allen and Unwin.

Gros, F. (2012) *Le principe sécurité*. Paris: Gallimard.

Gross, J. J. (2002) "Emotion Regulation: Affective, Cognitive, and Social Consequences." *Psychophysiology* 39(3): 281–291.

Guillemin, J. (2005) *Biological Weapons: From the Invention of State-Sponsored Programs to Contemporary Bioterrorism*. New York: Columbia University Press.

Gusfield, J. R. (1996) *Contested Meanings: The Construction of Alcohol Problems*. Madison: University of Wisconsin Press.

Gusterson, H. (2005) "Spies in Our Midst." *Anthropology News* 46(6): 39–40.

Gusterson, H., and Besteman, C. (eds.) (2009) *The Insecure American: How We Got Here and What We Should Do about It*. Berkeley: University of California Press.

Guzman, A. (2012) *The Consent Problem in International Law*. Berkeley Law School, University of California: www.escholarship.org/uc/blewp (accessed March 5, 2012).

Guzzini, S. (2000) "A Reconstruction of Constructivism in International Relations." *European Journal of International Relations* 6(2): 147–182.

Habermas, J. (1968) *Erkenntnis und Interesse*. Frankfurt a.M: Surkamp.

Hadjimatheou, K. (2014) "The Relative Moral Risks of Untargeted and Targeted Surveillance." *Ethic Theory Moral Practices* 17: 187–201.

Haggman, B. (1998) "Rudolf Kjellen and Modern Swedish Geopolitics." *Geopolitics* 3(2): 99–112.

Haglund, D. G. (1986) "The New Geopolitics of Minerals: An Inquiry into the Changing International Significance of Strategic Minerals." *Political Geography Quarterly* 5(3): 221–240.

Hagmann, J., and Dunn Cavelty, M. (2012) "National Risk Registers: Security Scientism and the Propagation of Permanent Insecurity." *Security Dialogue* 43(1): 80–97.

Hajjar, L. (2013) *Torture*. New York: Routledge.

Hale, C. R. (2008) "Introduction." In Hale, C. R. (ed.) *Engaging Contradictions: Theory, Politics and Methods of Activist Scholarship*. Berkeley: University of California Press, 1–30.

Halperin, E., and Gross, J. J. (2011) "Emotion Regulation in Violent Conflict: Reappraisal, Hope, and Support for Humanitarian Aid to the Opponent in Wartime." *Cognition and Emotion* 25(7): 1228–1236.

Hamilton, D. L., and Sherman, S. J. (1996) "Perceiving Persons and Groups." *Psychological Review* 103(2): 336.

Hamilton, J. A., and Placas, A. J. (2011) "Anthropology Becoming ... ? The 2010 Sociocultural Anthropology Year in Review." *American Anthropologist* 113(2): 246–261.

Hammond, M. (1963) "Res olim dissociabiles: Principatus ac Libertas: Liberty under the Early Roman Empire." *Harvard Studies in Classical Philology* 67: 93–113.

Hansen, L. (2006) *Security As Practice: Discourse Analysis and the Bosnian War*. London: Routledge.

(2012) "Reconstructing Desecuritisation: The Normative-Political in the Copenhagen School and Directions for How to Apply It." *Review of International Studies* 38(6): 525–546.
Harcourt, B. (2001) *Illusion of Order: The False Promise of Broken Windows Policing*. Cambridge, MA: Harvard University Press.
(2012) *Symposium of the Future of Risk*. Chicago Centre for Contemporary Theory, May 11, 2012: www.youtube.com/watch?v=PBDPubwsDXo (accessed July 9, 2014).
Hardy, M., and Hazelrigg, L. (2010) *Pension Puzzles: Social Security and the Great Debate*. New York: Russell Sage Foundation.
Hart, H. (1961) *The Concept of Law*. Oxford: Oxford University Press.
Harvey, D. (2006) "Space as a Keyword." In Castree, N., and Gregory, D. (eds.) *David Harvey: A Critical Reader*. Oxford: Blackwell, 270–293.
Hawi, D. R., Saguy, T., Dovidio, J. et al. (2012) *When Positive Expectations Are Not Met*. Symposium presentation at the annual meeting of the Society for Experimental Social Psychology (SESP), Austin, Texas.
Hayes, J. (2009) "Identity and Securitization in the Democratic Peace: The United States and the Divergence of Response to India and Iran's Nuclear Programs." *International Studies Quarterly* 53(4): 977–999.
Hedstrom, P., and Swedberg, R. (eds.) (1998) *Social Mechanisms: An Analytical Approach to Social Theory*. Cambridge: Cambridge University Press.
Hegel, G. F. (1952) *Philosophy of Right*. Oxford: Oxford University Press Translation.
(1967) *The Philosophy of Right*. Oxford: Oxford University Press.
(1975) *Lectures on the Philosophy of World History: Introduction* (translated by H. B. Nisbet). Cambridge: Cambridge University Press.
Heidegger, M. (1977) *The Question Concerning Technology* (translated by W. Lovitt). New York: Harper & Row.
Heimer, C. (1989) *Reactive Risk and Rational Action: Managing Moral Hazard in Insurance Contracts*. San Francisco: University of California Press.
Henrich, J., Heine, S. J., and Norenzayan, A. (2010) "The Weirdest People in the World?" *Behavioral and Brain Sciences* 33(2–3): 61–83.
Herbert, D. T. (1982) *The Geography of Urban Crime*. London: Longman.
Herbert, S. (1996) "Morality in Law Enforcement: Chasing 'Bad Guys' with the Los Angeles Police Department." *Law and Society Review* 30(4): 799–818.
Herington, J. (2012) "The Concept of Security." In Enemark, C., and Selgelid, M. J. (eds.) *Ethics and Security Aspects of Infectious Disease Control: Interdisciplinary Perspectives*. Aldershot: Ashgate, 7–26.

Herz, J. (1951) *Political Realism and Political Idealism: A Study in Theories and Realities.* Chicago: University of Chicago Press.

Heske, H. (1987) "Karl Haushofer: His Role in German Geopolitics and in Nazi politics." *Political Geography Quarterly* 6(2): 135–144.

Hewstone, M., Cairns, E., Voci, A. et al. (2006) "Intergroup Contact, Forgiveness, and Experience of 'The Troubles' in Northern Ireland." *Journal of Social Issues* 62(1): 99–120.

Hewstone, M., Rubin, M., and Willis, H. (2002) "Intergroup Bias." *Annual Review of Psychology* 53(1): 575–604.

Hicks, A. (2000) *Social Democracy and Welfare Capitalism: A Century of Income Security Politics.* Ithaca, NY: Cornell University Press.

Higgins, R. (1994) *Problems and Process: International Law and How We Use It.* Oxford: Oxford University Press.

Hillier, A. E. (2005) "Residential Security Maps and Neighborhood Appraisals: The Home Owners' Loan Corporation and the Case of Philadelphia." *Social Science History* 29(2): 207–233.

Hillyard, P., Pantazis, C., Tombs, S. et al. (2004) *Beyond Criminology: Taking Harm Seriously.* London: Pluto Press.

Hobbes, T. (1651/1968) *Leviathan.* London: Penguin.

(1994) "De Corpore Politico." In Gaskin, J. C. (ed.) *Human Nature and De Corpore Politico.* Oxford: Oxford University Press, 183–228.

Hobden, S., and Wyn Jones, R. (2011) "Marxist Theories of International Relations." In Baylis, J., Smith, S., and Owens, P. (eds.) *The Globalization of World Politics.* Oxford: Oxford University Press, 130–147.

Hobson, J. A. (1988 [1938, 1902]) *Imperialism: A Study*, 3rd ed. London: Unwin Hyman.

Hogg, M. A. (2003) "Social Identity." In Leary, M. R., and Tangney J. (eds.) *Handbook of Self and Identity.* New York: Guilford Press, 462–479.

(2007) "Uncertainty-Identity Theory." In Zanna, M. P. (ed.) *Advances in Experimental Social Psychology, Vol. 39.* San Diego: Elsevier Academic Press, 39–62.

(2010) "Human Groups, Social Categories, and Collective Self: Social Identity and the Management of Self-Uncertainty." In Arkin, R. M., Oleson, K. C., and Carroll P. J. (eds.) *Handbook of the Uncertain Self.* New York: Psychology Press, 401–420.

Hogg, M. A., and Abrams, D. (1988) *Social Identifications: A Social Psychology of Intergroup Relations and Group Processes.* London: Routledge.

Hogg, M. A., and Adelman, J. (2013) "Uncertainty–Identity Theory: Extreme Groups, Radical Behavior, and Authoritarian Leadership." *Journal of Social Issues* 69(3): 436–454.

Holbaard, M., and Pedersen, M. A. (eds.) (2013) *Times of Security: Ethnographies of Fear, Protest and the Future.* London: Routledge.

Hollenberg, S. (2013) *Challenges and Opportunities for Judicial Protection of Human Rights against Decisions of the United Nations Security Council.* Dissertation, Faculty of Law, University of Amsterdam.

Hollis, M., and Smith, S. (1990) *Explaining and Understanding International Relations.* Oxford: Oxford University Press.

Holmes, J. (2008) "Space and the Secure Base in Agoraphobia: A Qualitative Survey." *Area* 40(3): 375–382.

Homer-Dixon, T. F. (1999) *Environment, Scarcity and Violence.* Princeton, NJ: Princeton University Press.

Homer-Dixon, T. F., and Blitt, J. (eds.) (1998) *Ecoviolence: Links among Environment, Population and Security.* Lanham, MD: Rowan & Littlefield.

Homolar, A. (2010) "The Political Economy of National Security." *Review of International Political Economy* 17(2): 410–423.

Honig, B. (2001) *Democracy and the Foreigner.* Princeton, NJ: Princeton University Press.

Hönke, J., and Müller, M. (2012) "Governing (In)Security in a Postcolonial World: Transnational Entanglements and the Worldliness of 'Local' Practice." *Security Dialogue* 43(5): 383–401.

Hoogensen, G., and Stuvøy, K. (2006) "Gender, Resistance and Human Security." *Security Dialogue* 37(2): 207–228.

Hooks, G., and Mosher, C. (2005) "Outrages against Personal Dignity: Rationalizing Abuse and Torture in the War on Terror." *Social Forces* 83: 1627–1646.

Hornsey, M. J., and Hogg, M. A. (2000) "Assimilation and Diversity: An Integrative Model of Subgroup Relations." *Personality and Social Psychology Review* 4(2): 143–156.

Huddy, L., Feldman, S., and Weber, C. (2007) "The Political Consequences of Perceived Threat and Felt Insecurity." *Annals of the American Academy of Political and Social Science* 614(1): 131–153.

Huddy, L., Feldman, S., Taber, C. et al. (2005) "Threat, Anxiety, and Support of Antiterrorism Policies." *American Journal of Political Science* 49(3): 593–608.

Huddy, L., Khatib, N., and Capelos, T. (2002) "Trends: Reactions to the Terrorist Attacks of September 11, 2001." *The Public Opinion Quarterly* 66(3): 418–450.

Hughes, J., Rohloff, A., David, M. et al. (2011) "Foreword: Moral Panics in the Contemporary World." *Crime, Media, Culture: An International Journal* 7(3): 211–214.

Huish, R. (2008) "Human Security and Food Security in Geographical Study: Pragmatic Concepts or Elusive Theory?" *Geography Compass* 2(5): 1386–1403.

Hurd, I. (2007) *After Anarchy: Legitimacy and Power in the United Nations Security Council.* Princeton, NJ: Princeton University Press.

Huysmans, J. (2006) *The Politics of Insecurity: Fear, Migration and Asylum in the EU.* London: Routledge.

(2014) *Security Unbound: Enacting Democratic Limits.* London: Routledge.

Hwang, J., and Sampson, R. J. (2014) "Divergent Pathways of Gentrification Racial Inequality and the Social Order of Renewal in Chicago Neighborhoods." *American Sociological Review* 79(4): 726–751.

Hyndman, J. (2000) *Managing Displacement: Refugees and the Politics of Humanitarianism.* Minneapolis: University of Minnesota Press.

(2004) "Mind the Gap: Bridging Feminist and Political Geography through Geopolitics." *Political Geography* 23(3): 307–322.

(2007) "The Securitization of Fear in Post-Tsunami Sri Lanka." *Annals of the Association of American Geographers* 97(2): 361–372.

Hyndman, J., and De Alwis, M. (2004) "Bodies, Shrines, and Roads: Violence, (Im)Mobility and Displacement in Sri Lanka." *Gender, Place and Culture* 11(4): 535–557.

Ingram, A. (2008) "Pandemic Anxiety and Global Health Security." In Pain, R. and Smith, S. J. (eds.) *Fear: Critical Geopolitics and Everyday Life.* London: Ashgate, 75–85.

Ingram, A., and Dodds, K. (2012) *Spaces of Security and Insecurity: Geographies of the War on Terror.* Farnham: Ashgate.

(eds.) (2009) *Spaces of Security and Insecurity: Geographies of the War on Terror.* Farnham: Ashgate.

Iyer, A., Leach, C., and Crosby, F. J. (2003) "White Guilt and Racial Compensation: The Benefits and Limits of Self-Focus." *Personality and Social Psychology Bulletin* 29(1): 117–129.

Jackson, P. T. (2011) *The Conduct of Enquiry in International Relations.* London: Routledge.

Jackson, R. H., and Sørensen, G. (2007) *Introduction to International Relations: Theories and Approaches.* Oxford: Oxford University Press.

Jacobs, J. (1970) *The Economy of Cities.* New York: Random House.

Jaffe, R. (2012) "Criminal Dons and Extralegal Security Privatization in Downtown Kingston, Jamaica." *Singapore Journal of Tropical Geography* 33: 184–197.

Jervis, R. (1976) *Perception and Misperception in International Politics.* Princeton, NJ: Princeton University Press.

(1978) "Cooperation Under the Security Dilemma." *World Politics* 167–214.

John, S. (2011) "Security, Knowledge and Well-Being." *Journal of Moral Philosophy* 8(1): 68–91.
Johns, F. (2013) *Non-Legality in International Law: Unruly Law*. Cambridge: Cambridge University Press.
Johnson, B. R., Onwuegbuzie, A. J., and Turner, L. A. (2007) "Toward a Definition of Mixed Methods Research." *Journal of Mixed Methods Research* 1(2): 112–133.
Johnson, E., Morehouse, H., and Dalby, S. *et al.* (2014) "After the Anthropocene Politics and Geographic Inquiry for a New Epoch." *Progress in Human Geography* 38(3): 439–456.
Johnston, L., and Shearing, C. (2003) *Governing Security: Explorations of Policing and Justice*. London: Routledge.
Johnston, R. (2010) "Sixty Years of Change in Human Geography." In Backhouse, R., and Fontaine, P. (eds.) *The History of Social Sciences since 1945*. Cambridge: Cambridge University Press: 155–182.
Jonas, E., and Fritsche, I. (2013) "Destined to Die but Not to Wage War: How Existential Threat Can Contribute to Escalation or De-Escalation of Violent Intergroup Conflict." *American Psychologist* 68: 543–558.
Kagan, S. (2009) "Well-Being as Enjoying the Good." *Philosophical Perspectives* 23: 253–272.
Kahl, C. H. (2005) "Plight or Plounder? Natural Resources and Civil War." In Dombrowski, P. (ed.) *Guns and Butter – the Political Economy of International Security*. Boulder, CO: Lynne Rienner.
Kahler, M. (1998) "Rationality in International Relation." *International Organisation* 52(4): 919–941.
Kammerhofer, J. (2009) "Gaps, the Nuclear Weapons Advisory Opinion and the Structure of International Legal Argument between Theory and Practice." *British Yearbook of International Law* (2009) 80(1): 333–360.
Kaplan, R. (2012) *The Revenge of Geography: What the Map Tells Us about Coming Conflicts and the Battle against Fate*. New York: Random House.
Kapstein, E. (1989–1990) "Losing Control: National Security and the Global Economy." *The National Interest* 18: 85–90.
Katz, C. (2008) "Me and My Monkey: What's Hiding in the Security State." In Pain, R., and Smith, S. (eds.) *Fear: Critical Geopolitics and Everyday Life*. Farnham: Ashgate, 59–72.
Katzenstein, P. J. (ed.) (1996) *The Culture of National Security: Norms and Identity in World Politics*. New York: Columbia University Press.
Kelsen, H. (1960) *Reine Rechtslehre*. Wien: Deuticke Verlag.

Kelty, C. (2005) "Geeks, Social Imaginaries, and Recursive Publics." *Cultural Anthropology* 20(2): 185–214.

Kemp, A., Raijman, R., Resnik, J. *et al.* (2010) "Contesting the Limits of Political Participation: Latinos and Black African Migrant Workers in Israel." *Ethnic and Racial Studies* 23(1): 94–119.

Kennedy, D. (1987) *International Legal Structures*. Baden Baden: Nomos.

Kennedy, P. (1984) "The First World War and the International Power System." *International Security* 9(1): 7–40.

Kent, A. (2006) "Reconfiguring Security: Buddhism and Moral Legitimacy in Cambodia." *Security Dialogue* 37(3): 343–361.

Keohane, R. O. and Nye, J. S. (1977) *Power and Interdependence: World Politics in Transition*. Boston: Little, Brown.

Kessler, O. (2011) "Beyond Sectors, before the World: Finance, Security and Risk." *Security Dialogue* 42(2): 197–215.

Kestnbaum, M. (2009) "The Sociology of War and the Military." *Annual Review of Sociology* 35: 235–254.

Khimm, S. (2012) *Obama is Deporting Immigrants Faster than Bush: Republicans Don't Think That's Fast Enough*. Washington Post blog, August 27: www.washingtonpost.com/blogs/wonkblog/wp/2012/08/27/obama-is-deporting-more-immigrants-than-bush-republicans-dont-think-thats-enough/ (accessed October 27, 2012).

Kindleberger, C. P. (2013) *The World in Depression 1929–1939*, 40th ed. Oakland: University of California Press.

King, G., Keohane, R., and Verba, S. (1994) *Designing Social Inquiry: Scientific Inference in Qualitative Research*. Princeton, NJ: Princeton University Press.

King, G., and Murray, C. J. L. (2001) "Rethinking Human Security." *Political Science Quarterly* 116: 585–610.

Kinnvall, C. (2004) "Globalization and Religious Nationalism: Self, Identity, and the Search for Ontological Security." *Political Psychology* 25(5): 741–767.

Kirshner, J. (1998) "Political Economy in Security Studies after the Cold War." *Review of International Political Economy* 5(1): 64–91.

(2007) *Appeasing Bankers: Financial Caution on the Road to War*. Princeton, NJ: Princeton University Press.

Klabbers, J. (2009) "The Bridge Crack'd: A Critical Look at Interdisciplinary Relation." *International Relations* 23(1): 119–125.

Klinenberg, E. (2002) *Heat Wave: A Social Autopsy of Disaster in Chicago*. Chicago: University of Chicago Press.

Klinkenberg, B. (2007) "Geospatial Technologies and the Geographies of Hope and Fear." *Annals of the Association of American Geographers* 97(2): 350–360.

Knorr, K. (1957) "The Concept of Economic Potential for War." *World Politics* 10(1): 49–62.
  (1973) *Power and Wealth: The Political Economy of National Power*. London: Macmillan.
  (1975) *The Power of Nations*. New York: Basic Books.
  (1978) *Economic Issues and National Security*. Lawrence: University Press of Kansas.
Konrad, V., and Nicol, H. N. (2011) "Border Culture, the Boundary between Canada and the United States of America, and the Advancement of Borderlands Theory." *Geopolitics* 16(1): 70–90.
Koopman, S. (2011) "Alter-Geopolitics: Other Securities Are Happening." *Geoforum* 42(3): 274–284.
Kopinak, J. K. (1999) "The Use of Triangulation in the Study of Refugee Well-Being." *Quality Quantity* 33(2): 169–183.
Koskenniemi, M. (2004) *The Gentle Civilizer of Nations: The Rise and Fall of International Law 1870–1960*. Cambridge: Cambridge University Press.
  (2005) *From Apology to Utopia, the Structure of International Legal Argument*. Cambridge: Cambridge University Press (originally published in 1989 with Finnish Lawyers' Publishing Company; reissued with a new epilogue in 2005).
  (2010) Methodology of International Law, *Max Planck Encyclopedia of Public International Law*, Heidelberg and Oxford: www.mpepil.com/subscriber_article?script=yesand id=/epil/entries/law-9780199231690-e1440and recno=34and letter=M (accessed July 25, 2010).
Kosterman, R., and Feshbach, S. (1989) "Toward a Measure of Patriotic and Nationalistic Attitudes." *Political Psychology*, 10(2): 257–274.
Kramer, R. M., and Messick, D. M. (1998) Getting By with a Little Help from Our Enemies: Collective Paranoia and Its Role in Intergroup Relations. In Sedikides, C., Schopler, J., and Insko, C. A. (eds.) *Intergroup Cognition and Intergroup Behavior*. New York: Psychology Press, 233–255.
Kramer, R. M., and Wei, J. (1999) Social Uncertainty and the Problem of Trust in Social Groups: The Social Self in Doubt. In Tyler, T. R, Kramer, R. M., and John, O. P. (eds.) *The Psychology of the Social Self*. Mahwah, NJ: Lawrence Erlbaum Associates, 145–168.
Krasner, S. D. (1976) "State Power and the Structure of International Trade." *World Politics* 28(3): 317–347.
Kratochwil, F. (1989) *Rules, Norms and Decisions*. London: Cambridge University Press.
Krause, K., and Williams, M. C. (1997) *Critical Security Studies: Concepts and Cases*. Minneapolis: University of Minnesota Press.

Krause, K. (1998) "Critical Theory and Security Studies: The Research Programme of 'Critical Security Studies.'" *Cooperation and Conflict* 33(3): 298–333.

Kretsedemas, P. (2008) "Immigration Enforcement and the Complication of National Sovereignty: Understanding Local Enforcement as an Exercise in Neoliberal Governance." *American Quarterly* 60: 553–573.

Kupchik, A. (2010) *Homeroom Security: School Discipline in an Age of Fear*. New York: New York University Press.

Kurzman, C. (2011) *The Missing Martyrs: Why There Are So Few Muslim Terrorists*. Oxford: Oxford University Press.

Kuus, M. (2002) "European Integration in Identity Narratives in Estonia: A Quest for Security." *Journal of Peace Research* 39(1): 91–108.

(2002) "Sovereignty for Security? The Discourse of Sovereignty in Estonia." *Political Geography* 21(3): 393–412.

Kydd, A. H. (2005) *Trust and Mistrust in International Relations*. Princeton, NJ: Princeton University Press.

Lacoste, Y. (1976) *La géographie, ça sert, d'abord, à faire la guerre*. Paris: Éditions François Maspéro.

Lafree, G., and Dugan, L. (2004) "How Does Studying Terrorism Compare to Studying Crime?" In Deflem, M. (ed.) *Terrorism and Counter-Terrorism: Criminological Perspectives*. Amsterdam: Elsevier, 53–74.

Laitin, D. D. (2002) Comparative Politics: The State of the Subdiscipline. In Katznelson, I., and Miller, H. V. (eds.) *Political Science: The State of the Discipline*. New York: Norton.

Lakoff, A., and Collier, S. J. (eds.) (2008) *Biosecurity Interventions: Global Health and Security in Question*. New York: Columbia University Press.

Lakoff, A. (2007) "Preparing for the Next Emergency." *Public Culture* 19: 247–271.

(2008) "The Generic Biothreat; or, How We Became Unprepared." *Cultural Anthropology* 23: 399–428.

Lamphere, L. (2003) "The Perils and Prospects of an Engaged Anthropology." *Social Anthropology* 11(2): 153–168.

Lancaster, R. N. (2011) *Sex Panic and the Punitive State*. Berkeley: University of California Press.

Lane, J., Rader, N. E., Henson, B. et al. (2014) *Fear of Crime in the United States: Causes, Consequences, and Contradictions*. Durham, NC: Carolina Academic Press.

Larchanché, S. (2012) "Intangible Obstacles: Health Implications of Stigmatization, Structural Violence, and Fear among Undocumented Immigrants in France." *Social Science and Medicine* 74: 858–863.

Lasswell, H. D. (1950) *National Security and Individual Freedom*. New York: McGraw-Hill.
Latour, B. (2013) *War and Peace in an Age of Ecological Conflicts*. Lecture prepared for the Peter Wall Institute, Vancouver, September 23.
Lawrence, G., Lyons, K., and Wallington, T. (eds.) (2013) *Food Security, Nutrition and Sustainability*. London: Earthscan.
Laycock, G. (2003) *Launching Crime Science*. London: Jill Dando Institute of Crime Science, University College London.
Lazreg, M. (2008) *Torture and the Twilight of Empire: From Algiers to Baghdad*. Princeton, NJ: Princeton University Press.
Le Billon, P. (2012) *Wars of Plunder: Conflicts, Profits and the Politics of Resources*. New York: Columbia University Press.
Leach, C., Iyer, A., and Pedersen, A. (2006) "Anger and Guilt about Ingroup Advantage Explain the Willingness for Political Action." *Personality and Social Psychology Bulletin* 32(9): 1232–1245.
Legg, S. (2005) "Foucault's Population Geographies: Classifications, Biopolitics and Governmental Spaces." *Population, Space and Place* 11(3): 137–156.
Legro, J. W. and Moravcsik, A. (1999) "Is Anybody Still a Realist?" *International Security* 24(2): 5–55.
Leibniz, G. W. (1864) *Letter of 1705, Die Werke von Leibniz*. Klindworth: Hannover.
Leidner, B., and Castano, E. (2012) "Morality Shifting in the Context of Intergroup Violence." *European Journal of Social Psychology* 42(1): 82–91.
Leidner, B., Castano, E., Zaiser, E. *et al.* (2010) "Ingroup Glorification, Moral Disengagement, and Justice in the Context of Collective Violence." *Personality and Social Psychology Bulletin* 36(8): 1115–1129.
Leidner, B., Tropp, L. R., and Lickel, B. (2013) "Bringing Science to Bear—on Peace, Not War: Elaborating on Psychology's Potential to Promote Peace." *American Psychologist* 68(7): 514–526.
Leman-Langlois, S., and Shearing, C. (2004) "Repairing the Future: The South African Truth and Reconciliation Commission at Work." In Gilligan, G., and Pratt, J. (eds.) *Crime, Truth and Justice: Official Enquiry, Discourse, Knowledge*. Cullompton: Willan, 222–242.
Lemert, E. F. (2010) "Secondary Deviance." In Williams III, F.P., and McShane, M.D. (eds.) *Criminology Theory: Selected Classic Readings*. Oxford: Elsevier 199–204.
Léonard, S. (2010) "EU Border Security and Migration in the European Union: FRONTEX and Securitization through Practices." *European Security* 19(2): 231–254.

Lerner, J. S., Gonzalez, R. M., Small, D. A. *et al.* (2003) "Effects of Fear and Anger on Perceived Risks of Terrorism: A National Field Experiment." *Psychological Science* 14(2): 144–150.

Lessig, L. (1996) "The Zones of Cyberspace." *Stanford Law Review* 48(5): 1403–1411.

Leverentz, A. (2012) "Narratives of Crime and Criminals: How Places Socially Construct the Crime Problem." *Sociological Forum* 27(2): 348–371.

Levin, S., van Laar, C., and Sidanius, J. (2003) "The Effects of Ingroup and Outgroup Friendship on Ethnic Attitudes in College: A Longitudinal Study." *Group Processes and Intergroup Relations* 6(1): 76–92.

LeVine, R. A., and Campbell, D. T. (1972) *Ethnocentrism: Theories of Conflict, Ethnic Attitudes, and Group Behavior*. Oxford: John Wiley & Sons.

Levy, J. S. (1997) "Prospect Theory, Rational Choice, and International Relations." *International Studies Quarterly* 41(1): 87–112.

Levy, J. S., and W. R. Thompson (2010) "Balancing on Land and at Sea: Do States Ally against the Leading Global Power?" *International Security* 35(1): 7–43.

Lickel, B. (2012) "Retribution and Revenge." In Tropp, L. R. (ed.) *The Oxford Handbook of Intergroup Conflict*. New York: Oxford University Press, 89–105.

Lickel, B., Miller, N., Stenstrom, D. M. *et al.* (2006) "Vicarious Retribution: The Role of Collective Blame in Intergroup Aggression." *Personality and Social Psychology Review* 10(4): 372–390.

Liddell, H. G., and Scott, R. (1940) *A Greek-English Lexicon*, 9th ed. Oxford: Clarendon Press.

Liebes, T. (1992) "Decoding Television News: The Political Discourse of Israeli Hawks and Doves." *Theory and Society* 21: 357–381.

Light, J. (2003) *From Warfare to Welfare: Defense Intellectuals and Urban Problems in Cold War America*. Johns Hopkins University Press.

Lim, C. L., and Elias O. A. (1998) *The Paradox of Consensualism in International Law*. Den Haag: Kluwer.

Linklater, A., and Suganami, H. (2006) *The English School of International Relations: a Contemporary Reassessment*. Cambridge: Cambridge University Press.

List, C. (2006) "Republican Freedom and the Rule of Law." *Politics Philosophy Economics* 5: 201–220.

Loader, I. (2009) "Ice Cream and Incarceration: On Appetites for Security and Punishment." *Punishment and Society* 11(2): 241–257.

Loader, I., and Walker, N. (2007) *Civilizing Security*. Cambridge: Cambridge University Press.

Lobell, S. E., Ripsman, N. M., and Taliaferro, J. W. (eds.) (2009) *Neoclassical Realism, the State, and Foreign Policy*. Cambridge: Cambridge University Press.

Lobo-Guerrero, L. (2008) "'Pirates,' Stewards, and the Securitisation of Global Circulation." *International Political Sociology* 3(2): 219–235.

Locke, J. (1690) *Two Treatises of Government, Everyman's Library*. London: J. M. Dent and Sons.

Lotfi, S., and Koohsari, M. J. (2009) "Analyzing Accessibility Dimension of Urban Quality of Life: Where Urban Designers Face Duality between Subjective and Objective Reading of Place." *Social Indicators Research* 94(3): 417–435.

Low, S. M. (1997) "Urban Fear: Building the Fortress City." *City and Society* 9(1): 53–71.

(2003) *Behind the Gates: Life, Security, and the Pursuit of Happiness in Fortress America*. New York: Routledge.

(2004) *Behind the Gates: Life, Security, and the Pursuit of Happiness in Fortress America*. New York: Routledge.

Low, S. M., and Merry, S. E. (2010) "Engaged Anthropology: Diversity and Dilemmas." *Current Anthropology* 51(Supplement 2): S203–S226.

Löwenheim, O., and Heimann, G. (2008) "Revenge in International Politics." *Security Studies* 17(4): 685–724.

Lowry, R. P. (1972) "Toward a Sociology of Secrecy and Security Systems." *Social Problems* 19(4): 437–450.

Lupton, D., and Tulloch, J. (1999) "Theorizing Fear of Crime: Beyond the Rational/Irrational Opposition." *The British Journal of Sociology* 50 (3): 507–523.

Luthar, S. S. (ed.) (2003) *Resilience and Vulnerability: Adaptation in the Context of Childhood Adversities*. Cambridge: Cambridge University Press.

Lutz, C. (2001) *Homefront: A Military City and the American Twentieth Century*. Boston: Beacon.

Lynch, F. R. (2011) *One Nation under AARP: The Fight over Medicare, Social Security, and America's Future*. Berkeley: University of California Press.

Lynch, M., and Stretesky, P. (2011) "Similarities between Green Criminology and Green Science: Towards a Typology of Green Criminology." *International Journal of Comparative and Applied Criminal Justice* 35(4): 293–306.

(2014) *Exploring Green Criminology*. Farnham, UK: Ashgate.

Lyon, D., and Murakami Wood, D. (2012) "Security, Surveillance, and Sociological Analysis." *Canadian Review of Sociology/Revue Canadienne de Sociologie* 49(4): 317–327.

MacKenzie, M. (2009) "Securitization and Desecuritization: Female Soldiers and the Reconstruction of Women in Post-Conflict Sierra Leone." *Security Studies* 18(2): 241–261.

Macmillan, J. (2004) "Liberalism and the Democratic Peace." *Review of International Studies* 30(2): 179–200.

Maguire, M., Frois, C., and Zurawski, N. (eds.) (2014) "Introduction." *The Anthropology of Security: Perspectives from the Frontline of Policing, Counter-terrorism and Border Control*. London: Pluto, 118–138.

Maguire, M. (2009) "The Birth of Biometric Security." *Anthropology Today* 25: 9–14.

(2014) Counter-Terrorism in European Airports. In Maguire, M., Frois, C., and Zurawski, N. (eds.) *The Anthropology of Security: Perspectives from the Frontline of Policing, Counter-Terrorism and Border Control*. London: Pluto, 118–138.

Malesevic, S. (2010) *The Sociology of War and Violence*. Cambridge: Cambridge University Press.

Maliniak, D., Peterson, S., and Tierney, M. J. (2012) *TRIP Around the World: Teaching, Research, and Policy Views of International Relations Faculty in 20 Countries*. Williamsburg, VA: College of William and Mary.

Malinowski, B. (1922) *Argonauts of the Western Pacific*. London: George Routledge and Sons.

Mallard, G., and Lakoff, A. (2011) "How Claims to Know the Future Are Used to Understand the Present." In Camic, C., Gross, N., and Lamont, M. (eds.) *Social Knowledge in the Making*. Chicago: University of Chicago Press, 339–378.

Mamadouh, V. (2004) "Geography and War, Geographers and Peace." In Flint, C. (ed.) *The Geography of War and Peace: from Death Camps to Diplomats*. Oxford: Oxford University Press: 26–60.

Maoz, I., and McCauley, C. (2008) "Threat, Dehumanization, and Support for Retaliatory Aggressive Policies in Asymmetric Conflict." *Journal of Conflict Resolution* 52(1): 93–116.

Marcus, G. E., Sullivan, J. L., Theiss-Morse, E. *et al.* (1995) *With Malice Toward Some: How People Make Civil Liberties Judgments*. New York: Cambridge University Press.

Marigold, D. C., McGregor, I., and Zanna, M. P. (2010) "Defensive Conviction as Emotion Regulation: Goal Mechanisms and Interpersonal Implications." In Arkin, R. M., Oleson, K. C., and Carroll, P. J. (eds.) *Handbook of the uncertain self*. New York: Psychology Press, 232–248.

Martin, N., Morales, S., and Theodore, N. (2007) "Migrant Worker Centers: Contending with Downgrading in the Low-Wage Labor Market." *Geojournal* 68: 155–165.

Martin, P. L. (2003) *Promise Unfulfilled: Unions, Immigration, and the Farm Workers*. Ithaca, NY: ILR Press.

Maruyama, G., and Ryan, C. S. (2014) *Research Methods in Social Relations*, 8th ed. West Sussex: Wiley-Blackwell.

Masco, J. (2006) *The Nuclear Borderlands: The Manhattan Project in Post-Cold War New Mexico*. Princeton, NJ: Princeton University Press.

(2010) "Response to "Toward a Critical Anthropology of Security." *Current Anthropology* 51.

Maslow, A. H. (1943) "A Theory of Human Motivation." *Psychological Review* 50(4): 370–396.

(1962) *Toward a Psychology of Being*. Princeton, NJ: D Van Nostrand.

Massaro, V., and Williams, J. (2013) "Feminist Geopolitics: Redefining the Geopolitical, Complicating (In) Security." *Geography Compass* 7(8): 567–577.

Massey, D. (1992) "Politics and Space/Time." *New Left Review* 192: 65–84.

(2005) *For Space*. London: Sage.

Mathew, G. (1943) "The Character of the Gallienic Renaissance." *The Journal of Roman Studies* 33: 65–70.

Mathews, J. T. (1989) "Redefining Security." *Foreign Affairs* 68(2): 162–177.

Matthew, R. A., Barnett, J., McDonald, B. *et al.* (2009) *Global Environmental Change and Human Security*. Cambridge, MA: MIT Press.

Mayall, J. (1990) *Nationalism and International Society*. Cambridge: Cambridge University Press.

McDonald, M. (2008) "Securitization and the Construction of Security." *European Journal of International Relations* 14(4): 563–587.

(2013) "Discourses of Climate Security." *Political Geography* 33: 42–51.

McFate, M. (2005) "The Military Utility of Understanding Adversary Culture." *Joint Force Quarterly* 38: 42–48.

McGhee, D. (2010) *Security, Citizenship and Human Rights: Shared Values in Uncertain Times*. Basingstoke: Palgrave Macmillan.

McGregor, I., Haji, R., and Kang, S. (2008) Can Ingroup Affirmation Relieve Outgroup Derogation? *Journal of Experimental Social Psychology* 44(5): 1395–1401.

McGregor, I., Haji, R., Nash, K. A. *et al.* (2008) "Religious Zeal and the Uncertain Self." *Basic and Applied Social Psychology* 30(2): 183–188.

McMahan, J. (2002) *The Ethics of Killing: Problems at the Margins of Life*. Oxford: Oxford University Press.

McNamara, L. A., and Rubinstein, R. A. (2011) "Introduction: Scholars, Security, Citizenship: Anthropology and the State at War." In McNamara, L. A., and Rubinstein, R. A. (eds.) *Dangerous Liaisons:*

Anthropologists and the National Security State. Santa Fe, NM: SAR Press, xiii–xxxiv.

McNevin, A. (2006) "Political Belonging in a Neoliberal Era: The Struggle of the Sans-Papiers." *Citizenship Studies* 10(2): 135–151.

McSweeney, B. (1999) *Security, Identity and Interests: A Sociology of International Relations.* Cambridge: Cambridge University Press.

Meade, M. (2012) "The Geography of Life and Death: Deeper, Broader, and Much More Complex." *Annals of the Association of American Geographers* 102(5): 1219–1227.

Mearsheimer, J. J. (1990) "Back to the Future: Instability in Europe after the Cold War." *International Security* 15(1): 5–56.

(1994–1995) "The False Promise of International Institutions." *International Security* 19(3): 5–49.

(2001) *The Tragedy of Great Power Politics.* New York: W. W. Norton.

Megoran, N. (2006) "For Ethnography in Political Geography: Experiencing and Re-Imagining Ferghana Valley Boundary Closures." *Political Geography* 25(6): 622–640.

Meikle, S. (1996) "Aristotle on Business." *The Classical Quarterly* 64(1): 138–151.

Mencken, H. L. (1918) *In Defence of Women.* New York: Octagon.

Menjívar, C. (2006) "Liminal Legality: Salvadoran and Guatemalan Immigrants' Lives in the United States." *American Journal of Sociology* 111: 999–1037.

Mercer, J. (1995) "Anarchy and Identity." *International Organization* 49(2): 229–252.

(2005) "Rationality and Psychology in International Politics." *International Organization* 59(1): 77–106.

(2010) "Emotional Beliefs." *International Organization* 64(1): 1–31.

Metzl, J. M. (2010) *The Protest Psychosis: How Schizophrenia Became a Black Disease.* Boston: Beacon.

Miethe, T. D. (1995) "Fear and Withdrawal from Urban Life." *Annals of the American Academy of Political and Social Science* 539: 14–27.

Mildner, S. A. (2011) *Konfliktrisiko Rohstoffe? Herausforderungen und Chancen im Umgang mit knappen Ressourcen* (Resources as conflict risk? Challenges and opportunities in dealing with scarce resources). *Berlin: Studie der Stiftung Wissenschaft und Politik.*

Mill, J. S. (1991) "Utilitarianism." In Gray, J. (ed.) *On Liberty and Other Essays.* Oxford: Oxford University Press.

Miller, D., and Mills, T. (2009) "The Terror Experts and the Mainstream Media: The Expert Nexus and Its Dominance in the News Media." *Critical Studies on Terrorism* 2(3): 414–437.

Miller, S. E. (2010) "The Hegemonic Illusion? Traditional Strategic Studies in Context." *Security Dialogue* 41(6): 639–648.

Milner, H. V. (1998) "Rationalizing Politics: The Emerging Synthesis of International, American, and Comparative Politics." *International Organisation* 52(4): 759–786.
Milward, A. S. (1977) *War, Economy and Society*. Berkeley: University of California Press.
Mintz, A., Redd, S. B., and Vedlitz, A. (2006) "Can We Generalize from Student Experiments to the Real World in Political Science, Military Affairs, and International Relations?" *Journal of Conflict Resolution* 50 (5): 757–776.
Mitzen, J. (2006) "Ontological Security in World Politics: State Identity and the Security Dilemma." *European Journal of International Relations* 12(3): 341–370.
Mize, R. L., and Swords, A. C. S. (2010) *Consuming Mexican Labor: From the Bracero Program to NAFTA*. Toronto: University of Toronto Press.
Mohr, J. W., Wagner-Pacifici, R., Breiger, R. L. *et al.* (2013) "Graphing the Grammar of Motives in National Security Strategies: Cultural Interpretation, Automated Text Analysis and the Drama of Global Politics." *Poetics* 41(6) 670–700.
Molden, D. C., Lee, A. Y., and Higgins, E. (2008) "Motivations for Promotion and Prevention." In Shah, J. Y., and Gardner, W. L. (eds.) *Handbook of Motivation Science*. New York: Guilford Press, 169–187.
Molotch, H. (2012) *Against Security: How We Go Wrong at Airports, Subways, and Other Sites of Ambiguous Danger*. Princeton, NJ: Princeton University Press.
Monahan, T. (ed.) (2006) *Surveillance and Security: Technological Politics and Power in Everyday Life*. New York: Routledge.
Monteith, M. J., and Spicer, C. (2000) "Contents and Correlates of Whites' and Blacks' Racial Attitudes." *Journal of Experimental Social Psychology* 36(2): 125–154.
Mooney, P. H., and Hunt, S. A. (2000) "Food Security: The Elaboration of Contested Claims to a Consensus Frame." *Rural Sociology* 74(4): 469–497.
Moran, T. H. (1990) "The Globalisation of America's Defense Industries: Managing the Threat of Foreign Dependence." *International Security* 15(1): 57–99.
Moravcsik, A. (1997) "Taking Preferences Seriously: A Liberal Theory of International Politics." *International Organization* 51(4): 513–553.
Morgan, P. M. (2003) *Deterrence Now*. Cambridge: Cambridge University Press.
Morgenthau, H. J. (1929) *Die internationale Rechtspflege, ihr Wesen und ihre Grenzen*. Leipzig: Universitätsverlag von Noske.
 (1965) *Politics Among Nations: The Struggle for Power and Peace*, 4th ed. New York: Knopf.

(1978) *Politics among Nations*, 5th rev. ed. New York: Knopf.
(1985) *Politics among Nations*, 6th ed. New York: Knopf.
Mountz, A., and Hyndman, J. (2006) "Feminist Approaches to the Global Intimate." *Women's Studies Quarterly* 4(1): 446–463.
Muffels, R. J. A. (ed.) (2008) *Flexibility and Employment Security in Europe: Labour Markets in Transition*. Northampton, MA: Edward Elgar.
Mummendey, A., and Wenzel, M. (1999) "Social Discrimination and Tolerance in Intergroup Relations: Reactions to Intergroup Difference." *Personality and Social Psychology Review* 3(2): 158–174.
Murphy, K. (2004) "The Role of Trust in Nurturing Compliance: A Study of Accused Tax Avoiders." *Law and Human Behavior* 28(2): 187–209.
Mutimer, D., Grayson, K., and Beier, J. M. (2013) "Critical Studies on Security: An Introduction." *Critical Studies on Security* 1(1): 1–12.
Nadler, A., and Shnabel, N. (2008) "Instrumental and Socioemotional Paths to Intergroup Reconciliation and the Needs-Based Model of Socioemotional Reconciliation." In Nadler, A., Malloy, T. E., and Fisher, J. D. (eds.) *The Social Psychology of Intergroup Reconciliation*. New York: Oxford University Press, 37–56.
Nagel, J. (2011) "Climate Change, Public Opinion, and the Military Security Complex." *The Sociological Quarterly* 52(2): 203–210.
Nally, D. (2008) "'That Coming Storm': The Irish Poor Law, Colonial Biopolitics, and the Great Famine." *Annals of the Association of American Geographers* 98(3): 714–741.
Narang, V. (2014) *Nuclear Strategy in the Modern Era: Regional Powers and International Conflict: Regional Powers and International Conflict*. Princeton, NJ: Princeton University Press.
Narizny, K. (2007) *The Political Economy of Grand Strategy*. Ithaca, NY: Cornell University Press.
Neocleous, M. (2008) *Critique of Security*. Edinburgh: Edinburgh University Press.
Neumann, I. B. (2002) "Returning Practices to the Linguistic Turn: The Case of Diplomacy." *Millennium: Journal of International Studies* 31(3): 627–651.
Neumann, R. P. (2004) "Moral and Discursive Geographies in the War for Biodiversity in Africa." *Political Geography* 23(7): 813–837.
Newcomb, T. M. (1943) *Personality and Social Change*. New York: Dryden.
Newman, O. (1972) *Defensible Space*. New York: Macmillan.
Newnham, R. E. (2002) *Deutsche Mark Diplomacy: Positive Economic Sanctions in German-Russian Relations*. University Park: Pennsylvania State University Press.

Newton, L. (2008) *Illegal, Alien or Immigrant: The Politics of Immigration Reform*. New York: New York University Press.

Ngoc, A. C., and Wyatt, T. (2012) "A Green Criminological Exploration of Illegal Wildlife." *Asian Criminology* 8(2): 129–142.

Niou, E. M. S., Ordeshook, P. C., and Rose, G. F. (1989) *The Balance of Power*. Cambridge: Cambridge University Press.

Nissenbaum, H. (1998) "Protecting Privacy in an Information Age: The Problem of Privacy in Public." *Law and Philosophy* 17: 559–596.

Noble, G. (2005) "The Discomfort of Strangers: Racism, Incivility and Ontological Security in a Relaxed and Comfortable Nation." *Journal of Intercultural Studies* 26(1–2): 107–120.

Nollkaemper, A. (2002) "Review of Security Council Decisions by National Court." *German Yearbook of International Law* 165–202.

Nyers, P. (ed.) (2009) *Securitizations of Citizenship*. London: Routledge.

(2003) "Abject Cosmopolitanism: The Politics of Protection in the Anti-Deportation Movement." *Third World Quarterly* 24(6): 1069–1093.

(2010) "No One Is Illegal between City and Nation." *Studies in Social Justice* 4(2): 127–143.

O'Connell, M. E. (2012) "Cyber Security without Cyber War." *Journal of Conflict and Security Law* 17(2): 187–209.

(2013) The International Law of Drones, *ASIL Insights*, American Society of International Law: www.asil.org/insights/volume/14/issue/37/international-law-drones;

Öhman, A., and Mineka, S. (2001) "Fears, phobias, and preparedness: toward an evolved module of fear and fear learning." *Psychological Review* 108(3), 483.

O'Loughlin, J., and Heske, H. (1991) "From 'Geopolitik' to 'Géopolitique': Converting a Discipline for War to a Discipline for Peace." In Kliot, N., and Waterman, S. (eds.) *The Political Geography of Conflict and Peace*. London Bellhaven Press, 37–59.

O'Neill, K. L., and Kedron, T. (eds.) (2013) *Securing the City: Neoliberalism, Space, and Insecurity in Postwar Guatemala*. Durham, NC: Duke University Press.

O'Tuathail, G. (1996) "An Anti-Geopolitical Eye: Maggie O'Kane in Bosnia, 1992–93." *Gender, Place and Culture: A Journal of Feminist Geography* 3(2): 171–186.

(1996) *Critical Geopolitics: The Politics of Writing Global Space*. London: Routledge.

O'Donovan, A. M. (2005) "Immigrant Workers and Workers' Compensation after Hoffman Plastic Compounds, Inc. v. N.L.R.B." *NYU Review of Law and Social Change* 30: 299–324.

O'Malley, P. (2004) *Risk, Uncertainty and Government*. London: Glasshouse Press.
  (2004) "The Uncertain Promise of Risk." *Australian and New Zealand Journal of Criminology* 37(3): 323–343.
  (2008) "Governmentality and Risk." In Jens, O., and Zinn, J. O. (eds.) *Social Theories on Risk and Uncertainty: An Introduction*. Oxford and Malden, MA: Blackwell, 52–76.
  (2009) *The Currency of Justice: Fines and Damages in Consumer Societies*. Routledge.
  (2000) "The Postmodern Geopolitical Condition: States, Statecraft, and Security at the Millennium." *Annals of the Association of American Geographers* 90(1): 166–178.
Ochs, J. (2011) *Security and Suspicion: An Ethnography of Everyday Life in Israel*. Philadelphia: University of Pennsylvania Press.
Ogata, S., and Sen, A. (2003) *Human Security Now: Final Report of the Commission on Human Security*. New York: Commission on Human Security.
Oliner, S. P., and Oliner, P. M. (1988) *The Altruistic Personality: Rescuers of Jews in Nazi Europe*. New York: Free Press.
Ong, A. (1999) *Flexible Citizenship*. Durham, NC: Duke University Press.
Onuf, N. G. (1989) *World of Our Making: Rules and Rule in Social Theory and International Relations*. Columbia: University of South Carolina Press.
Orend, B. (2013) *The Morality of War*, 2nd ed. Peterborough: Broadview Press.
Owczarzak, J. (2009) "Defining HIV Risk and Determining Responsibility in Postsocialist Poland." *Medical Anthropology Quarterly* 23: 417–435.
Owen, T. (2008) "Measuring Human Security: Methodological Challenges and the Importance of Geographically Referenced Determinants." In Liotta, P. H., Mouat, D. A., Kepner, W. G. et al. (eds.) *Environmental Change and Human Security: Recognizing and Acting on Hazard Impacts*. New York: Springer, 35–64.
Owen, T., and Martin, M. (eds.) (2014) *Routledge Handbook of Human Security*. London: Routledge.
  (2004) "Human Security-Conflict, Critique and Consensus: Colloquium Remarks and a Proposal for a Threshold-Based Definition." *Security Dialogue* 35(3): 373–387.
Oxford Latin Dictionary (1982) Oxford: Oxford University Press.
Paasche, T. F. (2013) "'The Softer Side of Security': The Role of Social Development in Cape Town's Policing Network." *Geoforum* 45: 259–265.

Pain, R., and Smith, S. J. (2012) *Fear: Critical Geopolitics and Everyday Life*. Farnham, UK: Ashgate.

Painter, J. (2008) *Geographies of Space and Power*. London: Sage.

Palacio, J. F. (2013) "Was Geopolitics Born 60 Years before Mahan and Mackinder? The Forgotten Contribution of Friedrich List." *L'Espace Politique. Revue en ligne de géographie politique et de géopolitique* (21).

Palan, R. (2013) "Introduction." In Palan, R. (ed.) *Global Political Economy: Contemporary Theories*, 2nd ed. London: Routledge, 1–18.

Paldam, M. (1998) "Does Economic Growth Lead to Political Stability?" In Borner, S. and Paldam, M. (eds.) *The Political Dimensions of Growth: IEA Conference*, New York: Macmillan, 171–190.

Paluck, E. (2009) "Reducing Intergroup Prejudice and Conflict Using the Media: A Field Experiment in Rwanda." *Journal of Personality and Social Psychology* 96(3): 574–587.

(2012) "Interventions Aimed at the Reduction of Prejudice and Conflict." In Tropp, L. R. (ed.) *The Oxford Handbook of Intergroup Conflict*. New York: Oxford University Press, 179–192.

Paluck, E., and Cialdini, R. (2014) "Field research methods." In Reis, H., and Judd, C. (eds.) *Handbook of Research Methods in Social and Personality Psychology*. New York: Cambridge University Press, 81–97.

Pape, R. A. (2005) "Soft Balancing against the United States." *International Security* 30(1): 7–45.

Parfit, D. (2011) *On What Matters*. Oxford: Oxford University Press.

Paris, R. (2001) "Human Security: Paradigm Shift or Hot Air?" *International Security* 26(2): 87–102.

(2004) "Still an Inscrutable Concept." *Security Dialogue* 35(3): 370–372.

Patomaeki, H. (ed.) (2008) *The Political Economy of Global Security*. New York: Routledge.

Paul, T. V. (2005) "Soft Balancing in the Age of US Primacy." *International Security* 30(1): 46–71.

Paulus, A. (2001) "International Law after Post-Modernity: Towards a Renewal or Decline of International." Law *Leiden Journal of International Law* (4):727–755.

Pedersen, M. A., and Holbraad, M. (2013) "Introduction: Times of Security." In *Times of Security: Ethnographies of Fear, Protest and the Future*. Holbraad, M., and Pedersen, M. A. (eds.) New York and London: Routledge, 1–27.

Peluso, N. L. (1993) "Coercing Conservation? The Politics of State Resource Control." *Global Environmental Change* 3(2): 199–217.

Peluso, N. L., and Watts, M. (2001) *Violent Environments*. Ithaca, NY: Cornell University Press.

Peluso, N. L., and Vandergeest, P. (2011) "Political Ecologies of War and Forests: Counterinsurgencies and the Making of National Natures." *Annals of the Association of American Geographers* 101(3): 587–608.

Pereira, C., Vala, J., and Costa-Lopes, R. (2010) "From Prejudice to Discrimination: The Legitimizing Role of Perceived Threat in Discrimination against Immigrants." *European Journal of Social Psychology* 40(7): 1231–1250.

Perrin, A. J. (2005) "National Threat and Political Culture: Authoritarianism, Antiauthoritarianism, and the September 11 Attacks." *Political Psychology* 26: 2: 167–194.

Perrow, C. (1984) *Normal Accidents: Living with High-Risk Technologies*. Princeton, NJ: Princeton University Press.

Petersen, K. L. (2012) "Risk Analysis – a Field within Security Studies?" *European Journal of International Relations* 18(4): 693–717.

Pettigrew, T. F. (1998) "Intergroup Contact Theory." *Annual Review of Psychology* 4: 965–985.

Pettigrew, T. F., and Tropp, L. R. (2008) "How Does Intergroup Contact Reduce Prejudice? Meta-Analytic Tests of Three Mediators." *European Journal of Social Psychology* 38(6): 922–934.

(2011) *When Groups Meet: The Dynamics of Intergroup Contact*. New York: Psychology Press.

Pettigrew, T. F., Wagner, U., and Christ, O. (2010) "Population Ratios and Prejudice: Modelling Both Contact and Threat Effects." *Journal of Ethnic and Migration Studies* 36(4): 635–650.

Pettit, P. (1991) "Consequentialism." In Singer, P. (ed.) *A Companion to Ethics*. Oxford: Blackwell, 230–240.

(1996) "Freedom as Antipower." *Ethics* 106: 576–604.

(1999) *Republicanism: A Theory of Freedom and Government*. Oxford: Oxford University Press.

(2008) "Freedom and Probability: A Comment on Goodin and Jackson." *Philosophy and Public Affairs* 36: 206–220.

Peutz, N. (2006) "Embarking on an Anthropology of Removal." *Current Anthropology* 47: 217–241.

Philo, C. (2012) "Security of Geography/Geography of Security." *Transactions of the Institute of British Geographers* 37(1): 1–7.

Pinter, B., and Greenwald, A. G. (2011) "A Comparison of Minimal Group Induction Procedures." *Group Processes and Intergroup Relations* 14(1): 81–98.

Pirages, D. (1997) "Demographic Change and Ecological Security." *Environmental Change and Security Project Report* 3: 37–46.

Plant, E. (2004) "Responses to Interracial Interactions over Time." *Personality and Social Psychology Bulletin* 30(11): 1458–1471.

Plant, E., and Devine, P. G. (2003) "The Antecedents and Implications of Interracial Anxiety." *Personality and Social Psychology Bulletin* 29(6): 790–801.
Posen, B. R. (1993) "The Security Dilemma and Ethnic Conflict." *Survival* 35(1): 27–47.
Pottier, J. (2000) *Anthropology of Food: The Social Dynamics of Food Security*. Cambridge: Polity Press.
Pouliot, V. (2008) "The Logic of Practicality: A Theory of Practice of Security Communities." *International Organization* 62(2): 257–288.
Powell, R. (1991) "Absolute and Relative Gains in International Relations Theory." *The American Political Science Review* 85(4): 1303–1320.
Price, D. (2011) *Weaponizing Anthropology: Social Science in Service of the Militarized State*. Oakland, CA: AK Press.
Price, R. (1997) *The Chemical Weapons Taboo*. Ithaca, NY: Cornell University Press.
Price, R., and Reus-Smit, C. (1998) "Dangerous Liaisons? Critical International Theory and Constructivism." *European Journal of International Relations* 4(3): 259–294.
Price, R., and Tannenwald, N. (1996) "Norms and Deterrence: The Nuclear and Chemical Weapons Taboos." In Katzenstein, P. J. (ed.) *The Culture of National Security: Norms and Identity in World Politics*. New York: Columbia University Press, 114–152.
Purcell, B. S. (2008) Undocumented and Working: Reconciling the Disconnect between U.S. Immigration Policy and Employment Benefits Available to Undocumented Workers. *University of San Francisco Law Review* 43: 197–226.
Purdie-Vaughns, V., Steele, C. M., Davies, P. G. et al. (2008) "Social Identity Contingencies: How Diversity Cues Signal Threat or Safety for African Americans in Mainstream Institutions." *Journal of Personality and Social Psychology* 94(4): 615–630.
Purser, G. (2013) "Precarious Work." *Contexts* 12(4): 74–76.
Quackenbush, S. L. (2006) "Not Only Whether but Whom: Three-Party Extended Deterrence." *Journal of Conflict Resolution* 50(4): 562–583.
Quadagno, J. (1998) "Creating a Capital Investment Welfare State: The New American Exceptionalism." *American Sociological Review* 64(1) 1–11.
Rabinow, P. (1984) *The Foucault Reader*. London: Penguin.
Radzinowicz, L. (1956) *A History of English Criminal Law and Its Administration from 1750*, Vol. 2. London: Stevens and Sons.
  (1957) *A History of English Criminal Law and Its Administration from 1750*, Vol. 3. London: Stevens and Sons.

(1968) *A History of English Criminal Law and Its Administration from 1750*, Vol. 4. London: Stevens and Sons.
Ragin, C. C., Nagel, J., and White, P. (2004) *Workshop on Scientific Foundations of Qualitative Research*. National Science Foundation. Chicago.
Raleigh, C., and Urdal, H. (2007) "Climate Change, Environmental Degradation and Armed Conflict." *Political Geography* 26(6): 674–694.
Raleigh, C., and Hegre, H. V. (2009) "Population Size, Concentration, and Civil War: A Geographically Disaggregated Analysis." *Political Geography* 28(4): 224–238.
Ramadan, A. (2013) "Spatialising the Refugee Camp." *Transactions of the Institute of British Geographers* 38(1): 65–77.
Ranasinghe, P. (2013) "Discourse, Practice and the Production of the Polysemy of Security." *Theoretical Criminology* 17: 89–107.
Rasler, K., and Thompson, W. (1983) "Global Wars, Public Debts, and the Long Cycle." *World Politics* 35(4): 489–516.
Rawls, J. (1971) *A Theory of Justice*. Cambridge, MA: Harvard University Press.
  (1985) "Justice as Fairness: Political not Metaphysical." *Philosophy and Public Affairs* 14: 223–251.
Raworth, K. (2012) "A Safe and Just Space for Humanity: Can We Live within the Doughnut." *Oxfam Policy and Practice: Climate Change and Resilience* 8(1): 1–26.
Reader, S. (2006) "Does a Basic Needs Approach Need Capabilities?" *Journal of Political Philosophy* 14: 337–350.
Reid-Henry, S. (2007) "Exceptional Sovereignty? Guantanamo Bay and the Re-Colonial Present." *Antipode* 39(4): 627–648.
Reis, H. T., and Gosling, S. D. (2010) "Social Psychological Methods Outside the Laboratory." In Fiske, S., Gilbert, D., and Lindzey, G. (eds.) *Handbook of Social Psychology*, 5th ed., Vol. 1. Hoboken, NJ: Wiley, 82–114.
Reus-Smit, C. (2004) *American Power and World Order*. Cambridge: Polity Press.
  (2003) "Politics and International Legal Obligation." *European Journal of International Relations* 9(4) 591–625.
Reynald, D. M. (2011) *Guarding against Crime: a Theoretical and Empirical Elaboration of the Routine Activity Concept*. London: Ashgate.
Reynolds, E. A. (1998) *Before the Bobbies: The Night Watch and Police Reform in Metropolitan London 1720–1830*. Stanford, CA: Stanford University Press.
Rhodes, L. A. (2004) *Total Confinement: Madness and Reason in the Maximum Security Prison*. Berkeley: University of California Press.

Riek, B. M., Mania, E. W., and Gaertner, S. L. (2006) "Intergroup Threat and Outgroup Attitudes: A Meta-Analytic Review." *Personality and Social Psychology Review* 10(4): 336–353.

Rigakos, G. (2002) *The New Parapolice: Risk Markets and Commodified Social Control*. Toronto: University of Toronto Press.

Ripsman, N. M. and Paul, T. V. (2005) "Globalisation and the National Security State: A Framework for Analysis." *International Studies Review* 7(2): 199–227.

Roccas, S., and Elster, A. (2012) "Group Identities." In Tropp, L. R. (ed.) *The Oxford Handbook of Intergroup Conflict*. New York: Oxford University Press, 106–122.

Roccas, S., Klar, Y., and Liviatan, I. (2006) "The Paradox of Group-Based Guilt: Modes of National Identification, Conflict Vehemence, and Reactions to the In-Group's Moral Violations." *Journal of Personality and Social Psychology* 91(4): 698–711.

Roccas, S., Sagiv, L., Schwartz, S. *et al.* (2008) "Toward a Unifying Model of Identification with Groups: Integrating Theoretical Perspectives." *Personality and Social Psychology Review* 12(3): 280–306.

Rocco, R. (1999) "The Formation of Latino Citizenship in Southeast Los Angeles." *Citizenship Studies* 3(2): 253–266.

Rockstrom, J., Steffen, W. L., Noone, K. *et al.* (2009) "Planetary Boundaries: Exploring the Safe Operating Space for Humanity." *Ecology and Society* 14(2): 32.

Roemer, J. E. (1983) "Unequal Exchange, Labor Migration, and International Capital Flows: A Theoretical Synthesis." In Desai, P. (ed.) *Marxism, Central Planning and the Soviet Economy*. Cambridge, MA: MIT Press.

Rogne, Leah, Estes, Carroll, Grossman, Brian R. *et al.* (eds.) (2009) *Social Insurance and Social Justice: Social Security, Medicare and the Campaign against Entitlements*. New York: Springer.

Ron, J. (2003) *Frontiers and Ghettos: State Violence in Serbia and Israel*. Berkeley: University of California Press.

Rose, G. (1998) "Neoclassical Realism and Theories of Foreign Policy." *World Politics* 51(1): 144–172.

Rosen, D. (2005) *Armies of the Young: Child Soldiers in War and Terrorism*. New Brunswick, NJ: Rutgers University Press.

Rosenhek, Z. (1999) "The Politics of Claims-Making by Labour Migrants in Israel." *Journal of Ethnic and Migration Studies* 25(4): 575–595.

Rossi, U. (2013) "On Life As a Fictitious Commodity: Cities and the Biopolitics of Late Neoliberalism." *International Journal of Urban and Regional Research* 37(3): 1067–1074.

Rothschild, E. (1995) "What Is Security." *Daedalus* 124(3): 53–98.

Rouhana, N. N., and Fiske, S. T. (1995) "Perception of Power, Threat, and Conflict Intensity in Asymmetric Intergroup Conflict: Arab and Jewish Citizens of Israel." *Journal of Conflict Resolution* 39(1): 49–81.

Routledge, P. (2003) "Anti-Geopolitics." In Agnew, J. Mitchell, K., and O'Tuathail, G. (eds). *A Companion to Political Geography*. Oxford: Blackwell, 236–248

Rubel, A. (2007) "Privacy and the USA Patriot Act: Rights, the Value of Rights, and Autonomy." *Law Philos* 26: 119–159.

Ruggie, J. G. (1983) "Continuity and Transformation in the World Polity: Toward a Neorealist Synthesis." *World Politics* 35(2): 261–285.

(1998) "What Makes the World Hang Together? Neo-Utilitarianism and the Social Constructivist Challenge." *International Organisation* 52(4): 855–885.

Russett, B. (1993) *Grasping the Democratic Peace*. Princeton, NJ: Princeton University Press.

(1968) *Economic Theories of International Politics*. Chicago: Markham.

Rutherford, P., and Rutherford, S. (2013a) "The Confusions and Exuberances of Biopolitics." *Geography Compass* 7(6): 412–422.

Rutherford, S. and Rutherford, P. (2013b) "Geography and Biopolitics." *Geography Compass* 7(6): 423–434.

Sacco, V. F. (1995) "Media Constructions of Crime." *Annals of the American Academy of Political and Social Science* 539: 141–154.

Sagan, S. D., and Waltz, K. N. (2012) *The Spread of Nuclear Weapons: An enduring debate*, 3rd ed. New York: W. W. Norton.

Saguy, T., Tausch, N., Dovidio, J. F. *et al.* (2009) "The Irony of Harmony: Intergroup Contact Can Produce False Expectations for Equality." *Psychological Science* 20(1): 114–121.

Saguy, T., Tropp, L. R., and Hawi, D. (2013) "The Role of Group Power in Intergroup Contact." In Hodson, G., and Hewstone, M. (eds.) *Advances in Intergroup Contact*. New York: Psychology Press, 113–131.

Salter, M. B. (2008) "Securitization and Desecuritization: Dramaturgical Analysis and the Canadian Aviation Transport Security Authority." *Journal of International Relations and Development* 11(4): 321–349.

Salter, M. B., and Mutlu, C. E. (2013) *Research Methods in Critical Security Studies: An Introduction*. London: Routledge.

Sanyal, R. (2012) "Refugees and the City: An Urban Discussion." *Geography Compass* 6(11): 633–644.

Sartori, A. E. (2005) *Deterrence by Diplomacy*. Princeton, NJ: Princeton University Press.

Scanlan, S. J. (2003) "Food Security and Comparative Sociology: Research, Theories, and Concepts." *International Journal of Sociology* 33(3): 88–111.

Schelling, T. C. (1960) *The Strategy of Conflict*. Cambridge, MA: Harvard University Press.

Schlatter, R. (1945) "Thomas Hobbes and Thucydides." *Journal of the History of Ideas* 6: 350–362.

Schmidt, B. (1998) *The Political Discourse of Anarchy: A Disciplinary History of International Relations*. Albany: State University of New York Press.

Schmitt, M. (2010) "The Interpretative Guide on the Notion of Direct Participation in Hostilities: A Critical Analysis", *National Security Journal*: http://harvardnsj.org/2010/05/the-interpretive-guidance-on-the-notion-of-direct-participation-in-hostilities-a-critical-analysis/ (accessed September 2014).

Schram, A., and van Riel, A. (1993) "Weimar Economic Decline, Nazi Economic Recovery, and the Stabilisation of Political Dictatorship." *Journal of Economic History* 53(1): 71–105.

Schur, E. F., and Maher, V. (1973) *Radical Nonintervention: Rethinking the Delinquency Problem*. Englewood Cliffs, NJ: Prentice-Hall.

Schuurman, N. (2006) "Formalization Matters: Critical GIS and Ontology Research." *Annals of the Association of American Geographers* 96(4): 726–739.

Schweller, R. L. (2004) "Unanswered Threats: A Neoclassical Realist Theory of Underbalancing." *International Security* 29(2): 159–201.

(2006) *Unanswered Threats: Political Constraints on the Balance of Power*. Princeton, NJ: Princeton University Press.

Schweller, R. L. and Wohlforth, W. C. (2000) "Power Test: Evaluating Realism in Response to the End of the Cold War." *Security Studies* 9(3): 60–107.

Selgelid, M. J., and Enemark, C. (2008) "Infectious Diseases, Security and Ethics: The Case of HIV/AIDS." *Bioethics* 22: 457–465.

Selmeski, B. R. (2007) "Who Are the Security Anthropologists?" *Anthropology News* 48: 11–12.

Shakespeare, W. (1988) *The Tragedy of Macbeth, William Shakespeare: The Complete Works*, compact ed. Oxford: Clarendon Press.

Shami, S., and Godoy-Anativia, M. (2007) "Did the Events of 9/11 Change the Field of Middle East Studies?" *International Journal of Middle East Studies* 39(3): 346–349.

Shamir, M., and Sagiv-Schifter, T. (2006) "Conflict, Identity, and Tolerance: Israel in the Al-Aqsa Intifada." *Political Psychology* 27(4): 569–595.

Sharp, J. P. (1993) "Publishing American Identity: Popular Geopolitics, Myth and the Reader's Digest." *Political Geography* 12(6): 491–503.
  (2000) "Remasculinising Geo-Politics? Comments on Gearoid O'Tuathail's 'Critical Geopolitics.'" *Political Geography* 19(3): 361–364.
  (2013) "Africa's Colonial Present: Development, Violence and Postcolonial Security." In Huggan, G. (ed.) *Oxford Handbook of Postcolonial Studies*. Oxford: Oxford University Press, 235–252.
Shaw, M. (2003) *International Law*, 6th ed. Cambridge: Cambridge University Press.
Shearing, C. (1989) "Decriminalising Criminology." *Canadian Journal of Criminology* 31(2): 169–178.
Shearing, C., and Stenning, P. C. (1987) "Say 'Cheese': The Disney Order That Is Not So Mickey Mouse." In Shearing, C., and Stenning, P. C. (eds.) *Private Policing*. Newbury, CA: Sage, 317–323.
Shearing, C., and Marks, M. (2011) "Criminology's Disney World: The Ethnographer's Ride of South African Criminal Justice." In Bosworth, M. and Hoyle, C. (eds.) *What Is Criminology*. Oxford: Oxford University Press, 125–140.
  (1980) "Snowflakes or Good Pinches? Private Security's Contribution to Modern Policing." In Donelan, R. (ed.) *The Maintenance of Order in Society*. Ottawa: Canadian Police College, 96–105.
Shearing, C., and Wood, J. (2007) *Imagining Security*. Cullompton: Willan.
Shepherd, L. J. (2008) *Gender, Violence and Security: Discourse as Practice*. London: Zeb Books.
  (2013) *Critical Approaches to Security: An Introduction to Theories and Methods*. London: Routledge.
Sherman, L. W. (2009) "Evidence and Liberty: The Promise of Experimental Criminology." *Criminology and Criminal Justice* 9(1): 5–28.
  (1995) "Public Regulation of Private Crime Prevention." *Annals of the American Academy of Political and Social Science* 539: 102–113.
Sherraden, M., and McBride, A. M. (2010) *Striving to Save: Creating Policies for Financial Security of Low-Income Families*. Ann Arbor: University of Michigan Press.
Shklar, J. (1986) *Legalism; Law, Morals and Political Trials*. Cambridge, MA: Harvard University Press (originally published in 1964).
Shnabel, N., Nadler, A., Ullrich, J. et al. (2009) "Promoting Reconciliation through the Satisfaction of the Emotional Needs of Victimized and Perpetrating Group Members: The Needs-Based Model of Reconciliation." *Personality and Social Psychology Bulletin* 35(8): 1021–1030.
Shue, H. (1980) *Basic Rights: Subsistence, Affluence, and US Foreign Policy*. Princeton, NJ: Princeton University Press.

Sidanius, J., Feshbach, S., Levin, S. *et al.* (1997) "The Interface between Ethnic and National Attachment: Ethnic Pluralism or Ethnic Dominance?" *Public Opinion Quarterly* 61(1): 102–133.

Silbey, S. S. (2009) "Taming Prometheus: Talk about Safety and Culture." *Annual Review of Sociology* 35: 341–369.

Silverman, D. (1997) *Qualitative Research: Theory, Method and Practice.* Thousand Oaks, CA: Sage.

Simko, C. (2012) "Rhetorics of Suffering : September 11 Commemorations as Theodicy." *American Sociological Review* 77: 880.

Simon, J. (2007) *Governing through Crime: How the War on Crime Transformed American Democracy and Created a Culture of Fear.* Oxford: Oxford University Press.

Singer, D. J., and Small, M. (1972) *The Wages of War, 1816–1965: A Statistical Handbook.* New York: John Wiley.

Sjoberg, L. (2013) *Gendering Global Conflict: Toward a Feminist Theory of War.* New York: Columbia University Press.

Skidmore, M. (2003) "Darker than Midnight: Fear, Vulnerability, and Terror Making in Urban Burma." *American Ethnologist* 30: 5–21.

(2008) "Scholarship, Advocacy, and the Politics of Engagement in Burma (Myanmar)." In V. Sanford and A. Angel-Ajani (eds.) *Engaged Observer: Anthropology, Advocacy, and Activism.* New Brunswick, NJ: Rutgers University Press, 42–59.

Skitka, L. J., Bauman, C. W., Aramovich, N. P. *et al.* (2006) "Confrontational and Preventative Policy Responses to Terrorism: Anger Wants a Fight and Fear Wants 'Them' to Go Away." *Basic and Applied Social Psychology* 28(4): 375–384.

Skogan, W. (1986) "Fear of Crime and Neighborhood Change." *Crime and Justice* 8: 203–229.

Smith, J. R., and Louis, W. R. (2008) "Do as We Say and as We Do: The Interplay of Descriptive and Injunctive Group Norms in the Attitude-Behaviour Relationship." *British Journal of Social Psychology* 47(4): 647–666.

Smith, N. (2003) *American Empire: Roosevelt's Geographer and the Prelude to Globalization*, Berkeley: University of California Press.

(2010) *Urban Politics, Urban Security.* Cambridge, MA: Harvard Graduate School.

Smith, S. (1996) "Positivism and Beyond." In Smith, S., Booth, K., and Zalewski, M. (eds.) *International Theory: Positivism and Beyond.* Cambridge: Cambridge University Press: 11–46.

(2005) "The Contested Concept of Security." In Booth, K. (ed.) *Critical Security Studies and World Politics.* Boulder, CO: Lynne Rienner.

Smith, T. W., Rasinski, K. A., and Toce, M. (2001) *America Rebounds: A National Study of Public Response to the September 11th Terrorist Attacks*. Chicago: NORC.

Sommerville, M., Essex, J., and Le Billon, P. (2014) "The 'Global Food Crisis' and the Geopolitics of Food Security." *Geopolitics* 19(2): 239–265.

Sorell, T. (2007) "Hobbes's Moral Philosophy." In Springborg, P. (ed.) *The Cambridge Companion to Hobbes's Leviathan*. Cambridge: Cambridge University Press, 128–156.

South, N., and Brisman, A. (2013) "Critical Green Criminology, Environmental Rights and Crimes of Exploitation." In Winlow, S., and Atkinson, R. (eds.) *New Directions in Crime and Deviancy*. London: Routledge, 99–110.

Spanovic, M., Lickel, B., Denson, T. F. et al. (2010) "Fear and Anger As Predictors of Motivation for Intergroup Aggression: Evidence from Serbia and Republika Srpska." *Group Processes and Intergroup Relations* 13(6): 725–739.

Sparke, M. B. (2006) "A Neoliberal Nexus: Economy, Security and the Biopolitics of Citizenship on the Border." *Political Geography* 25(2): 151–180.

(2007) "Geopolitical Fears, Geoeconomic Hopes, and the Responsibilities of Geography." *Annals of the Association of American Geographers* 97 (2): 338–349.

Springer, S. (2008) "The Nonillusory Effects of Neoliberalisation: Linking Geographies of Poverty, Inequality, and Violence." *Geoforum* 39(4): 1520–1525.

(2012) "Anarchism! What Geography Still Ought to Be." *Antipode* 44(5): 1605–1624.

Springer, S., Chi, H., Crampton, J. et al. (2012) "Leaky Geopolitics: The Ruptures and Transgressions of Wikileaks." *Geopolitics* 17(3): 681–711.

Sprout, H., and Sprout, M. (1957) "Environmental Factors in the Study of International Politics." *Journal of Conflict Resolution* 1(4): 309–328.

Spruyt, H. (1994) *The Sovereign State and Its Competitors: An Analysis of Systems Change*. Princeton, NJ: Princeton University Press.

Squires, G., and Hartman, C. (2006) *There Is No Such Thing as a Natural Disaster: Race, Class, and Hurricane Katrina*. New York: Routledge.

Staerklé, C., Sidanius, J., Green, E. T. et al. (2010) "Ethnic Minority-Majority Asymmetry in National Attitudes around the World: A Multilevel Analysis." *Political Psychology*, 31(4): 491–519.

Stampnitzky, L. 2013a. *Disciplining Terror: How Experts Invented Terrorism*. Cambridge: Cambridge University Press.
  2013b. "Toward a Sociology of 'Security.'" *Sociological Forum* 6: 281–333.
States, I. C. o. A. (1933) *Convention on the Rights and Duties of States (Inter-American). Montevideo Convention on the Rights and Duties of States*: www.oas.org/juridico/english/treaties/a-40.html.
Staub, E. (1997) "Blind versus Constructive Patriotism: Moving from Embeddedness in the Group to Critical Loyalty and Action." In Bar-Tal, D., and Staub, E. (eds.) *Patriotism: In the Lives of Individuals and Nations*. Chicago: Nelson-Hall, 213–228.
Steans, J. (1998) *Gender and International Relations: An Introduction*. Cambridge: Polity.
Steele, B. J. (2008) *Ontological Security in International Relations:Self-Identity and the IR State*. London: Routledge.
Steele, C. M., and Aronson, J. (1995) "Stereotype Threat and the Intellectual Test Performance of African Americans." *Journal of Personality And Social Psychology* 69(5): 797–811.
Steffen, W., Crutzen, P., and McNeill, J. (2007) "The Anthropocene: Are Humans Now Overwhelming the Great Forces of Nature." *Ambio* 36(8): 614–621.
Steffen, W., Persson, Å., Deutsch, L. *et al*. (2011) "The Anthropocene: From Global Change to Planetary Stewardship." *Ambio* 40: 739–761.
Steinmetz, G. (ed.) (2013) *Sociology and Empire: The Imperial Entanglements of a Discipline*. Durham, NC: Duke University Press.
Stephan, C., and Stephan, W. G. (2000) "The Measurement of Racial and Ethnic Identity." *International Journal of Intercultural Relations* 24(5): 541–552.
Stephan, W. G., and Renfro, C. (2002) "The Role of Threat in Intergroup Relations." In Mackie, D. M. and Smith, E. R. (eds.) *From Prejudice to Intergroup Emotions: Differentiated Reactions to Social Groups*. New York: Psychology Press, 191–207.
Stephan, W. G., Renfro, C., Esses, V. M. *et al*. (2005) "The Effects of Feeling Threatened on Attitudes Toward Immigrants." *International Journal of Intercultural Relations* 29(1): 1–19.
Stephan, W. G., and Stephan, C. W. (1985) "Intergroup Anxiety." *Journal of Social Issues* 41(3): 157–175.
Stephan, W. G., Ybarra, O., and Morrison, K. (2009) "Intergroup Threat Theory." In Nelson, T. D. (ed.) *Handbook of Prejudice, Stereotyping, and Discrimination*. New York: Psychology Press, 43–59.
Stepputat, F. (2012) "Knowledge Production in the Security-Development Nexus: An Ethnographic Reflection." *Security Dialogue* 43(5): 439–455.

Sterio, M. (2012) "The United States' Use of Drones in the War on Terror: The (Il)legality of Targeted Killings under International Law." *Case Western Reserve Journal of International Law* 45: 197–214.

Sterling, B. (2009) *The Caryatids*. New York: Del Rey.

Stinchcombe, A. L. (1963) "Institutions of Privacy in the Determination of Police Administrative Practice." *American Journal of Sociology* 69(2): 150–160.

Stokes, D. E. (1997) *Pasteur's Quadrant: Basic Science and Technological Innovation*. Washington, DC: Brookings Institution Press.

Stouffer, Samuel A., Lumsdaine, R., Williams, M. *et al.* (1949) *The American Soldier: Combat and Its Aftermath*. Princeton, NJ: Princeton University Press.

Strachan, H. (2013) *The Direction of War: Contemporary Strategy in Historical Perspective*. Cambridge: Cambridge University Press.

Strange, S. (1982) "Cave! Hic Dragones: A Critique of Regime Analysis." *International Organization* 36(2): 479–496.

(1988) *States and Markets*. New York: Basil Blackwell.

Striker, G. (1990) "Ataraxia: Happiness as Tranquility." *The Monist* 73: 97–110.

Stritzel, H. (2007) "Towards a Theory of Securitization: Copenhagen and Beyond." *European Journal of International Relations* 13(3): 357–383.

Stubbs, R., and Underhill, G. R. D. (eds.) (1994) *Political Economy and the Changing Global Order*. New York: St Martin's Press.

Sundberg, J. (2011) "Diabolic Caminos in the Desert and Cat Fights on the Rio: A Posthumanist Political Ecology of Boundary Enforcement in the United States–Mexico Borderlands." *Annals of the Association of American Geographers* 101(2): 318–336.

Sutton, B., and Norgaard, K. M. (2013) "Cultures of Denial: Avoiding Knowledge of State Violations of Human Rights in Argentina and the United States." *Sociological Forum* 28: 495–524.

Swanton, C. (1985) "On the 'Essential Contestedness' of Political Concepts." *Ethics* 95: 811–827.

Swart, H., Hewstone, M., Christ, O. *et al.* (2011) Affective Mediators of Intergroup Contact: A Three-Wave Longitudinal Study in South Africa. *Journal of Personality and Social Psychology* 101(6): 1221–1238.

Sweetser, C. (2009) "Humanity as Alpha and Omega of International Law, Four Replies to Anne Peters." *European Journal of International Law* 20: 545–567.

Swyngedouw, E. (1999) "Modernity and Hybridity: Nature, Regeneracionismo, and the Production of the Spanish Waterscape, 1890–1930." *Annals of the Association of American Geographers* 89(3): 443–465.

Sylvester, C. (2006) "Bare Life as a Development/Postcolonial Problematic." *The Geographical Journal* 172(1): 66–77.
  (2007a) "Anatomy of a Footnote." *Security Dialogue* 38(4): 547–558.
  (2007b) "Whither the International at the End of IR." *Millennium: Journal of International Studies* 35(3): 551–573.
Szeto, A. H., and Sorrentino, R. M. (2010) "Uncertainty Orientation: Myths, Truths, and the Interface of Motivation and Cognition." In Arkin, R. M., Oleson, K. C., and Carroll, P. J. (eds.) *Handbook of the Uncertain Self*. New York: Psychology Press, 101–121.
Tajfel, H., Billig, M. G., Bundy, R. P. *et al.* (1971) "Social Categorization and Intergroup Behaviour." *European Journal of Social Psychology* 1 (2): 149–178.
Tajfel, H., and Turner, J. C. (1986) "The Social Identity Theory of Intergroup Behaviour." In Worchel, S., and Austin, W. G. (eds.) *Psychology of Intergroup Relations*. Chicago: Nelson Hall, 7–24.
Taliaferro, J. W. (2000–2001) "Security Seeking under Anarchy: Defensive Realism Revisited." *International Security* 25(3): 128–161.
  (2004) *Balancing Risks: Great Power Intervention in the Periphery*. Ithaca, NY: Cornell University Press.
Tang, S. (2009) "The Security Dilemma: A Conceptual Analysis." *Security Studies* 18(3): 587–623.
Tannenwald, N. (1999) "The Nuclear Taboo: The United States and the Normative Basis of Nuclear Non-Use." *International Organization* 53(3): 433–468.
  (2007) *Nuclear Taboo: the United States and the Non-Use of Nuclear Weapons since 1945*. New York: Cambridge University Press.
Tarrant, M., Branscombe, N. R., Warner, R. H. *et al.* (2012) "Social Identity and Perceptions of Torture: It's Moral When We Do It." *Journal of Experimental Social Psychology*, 48(2): 513–518.
Taussig, M. 1984. "Culture of Terror–Space of Death: Roger Casement's Putumayo Report and the Explanation of Torture". *Comparative Studies in Society and History* 26(3): 467–497.
Taylor, I., Walton, P., and Young, J. (1975) *Critical Criminology*. London: Routledge. (reprinted 2011).
Taylor, R. B. (1995) "The Impact of Crime on Communities." *Annals of the American Academy of Political and Social Science* 539: 28–45.
Thoits, P. A. (1989) "The Sociology of Emotions." *Annual Review of Sociology* 15: 317–342.
Thomas, C. (2000) *Global Governance, Development and Human Security: The Challenge of Poverty and Inequality*. London: Pluto Press.
Thomas, N., and Tow, W. T. (2002) "The Utility of Human Security: Sovereignty and Humanitarian Intervention." *Security Dialogue* 33: 177–192.

Thongchai, W. (1994) *Siam Mapped: A History of the Geo-Body of a Nation*. Honolulu: University of Hawaii Press.

Thrift, N. J. (2011) "Lifeworld Inc.: And What to Do about It." *Environment and Planning D: Society and Space* 29(1): 5–26.

Thucydides (1843) *History of the Peloponnesian War*. London: Bohn.

Tickner, J. A. (1992) *Gender in International Relations: Feminist Perspectives on Achieving Global Security*. New York: Columbia University Press.

(1997) "You Just Don't Understand: Troubled Engagements between Feminists and IR Theorists." *International Studies Quarterly* 41(4): 611–632.

Ticktin, M. (2011) *Casualties of Care: Immigration and the Politics of Humanitarianism in France*. Berkeley: University of California Press.

Till, K. E., Sundberg, J., Pullan, W. et al. (2013) "Interventions in the Political Geographies of Walls." *Political Geography* 33: 52–62.

Tilly, C. (2006) "Terror as Strategy and Relational Process." *International Journal of Comparative Sociology* 46: 11–32.

(1992) *Coercion, Capital and European States, 990–1992*. Boston: Wiley-Blackwell.

Trawalter, S., Todd, A. R., Baird, A. A. et al. (2008) "Attending to threat: Race-based patterns of selective attention." *Journal of Experimental Social Psychology* 44(5): 1322–1327.

Trawalter, S. A., and Shelton, J. (2009) "Predicting Behavior during Interracial Interactions: A Stress and Coping Approach." *Personality and Social Psychology Review* 13(4): 243–268.

Tropp, L. R., Hawi, D. R., Van Laar, C. et al. (2012) "Cross-Ethnic Friendships, Perceived Discrimination, and Their Effects on Ethnic Activism over Time: A Longitudinal Investigation of Three Ethnic Minority Groups." *British Journal of Social Psychology* 51(2): 257–272.

Tropp, L. R., and Pettigrew, T. F. (2005) "Relationships between Intergroup Contact and Prejudice among Minority and Majority Status Groups." *Psychological Science* 16(12): 951–957.

Trubowitz, P. (1998) *Defining the National Interest: Conflict and Change in American Foreign Policy*. Chicago: University of Chicago Press.

Tucker, B. (2012) "Do Risk and Time Experimental Choices Represent Individual Strategies for Coping with Poverty or Conformity to Social Norms? Evidence from Rural Southwestern Madagascar." *Current Anthropology* 53(2): 149–180.

Turk, A. T. (2004) "Sociology of Terrorism." *Annual Review of Sociology* 30: 271–286.

Turner, J. C., Hogg, M. A., Oakes, P. J. et al. (1987) *Rediscovering the Social Group: A Self-Categorization Theory*. Cambridge, MA: Basil Blackwell.

Tyler, J. (2008) *The Killing of Cambodia: Geopolitics, Genocide and the Unmaking of Space*. London: Ashgate.

Tyler, T. (2006) *Why People Obey the Law*. Princeton, NJ: Princeton University Press.

Tyler, T. R., and Blader, S. L. (2003) "The Group Engagement Model: Procedural Justice, Social Identity, and Cooperative Behavior." *Personality and Social Psychology Review* 7(4): 349–361.

Tyner, J. A. (2012) *Genocide and the Geographical Imagination: Life and Death in Germany, China, and Cambodia*. Lanham, MD: Rowman & Littlefield.

Ullman, R. H. (1983) "Redefining Security." *International Security* 8: 129–153.

United Nations (1994) *Human Development Report: New Dimensions of Human Security*. New York: UNDP.

Valverde, M. (2001) "Governing Security, Governing through Security." In Daniels, R. J., Macklem, P., and Roach, K. (eds.) *The Security of Freedom: Essays on Canada's Anti-Terrorism Bill*. Toronto: University of Toronto Press.

(2011) "Questions of Security: A Framework for Research." *Theoretical Criminology* 15(1): 3–22.

Valverde, M., and Cirak, M. (2002) "Governing Bodies, Creating Gay Spaces: Security in 'Gay' Downtown Toronto." *British Journal of Criminology* 43: 102–121.

Valverde, M., and Wood, J. (2001) "In the Name of Security." *University of Toronto Bulletin* 16: 1.

Van den Bos, K. (2001) "Uncertainty Management: The Influence of Uncertainty Salience on Reactions to Perceived Procedural Fairness." *Journal of Personality and Social Psychology* 80(6): 931–941.

Van den Bos, K., and Lind, E. (2010) "The Social Psychology of Fairness and the Regulation of Personal Uncertainty." In Arkin, R. M., Oleson, K. C., and Carroll, P. J. (eds.) *Handbook of the Uncertain Self*. New York: Psychology Press, 122–141.

Van Evera, S. (1999) *Causes of War: Structures of Power and the Roots of International Conflict*. Ithaca, NY: Cornell University Press.

Varsanyi, M. (2006) "Interrogating 'Urban Citizenship' vis-à-vis Undocumented Migration." *Citizenship Studies* 10(2): 229–249.

Vaughn, D. (1997) *The Challenger Launch Decision: Risky Technology, Culture, and Deviance at NASA*. Chicago: University of Chicago Press.

Vélez-Torres, I. (2014) "Governmental Extractivism in Colombia: Legislation, Securitization and the Local Settings of Mining Control." *Political Geography* 38: 68–78.

Veneziani, R. "Global Capitalism and Imperialism Theory: Methodological and Substantive Insights from Rosa Luxemburg." *Review of Political Economy* 21(2): 195–211.

Vesselinov, E. (2008) "Members Only: Gated Communities and Residential Segregation in the Metropolitan United States." *Sociological Forum* 23 (3): 536–555.

Vollhardt, J. (2010) "Enhanced External and Culturally Sensitive Attributions after Extended Intercultural Contact." *British Journal of Social Psychology* 49(2): 363–383.

von Clausewitz, C. (1873) *On War* (translated by J. J. Graham). London: Trübner.

Von Hirsch, A. (1993) *Censure and Sanctions*. Oxford: Clarendon Press.

Vorauer, J. D. (2006) "An Information Search Model of Evaluative Concerns in Intergroup Interaction." *Psychological Review* 113(4): 862–886.

Vuori, J. A. (2008) "Illocutionary Logic and Strands of Securitization: Applying the Theory of Securitization to the Study of Non-Democratic Political Orders." *European Journal of International Relations* 14(1): 65–100.

(2011) "Religion Bites: Falungong, Securitization/Desecuritization in the People's Republic of China." In Balzacq, T. (ed.) *Securitization Theory: How Security Problems Emerge and Dissolve*. London: Routledge: 186–211.

(2014) *Critical Security and Chinese Politics: The Anti-Falungong Campaign*. London: Routledge.

Waever, O. (1993) *Securitization and Descecuritization*. Copenhagen: Centre for Peace and Conflict Research.

(1995) "Securitisation and De-Securitisation." In Lipschutz, R. D. (ed.) *On Security*. New York: Columbia University Press, 46–86.

(1996) "European Security Identities." *Journal of Common Market Studies* 34(1): 103–132.

Wagner, U., and Hewstone, M. (2012) "Intergroup Contact." In Tropp, L. R. (ed.) *The Oxford Handbook of Intergroup Conflict*. New York: Oxford University Press, 193–209.

Wagner-Pacifici, R. (1995) *Discourse and Destruction: The City of Philadelphia versus MOVE*. Chicago: University of Chicago Press.

Wahl, R. (2014) "Justice, Context, and Violence: Law Enforcement Officers on Why They Torture." *Law and Society Review* 48(4): 807–836.

Walby, K., and Lippert, R. (2014) *Corporate Security in the 21st Century: Theory and Practice in International Perspective*. Basingstoke: Palgrave Macmillan.

Walder, A. G. (2009) "Political Sociology and Social Movements." *Annual Review of Sociology* 35(1): 393–412.

Waldron, J. (2003) Security and Liberty: The Image of Balance. *The Journal of Political Philosophy* 11: 191–210.
  (2006) "Safety and Security." *Nebraska Law Review* 85(2): 454–507.
  (2009) "Security as a Basic Right (after 9/11)." In Beitz, C. R., and Goodin, R. E. (eds.) *Global Basic Rights*. Oxford: Oxford University Press., 207–226.
Walker, R. B. J. (1990) "Security, Sovereignty, and the Challenge of World Politics." *Alternatives* 15(1): 3–27.
  (1993) *Inside/Outside: International Relations as Political Theory*. Cambridge: Cambridge University Press.
  (1997) "The Subject of Security." *Critical Security Studies*. In Krause, K., and Williams, M. C. (eds.) Minneapolis: University of Minnesota Press, 61–82.
Walklate, S. (1998) "Crime and Community: Fear or Trust?" *The British Journal of Sociology* 49(4): 550–569.
Waller, I., and Sansfacon, D. (2000) *Investing Wisely in Crime Prevention: International Experiences*. US Department of Justice, Office of Justice Programs, Bureau of Justice Assistance.
Walt, S. M. (1987) *The Origins of Alliances*. Ithaca, NY: Cornell University Press.
  (1991) "The Renaissance of Security Studies." *International Studies Quarterly* 35(2): 211–239.
  (2002) "The Enduring Relevance of the Realist Tradition." *Political Science: the State of the Discipline*. Katznelson, I., and Miller, H. V. (eds.) New York: Norton: 197–234.
  (2009) "Alliances in a Unipolar World." *World Politics* 61(1): 86–120.
Walters, W. (2002) "Deportation, Expulsion, and the International Police of Aliens." *Citizenship Studies* 6(3): 265–292.
  (2004) "Secure Borders, Safe Haven, Domopolitics." *Citizenship Studies* 8(3): 237–260.
Waltz, K. N. (1959) *Man, the State, and War: A Theoretical Analysis*. New York: Columbia University Press.
  (1979) *Theory of International Politics*. Reading, MA: Addison-Wesley.
  (1981) "The Spread of Nuclear Weapons: More May Better." Adelphi Papers 171. London: International Institute for Strategic Studies.
  (1990) "Realist Thought and Neorealist Theory." *Journal of International Affairs* 44(1): 21–37.
Walzer, M. (2000) *Just and Unjust Wars: a Moral Argument with Historical Illustrations*, 3rd ed. New York: Basic Books.
  (2006) *Just and Unjust Wars. a Moral Argument with Historical Illustrations*, 4th ed. New York: Basic Books.

Waterston, A. (1997) *Street Addicts in the Political Economy.* Philadelphia: Temple University Press.
Weil, P. (1983) "Towards Relative Normativity in International Law?" *American Journal of International Law* 77(3): 413–442.
Weldes, J., Laffey, M., Gusterson, H. *et al.* (1999) *Cultures of Insecurity: States, Communities, and the Production of Danger.* Minneapolis: University of Minnesota Press.
Welker, M. A. (2009) "Corporate Security Begins in the Community: Mining, the Corporate Social Responsibility Industry, and Environmental Advocacy in Indonesia." *Cultural Anthropology* 24(1): 142–179.
Wendt, A. (1987) "The Agent-Structure Problem in International Relations Theory." *International Organization* 41(3): 335–370.
  (1992) "Anarchy Is What States Make of It: The Social Construction of Power Politics." *International Organization* 46(2): 391–425.
  (1994) "Collective Identity Formation and the International State." *American Political Science Review* 88(2): 384–396.
  (1995) "Constructing International Politics." *International Security*: 71–81.
  (1999) *Social Theory of International Politics.* Cambridge: Cambridge University Press.
Werner W. G., (2010) "The Use of Law in International Political Sociology." *International Political Sociology* (4): 3.
White, A. (2011) "The New Political Economy of Private Security." *Theoretical Criminology* 16(1): 85–101.
White, R. (2009) *Global Environmental Harm: Criminological Perspectives. Cullumpton*, Devon: Willan.
Wieviorka, M. (2009) *Violence: A New Approach* (translated by D. Macey). Los Angeles: Sage.
Wight, C. (2006) *Agents, Structures and International Relations: Politics as Ontology.* Cambridge: Cambridge University Press.
Wildavsky, A. (1988) *Searching for Safety.* New Brunswick, NJ: Transaction.
Wilder, D. A. (1984) "Intergroup Contact: The Typical Member and the Exception to the Rule." *Journal of Experimental Social Psychology* 20: 177–194.
  (1993) "The Role of Anxiety in Facilitating Stereotypic Judgments of Outgroup Behavior." In Mackie, D. M., and Hamilton, D. (eds.) *Affect, Cognition, and Stereotyping: Interactive Processes in Group Perception.* San Diego, CA: Academic Press, 87–109.
Wilkinson, C. (2011) "The Limits of Spoken Words: From Meta-Narratives to Experience in Security." In Balzacq, T. (ed.) *Securitization Theory: How Security Problems Emerge and Dissolve.* London: Routledge: 94–115.

Williams, B. (1981) *Moral Luck*. Oxford: Oxford University Press.
Williams, M. C. (2003) "Words, Images, Enemies: Securitization and International Politics." *International Studies Quarterly* 47(4): 511–531.
  (2007) *Culture and Security: Symbolic Power and the Politics of International Security*. London: Routledge.
  (2011) "Securitization and the Liberalism of Fear." *Security Dialogue* 42(4–5): 453–463.
Williams, M. C., and Krause, K. (1997) "Preface: Toward Critical Security Studies." *Critical Security Studies: Concepts and Cases*. Minneapolis: University of Minnesota Press, vvi–xxi.
Williams, M. J. (2008) "(In)Security Studies, Reflexive Modernization and the Risk Society." *Cooperation and Conflict* 43(1): 57–79.
Williams, P. (2013) *Security Studies: An Introduction*, 2nd ed. London: Routledge.
Williamson, O. E. (2000) "The New Institutional Economics: Taking Stock, Looking Ahead." *Journal of Economic Literature* 38(3): 595–613.
Wilson, R. A. (ed.) (2005) *Human Rights in the "War on Terror."* Cambridge: Cambridge University Press.
Wilson, S., and Ebert, N. (2013) "Precarious Work: Economic, Sociological and Political Perspectives." *The Economic and Labour Relations Review* 24(3): 263–278.
Wilson, T. D., Aronson, E., and Carlsmith, K. (2010) "The Art of Laboratory Experimentation." In Fiske, S. T., Gilbert, D. T., and Lindzey, G. (eds.) *Handbook of Social Psychology*, Vol. 1. Hoboken, NJ: Wiley, 51–81.
Wimmer, A. (2012) *Waves of War: Nationalism, State Formation, and Ethnic Exclusion in the Modern World*. Cambridge: Cambridge University Press.
Wishnie, M. J. (2003) "Immigrants and the Right to Petition." *NYU Law Review* 78: 667–748.
Wisner, B., Blaikie, P., Cannon, T. et al. (2004) *At Risk: Natural Hazards, People's Vulnerability and Disasters*, London: Routledge.
Wittgenstein, L. (1953) *Philosophical Investigations*. Oxford: Basil Blackwell.
Wohlforth, W. C. (1993) *The Elusive Balance: Power and Perceptions during the Cold War*. Ithaca, NY: Cornell University Press.
  (2009) "Statement from the New Editor-in-Chief." *Security Studies* 18(1): 1–3.
Wohlforth, W. C., Little, R., Kaufman, S. J. et al. (2007) "Testing Balance-of-Power Theory in World History." *European Journal of International Relations* 13(2): 155–185.
  (2011) "No-One Loves a Realist Explanation." *International Politics* 48 (4/5): 441–459.

(2009) "Realism and Security Studies." In Dunn Cavelty, M., and Mauer, V. (eds.) *The Routledge Handbook for Security Studies*. London: Routledge, 9–20.

Wolf, E. R. (1999) *Peasant Wars of the Twentieth Century*. Norman: University of Oklahoma Press.

Wolfers, A. (1952) "'National Security' as an Ambiguous Symbol." *Political Science Quarterly* 67(4): 481–502.

Wood, J., and Dupont, B. (eds.) (2006) *Democracy, Society and the Governance of Security*. Cambridge: Cambridge University Press.

Wood, J., and Shearing, C. (2007) *Imagining Security*. London: Routledge.

Woodward, R. (2005) "From Military Geography to Militarism's Geographies: Disciplinary Engagements with the Geographies of Militarism and Military Activities." *Progress in Human Geography* 29(6): 718–740.

Wright, M. W. (2013) "Feminicidio, Narcoviolence, and Gentrification in Ciudad Juarez: The Feminist Fight." *Environment and Planning D: Society and Space* 31(5): 830–845.

Wright, S. C., Aron, A., and Tropp, L. R. (2002) Including Others (and Groups) in the Self: Self-Expansion and Intergroup Relations. In Forgas, J. P., and Williams, K. D. (eds.) *The Social Self: Cognitive, Interpersonal and Intergroup Perspectives*. Philadelphia: Psychology Press, 343–363.

Yar, M. (2013) *Cybercrime and Society*. London: Sage.

Yarwood, R. (2007) "The Geographies of Policing." *Progress in Human Geography* 31(4): 447–465.

Zack, N. (2009) *Ethics for Disaster*. Lanham, MD: Rowman & Littlefield.

Zagare, F. C., and Kilgour, M. D. (2000) *Perfect Deterrence*. Cambridge: Cambridge University Presss.

Zalewski, M., and Enloe, C. (1995) "Questions about Identity in International Relations." In Booth, K. and Smith, S. (eds.) *International Relations Theory Today*. London: Polity, 279–305.

Zedner, L. (2003) "The Concept of Security: An Agenda for Comparative Analysis." *Legal Studies* 23: 153.

(2006) "Policing before and after the Police: The Historical Antecedents of Contemporary Crime Control." *British Journal of Criminology* 46(1): 78–96.

(2009) *Security*. London: Routledge.

Zeiderman, A. (2013) "Living Dangerously: Biopolitics and Urban Citizenship in Bogotá, Colombia." *American Ethnologist* 40(1): 71–87.

Zick, A., Pettigrew, T. F., and Wagner, U. (2008) "Ethnic Prejudice and Discrimination in Europe." *Journal of Social Issues* 64(2): 233–251.

Ziegler, J. N. (1991) "Semiconductors." *Daedalus* 120(4): 155–182.

Zilberg, E. (2011) *Spaces of Detention: The Making of a Transnational Gang Crisis between Los Angeles and San Salvador*. Durham, NC: Duke University Press.

Zürn, M., Binder, M., and Ecker-Ehrhardt, M. (2012) "International Authority and Its Politicization." *International Theory* 4(1): 69–106.

Reports

Council of Canadian Academies (2014) *Future of Canadian Policing Models*. Ottawa: Council of Canadian Academies.

Dutch Advisory Committee on Issues of Public International Law, Armed Drones, 2013: http://cms.webbeat.net/ContentSuite/upload/cav/doc/Main_conclusions_of_CAVV_advice_on_armed_drones.pdf.

Report of the Special Rapporteur on the promotion and protection of human rights and fundamental freedoms while countering terrorism, 18 September 2013, General Assembly, A/68/389;

Tallinn Manual on the International Law Applicable to Cyber Warfare: *Prepared by the International Group of Experts at the Invitation of the NATO Cooperative Cyber Defence Centre of Excellence*, Schmitt, Michael N. (general ed.) Cambridge: Cambridge University Press 2013.

Websites

American Society of International Law Website: www.asil.org/mission.cfm (accessed July 22, 2013)

African Society of International Law Website: www.aail-aadi.org/#!about-us/ch88 (accessed July 22, 2013)

Asian Society of International Law Website: http://asiansil-jp.org/en/ (accessed July 22, 2013)

Australian and New Zealand Society of International Law Website: http://anzsil.anu.edu.au/; (accessed July 22, 2013)

European Society of International Law Website, at: www.esil-sedi.eu/node/177 (accessed 22 July 2013)

Index

Agamben, Giorgio, 43, 46, 55, 73, 75, 219
agency, 36, 80
anarchy, 113, 120–2, 166
Anthropocene, 14, 79, 191–2, 194, 247, 271
asphaleia, 25, 38
asylum seekers, 57
ataraxia, 23, 25
audience, 76, 112, 209–10

Bentham, Jeremy, 27, 224
biopolitics, 1, 14, 74–6, 241, 251, 265, 270
Bolivia, 52, 240

Cambodia, 51, 248, 274–5
capitalism, 80, 169–74
civil war, 83, 162, 171, 227, 230, 264
climate change, 2, 79, 107–8
communities, 12, 31, 40, 48–9, 52, 56–9, 63–4, 70, 72, 74, 79, 97, 108, 123, 139, 154, 158, 220, 278; global, 48; political, 158
consensualism, 201–2
constructivism, 123, 126–8, 135, 157
Copenhagen school, 50, 210
critical theory, 81, 128, 135, 196
culture, 6, 45–6, 48–9, 51, 61, 98, 100, 103, 105, 135, 157, 182, 222, 237, 249, 269
cybersecurity, 48, 194
cyberspace, 6, 77, 117, 185, 193–4, 203, 238, 252

defensive realism, 114, 119–20
desecuritization, 9, 19, 190, 243
detention, 55, 57
deterrence, 120, 127, 131, 180, 263
drones, 62, 77, 197, 259, 281

embodiment, 82, 85
emergency, 28, 30, 40, 43–4, 116, 125, 185, 209
emotions, 83, 127, 137, 142, 144–5, 236
Enlightenment, 18, 24–7, 41, 223
Epicureans, 18, 22–3
epistemology, 17, 19, 112, 122, 128–9, 197
essentially contested concept, 18, 29
Estonia, 73, 250
ethnic relations, 6; ethnic cleansing, 101; ethnic policing, 101
ethnography, 15–16, 48, 52, 58, 61, 94, 97, 102, 109, 256
exception, logic of, 9, 210

fear, 10, 22, 25, 36–9, 49, 54, 76, 91, 94–6, 98, 115, 144, 177, 189, 244, 246, 248, 252, 269, 279
feminism, 62, 74, 80, 89, 122, 124
food security, 9, 48, 70, 79, 87, 93, 187, 193, 245
Foucault, Michel, 29, 46, 75, 81, 177–8, 188, 190, 236–7, 251, 263

Geographical Information Systems, 12, 65
global warming, 6
governance, 13–14, 20, 55–6, 75, 78, 80, 160, 170, 178, 181, 183–94, 228, 235, 238
governmentality, 72, 124, 190, 224
Gramsci, Antonio, 46

hegemonic stability theory, 163
Hobbes, Thomas, 18, 22, 25–6, 91, 164, 177, 179, 187–8, 221, 232, 244, 267, 270

Index

human rights, 39, 42, 52, 58, 90, 101, 106, 197, 209, 213–15, 241, 272, 281
human security, 11, 19, 28, 32–3, 35–6, 40, 63, 79, 87, 91, 115, 154, 177, 208, 223, 235, 260, 275
Human Terrain System, 6, 51, 68

immigration, 2, 6, 45–6, 53–7, 59, 75, 93, 98, 144, 224
imperialism, 62, 99, 157, 159, 164, 172
inductive, 65, 83, 130, 175
insecurity, 6, 18–20, 39, 41, 46–50, 52, 60, 62–3, 68, 79, 84, 92–5, 97–8, 104, 106, 109, 118–19, 137–9, 141, 143, 149, 151, 153, 155, 167, 225, 245–6
instrumentalization of security, 13–14
intersubjectivities, 12

Kant, Immanuel, 168, 223

legalism, 9, 21, 199, 211–13, 215
Lenin, Vladimir, 171–2
liberty, 2, 18, 22, 24, 28–9, 31, 34, 40–1, 135, 268, 277
Locke, John, 26, 41, 253

Marxism, 46, 169, 265
mercantilism, 157, 164
methodological pluralism, 5, 15–16
Mexico, 54, 84, 97–8, 220, 233, 238, 254–5, 272
military, 7, 10, 36, 50, 60, 62–3, 67–8, 70, 72–3, 78, 84, 89, 98, 100, 107–8, 112, 114, 119–22, 124, 148, 160, 162, 167, 172–3, 175, 197, 223, 241, 248, 280
modernity, 99, 103, 239
morality, 14, 211
multidisciplinary approach, 2–3, 5, 15, 20, 135–6

national security, 6–7, 13, 19, 25, 28, 31–2, 40, 48, 52–4, 62, 66, 71, 74, 108, 112–14, 116–17, 120, 122, 178, 208–9, 211, 219, 245
nationalism, 99, 113, 148, 172, 220
neoliberal, 13–14, 46, 50, 55–6, 73, 77, 85, 88, 167, 270

neorealism, 119, 121–3, 157–8, 162–3
new materialism, 86
nonconsensualism, 202
norms, 113, 123, 140, 147, 150, 197, 200–2, 214, 247, 269

objective security, 12, 37–8
offensive realism, 119–20, 126
ontological security, 10, 38
ontology, 127–9, 197, 267

paradigm, 2, 55, 93, 96, 114, 118, 126, 139, 192, 200
performance, 81, 164, 167, 210, 271
politicization, 9
populations, 49, 53–7, 59, 64, 67–9, 71, 75–6, 78, 87, 117, 140–1
positivism, 62, 65, 129, 131, 201
postcolonial theory, 80–1; post-colonial studies, 74
practices, 8–9, 14, 17–19, 21, 30, 32, 40, 42–3, 46, 49, 51, 57, 59, 62–4, 67, 70, 72, 78, 80–1, 83, 85–6, 88–9, 93, 98, 104–5, 108–9, 115, 117–18, 124–7, 189–91, 197, 207–8
precarity, 93
process-tracing, 129, 134
processual, 5, 8–9, 46, 50, 122
public media, 72, 74, 81

rational choice, 163, 216; rational actors, 114, 119
referent object, 6, 14, 19, 32, 69, 71, 74, 112–14, 116–17, 157
refugee, 57, 76, 264
resilience, 10, 109, 184, 224
routines, 80, 210

Said, Edward, 81
scientific realism, 129
securitas, 23–6, 28, 32
securitization, 2, 9, 14, 18, 21, 210, 231, 253
security dilemma, 119–20, 159, 173, 273
security narratives, 8, 63, 70, 74, 81
Shklar, Judith, 9, 211, 267
sovereignty, 55–6, 71–2, 74–5, 113, 122, 205, 230, 235, 250, 277
Sri Lanka, 76, 83, 246
statistical analysis, 15, 65, 68

surveillance, 2, 18, 42, 50, 53–4, 62, 73, 77, 85, 103, 117, 140, 179–80, 185

Tanzania, 74
territoriality, 1
terrorism, 41, 62, 72, 91, 96, 99–101, 103, 107, 112, 197, 206, 229, 241, 252, 254, 271, 281; terrorist attacks, 2, 101, 105, 140, 187, 245, 270
threats, 10–12, 19, 21–2, 35–6, 39, 45, 50, 54, 59, 62–5, 67, 70, 72–3, 75–7, 82, 85, 92, 95, 100, 103, 105, 107, 110, 116–17, 120, 126, 142–3, 145–6, 149, 151, 153, 161, 165, 195, 212; existential threats, 71; intergroup threats, 147; social threats, 28; symbolic threats, 146
Thucydides, 25, 267, 274
torture, 28, 40, 101, 106, 148, 214, 273
triangulation, 132, 134, 222

United Nations Security Council, 21, 199, 209, 211–15, 232, 245–6, 259
US homeland security, 66

violence, 1, 10, 14, 26–8, 32, 36–9, 52, 55, 63, 70, 74, 76, 78–80, 83, 88, 90, 99–101, 107, 117, 143, 145, 147–8, 170, 174, 176, 225, 236, 240–1, 251, 268, 270